WHEN CHRIST MEETS CHRIST

Homilies on the Just Word

WALTER J. BURGHARDT, S.J.

D1226125

PAULIST PRESS
New York/Mahwah

also by Walter J. Burghardt, S.J.
published by Paulist Press

GRACE ON CRUTCHES
LOVELY IN EYES NOT HIS
PREACHING: THE ART AND THE CRAFT
SEASONS THAT LAUGH OR WEEP
SIR, WE WOULD LIKE TO SEE JESUS
STILL PROCLAIMING YOUR WONDERS
TELL THE NEXT GENERATION
TO CHRIST I LOOK
DARE TO BE CHRIST

Illustrations by Nancy Rakoczy Myette

Acknowledgments

Excerpts from *Letters and Papers from Prison,* revised, enlarged edition by Dietrich Bon-hoeffer, copyright © 1953, 1967, 1971 by SCM Press, are reprinted by permission of Macmillan Publishing Company. Excerpts from *Listen to the Warm* by Rod McKuen, copyright © 1967 by Rod McKuen, are reprinted by permission of Random House, Inc. The excerpt from "One Hand, One Heart" from *West Side Story,* music by Leonard Bernstein, lyrics by Stephen Sondheim, copyright © 1956, 1957 by Leonard Bernstein and Stephen Sondheim, is reprinted by permission of Jalni Publications, Inc. (U.S. and Canadian Publisher) and G. Schirmer, Inc. (worldwide print rights and publisher for the rest of the world). International copyrights secured. All rights reserved.

Library of Congress Cataloging-in-Publication Data

Burghardt, Walter J.
    When Christ meets Christ: homilies on the just Word/Walter J. Burghardt.
        p.   cm.
    Includes bibliographical references.
    ISBN 0-8091-3373-3
    1. Catholic Church—Sermons.   2. Sermons, American.
    3. Christianity and justice—Catholic Church—Sermons.   I. Title.
BX1756.B828W48   1993
252'.6—dc20   92-46434
                                                                                                        CIP

Published by Paulist Press
997 Macarthur Boulevard
Mahwah, NJ 07430

Printed and bound in the
United States of America

TABLE OF CONTENTS

FROM ADVENT TO EASTER

ORDINARY TIME

WEDDING HOMILIES

ANNIVERSARIES

MEDLEY

PREFACE

This, the eighth collection of my homilies published by the Paulist Press since 1980, takes its title and subtitle from the strong emphasis I have been placing in recent years on what I call "the just Word." I mean the stress in Scripture, from Genesis to Revelation, on the faith that does justice. Today, as rarely before, Christians are recovering a biblical heritage that is summed up in the prophet Micah's stunning question and answer: "What does the Lord require of you? Act justly, love steadfastly, and walk humbly with your God" (Mic 6:8).

These 36 homilies constitute my effort to demonstrate that "the just Word" is not limited to a small number of biblical texts such as Isaiah 58:6 ff. ("Is not this the fast that I choose, to loose the bonds of injustice . . . ?") and Luke 4:18 ("The Spirit of the Lord has anointed me to bring good news to the poor . . ."). The *whole* of Scripture is social, oriented to community, bent on expressing and effecting fidelity to a relationship within humans and with the earth stemming from a covenant with God—a God who declares to each woman and man divinely shaped, "You are precious in my sight and I love you" (Isa 43:4).

In line with this conviction, the present set of homilies preaches the just Word in Advent and Lent, in Eastertide and ordinary time, at nine weddings and seven anniversaries, at a medley of occasions from baptisms to baccalaureates. Never have I experienced so profoundly the power of God's just Word.

Walter J. Burghardt, S.J.

1

Prologue

PREACHING THE JUST WORD: PROBLEM, PREACHER, PROJECT

Recently, a remarkably creative Old Testament scholar, Walter Brueggemann, addressed the problem of "scandal" in the preaching of social, political, and economic issues:

> In Luke 7, after John the Baptist raises his christological question through his disciples whether Jesus is the Christ, and after Jesus answers with specificity that "the blind see, the lame walk, lepers are cleansed, the dead are raised, and the poor rejoice," Jesus adds, "blessed is the one who is not scandalized by me" (v. 23). Or as I have rendered it, "Lucky are you, if you are not upset." The theological scandal of biblical faith, when rendered into political, economic issues, is indeed upsetting.
>
> How is a pastor to give voice to this scandal in a society that is hostile to it, and when we ourselves as teachers and pastors of the church are somewhat queasy about the scandal as it touches our own lives? How can the radical dimension of the Bible as it touches public reality be heard in the church?[1]

How can the social dimension of Scripture, so scandalous to pious ears, be given a persuasive voice within the Church? Three swift points: (1) the problem, (2) the preacher, (3) the project.

I

First, the problem. It stems from at least two sources: the pews and the pulpit. The pews, in that all too many Christians, Roman Catholics included, insist that justice issues, the "social gospel," are

5

not a legitimate concern of the Church, and surely do not belong in the pulpit. To preach justice, they claim, is to preach politics, to get mired in sociology, to trespass on economics. Others declare that Christ entered the human scene not to relieve suffering but to forgive sins. Similarly, the Church of Christ should concentrate not on violations of social justice but on the hardness of human hearts we call sin. Still others assert that Christ preached a personal rather than a social morality. By nature, therefore, his Church is exclusively concerned with the relationship of the soul to eternity. In sum, the Church is a spiritual institution, and its mission is sheerly spiritual. Such attitudes find confirmation in a scholarly effort to show that "social justice" is an attempt to wrest control of the economy from the citizen and thereby strengthen the state.

These convictions are not easily overcome. Many a Catholic, like myself, grew up with the catechism imperative, "God made us to praise, reverence, and serve Him in this life and to be happy with Him for ever in the next." The ultraliteral interpretation of that maxim has contributed to an excessive me-and-Jesus spirituality that is not integrated with social justice, even when much charitable activity is taking place.

It is true, Christianity is not sheer socialization, liberation from oppressive structures, an end to poverty, to racism, to violence. The Church has for primary purpose to fashion the human person in the image of God, in the likeness of Christ; short of this there is no salvation. The essential liberation is freedom from the slavery that is sin. It is in harmony with this conviction that Pius XII could say in a 1956 allocution, "The goal which Christ assigns to [the Church] is strictly religious. . . . The Church must lead men and women to God, in order that they may give themselves over to God unreservedly. . . ."[2]

Still, salvation takes place within community—the community of humankind shaped by God in the beginning, and the community of believers shaped by Christ in the covenant of his blood. It is in this context that a traditional axiom makes sense: No man gets to heaven by himself, no woman by herself. No one can say to any other, "I have no need of you" (see 1 Cor 12:21). Not only need for prayers; need for help in developing the whole person that is to be saved. That is why the Second Vatican Council could declare resoundingly in its Decree on the Apostolate of the Laity:

> Christ's redemptive work, while of its nature directed to the salvation of men and women, involves also the renewal of the whole temporal order. The Church has for mission, therefore, not only to

bring to men and women the message of Christ and his grace, but also to saturate and perfect the temporal sphere with the spirit of the gospel. . . . The two spheres [spiritual and temporal], distinct though they are, are so linked in the single plan of God that He Himself purposes in Christ to take up the whole world again into a new creation, initially here on earth, completely on the last day.[3]

This is the vision of the 1971 Synod of Bishops in its message "On Justice in the World": The vindication of justice and participation in the process of transforming the world is "a constitutive element of the preaching of the gospel."[4] This is the vision that emerged from the 1974 Synod of Bishops in a significant statement on "Human Rights and Reconciliation." Said the bishops in common;

Human dignity is rooted in the image and reflection of God in each of us. It is this which makes all persons essentially equal. The integral development of persons makes more clear the divine image in them. In our time the Church has grown more deeply aware of this truth; hence she believes firmly that the promotion of human rights is required by the gospel and is central to her ministry.[5]

In 1976 the International Theological Commission (an advisory body serving the pope) argued that God's grace should sharpen the conscience of Christians, should help us build a more just world. Not simply by spiritual reformation; not simply by assisting individuals;

for there is a kind of "injustice that assumes institutional shape," and as long as this obtains, the situation itself calls for a greater degree of justice and demands reforming. . . .

We may argue how legitimate it is to speak of "institutional sin" or of "sinful structures," since the Bible speaks of sin in the first instance in terms of an explicit, personal decision that stems from human freedom. But it is unquestionable that by the power of sin injury and injustice can penetrate social and political institutions. That is why . . . even situations and structures that are unjust have to be reformed.

Here we have a new consciousness, for in the past these responsibilities could not be perceived as distinctly as they are now. . . . [6]

A new consciousness. Not that the Prior Testament and the New are silent on social issues. Those who read in Scripture a sheerly personal morality have not sung the Psalms or been burned by the prophets, have not perceived the implications of Jesus' message. Through Isaiah and Hosea, through Amos and Micah and Jeremiah, it becomes startlingly clear that God was not satisfied with Israel's burnt offerings and feasts, incense and prayers, melody of harps and rivers of oil, even Israel's first-born. What, then, could God possibly want? Love steadfastly and act justly (cf. Isa 1:11–18; 42:1–4; Hos 2:18–20; 6:6; Amos 5:18–25; Mic 6:6–8; Jer 7:5–7).

Remember, however, that justice, for the Jew, was not simply a question of human deserving, of human law. The Jews were to give to others what they had been given by God, were to act toward one another—and even toward the stranger, the outsider—as God had acted toward them—and precisely because God had acted this way. Their justice was to image not the justice of man and woman but the justice of God. For Israel, the practice of justice was an expression, a demand, of steadfast love—God's love and their own love. Not to execute justice was not to worship God.

This is the tradition that sparked the ministry of Jesus: "I will put my Spirit upon him, and he shall proclaim justice to the Gentiles. . . . He will not break a bruised reed or quench a smoldering wick till he brings justice to victory" (Mt 12:18–20). In harmony with Hosea, he wants not sacrifice but compassion, mercy (cf. Mt 12:7; 23:23). And the just man, the just woman is not primarily someone who gives to another what that other *deserves*. The just man, the just woman has covenanted with God; this covenant demands that we treat other human persons as *God* wants them treated in God's covenant plan.

The early Christians seem to have grasped that. If *anyone* is hungry or thirsty, naked or a stranger, sick or in prison, it is always Christ who clamors for bread or water, Christ who cries to be clothed or welcomed, Christ whom you visit on a bed of pain or behind bars (cf. Mt 25:31–46). And the first letter of John is terribly uncompromising: "If anyone has the world's goods and sees his brother [or sister] in need, yet closes his heart against him [or her], how does God's love abide in him?" (1 Jn 3:17). For the Christian, social justice means playing out the second great commandment of the law and the gospel: You shall love your brothers and sisters at least as much as you love yourself. In fact, you should love them as Jesus does—even unto crucifixion.

The second problem, the pulpit, compounds the first. How is it possible to handle with competence from the pulpit issues as complex as insider trading, a billion of God's human images falling asleep hungry, the rape of the earth, sexual abuse, unequal opportunities for education, 37 million Americans without access to healthcare, coke and crack king of our streets, black and white in a tenuous truce, women's demands for justice in society and church? Is it actually possible to preach a 15-minute social-justice homily that is woven of competence and compassion, a homily that strikes fire in the hearts of hearers?

Basic to this problem is massive ignorance. Catholicism's rich tradition of social doctrine has been termed our best-kept secret. Even our Catholic clergy are in large measure not immune to the charge leveled more generally by Lawrence Cunningham when he was professor of religion at Florida State University. He found himself frustrated in the classroom

> because students lack any sense of the historical perspective of Western culture in general and the part Catholicism played in the formation of that culture in particular. They . . . have no sense of the kind of church which existed before the Second Vatican Council. Students have this strong conviction that what is important happens now and the "now" has little or no link with the past. They tend to see the life of the church rather as they see the surface of a video game screen: active, immediate and graspable as a whole.[7]

This lamentation is not irrelevant to social justice. Our postimmigrant Church, including a fair proportion of the ordained, is incredibly ignorant of 20 centuries of rich social doctrine: from Christ's proclamation of "good news to the poor" (Lk 4:18) to John Paul II's warning against an unbridled capitalism; from the insistence of early Fathers of the Church that God's good earth was given to all men and women, not a favored few, to the U.S. bishops' pastoral plea for "economic justice for all." Without some such appreciation it is not likely that our preaching will affect our divided Catholic community. I mean the American Catholic "center," the "postimmigrant" Catholic community, "a church pervasively present in white, upper-income suburbs," and the "newly immigrant church . . . persistently present in inner-city communities, largely black and Hispanic."[8]

To pursue this facet of the problem, let me attempt a more positive presentation of the preacher's possibilities in the area of social justice.

II

Some years ago the learned French Dominican Yves Congar pointed out that the specific function of the homily is not only to explain the liturgical mystery but to bring the faithful into the mystery "by throwing light on their life so that they can unite it to this mystery. When this happens, the sermon is a word which prompts a response."[9] The liturgy's insights are rarely obvious; liturgical texts and forms tend to get fixed and rigid, are not more different in Buenos Aires than in Buffalo. What the homily does is extend the immemorial symbols to a particular time and place, a particular people, a people's needs and hungers. If they need to act justly or if they hunger for justice (both are inescapably present on the human and Christian scene), a liturgy that on principle should express their faith and mold their faith forbids the preacher to keep silent. To say nothing is to say something. Homilies that avoid concrete applications risk saying nothing. To limit myself to abstract principle is to risk what Karl Rahner called "a terrifying sterility."[10]

If I mount the pulpit with "Scripture alone" in my hands, if I limit my preaching to the broad biblical imperatives, if I simply repeat scriptural slogans like "Man does not live on bread alone," "My peace I give to you," "Seek first the kingdom of God," "Love your neighbor as you love yourself," "Wives, be subject to your husbands," hungry stomachs will stay bloated, the arms race will escalate, dissidents will rot in political prisons, blacks will return to their slavery, and women will continue to be second-class citizens in much of the world. After all, it is not only the heathen who are responsible for oppression. The oppressors, large and small, often break Eucharistic bread with us. In fact, who among us is not, by act or silence, an oppressor of our sisters and brothers?

But how concrete dare I get? At times the issue is so clear that trenchant language is a must. The riots and looting, the burning and killing that devastated south-central Los Angeles in April 1992 demanded from the pulpit not general exhortations on loving the neighbor but serious reflection on the second-class citizenship of African-Americans. The critical situation of children in the United States as I write (infant mortality, poverty, neglect, sexual abuse) compels us to preach at least what the U.S. bishops presented in their 1991 statement "Putting Children and Families First: A Challenge for Our Church, Nation and World."[11]

Not that a homily is a clear-cut strategy for the solution of a complex issue such as poverty or the environment. Strategies call for specific expertise, broad consultation, prolonged discussion. A preacher's delicate, indispensable task is to *help form Christian consciences.* Not force; form. This does not mean barring the controversial from the pulpit; the more complex an issue, the more open to controversy. It does mean that "the pulpit, as a general rule, is not the proper forum in which to pontificate on complicated and highly controversial political and socio-economic issues."[12] Here the crucial word is "pontificate." On such issues, in a short span of time, with no room for counterargument, I dare not speak in dogmatic fashion, as if I alone am the trumpet of the Lord. But if I dare not dogmatize, I may still raise the issues, lay them out, even say where I stand and why. Not to impose my convictions as gospel, but as a spur to personal and communal reflection.

I may not take unfair advantage of a captive audience, especially since the expertise in the pews often exceeds my own. Inasmuch as the suffering faithful, however sorely provoked, are expected by immemorial custom to hold their tongues as I empty my quiver against unbridled capitalism and the rapists of our environment, I should provide another forum, such as discussion groups, where controversial issues and strategies may be properly debated. For I must guard against a persistent priestly peril, where I see the ordained minister as alone bearing the burden of Christian guidance, of pastoral counseling. Here Vatican II was clear, concise, compelling—a sentence to be scotch-taped to every rectory refrigerator: "Let the laity not imagine that their pastors are always such experts that to every problem which arises, however complicated, they can readily give a concrete solution, or even that such is their mission."[13] We are in this together; all of us, pope and bishops included, belong to a church that is for ever learning.

III

It is in this context that I have designed a long-range project. A half century of preaching across the country, almost 45 years as managing editor/editor-in-chief of the scholarly journal *Theological Studies,* 32 years of engagement with the Fathers of the Church as scholar and professor, two decades of intensive ecumenical activity, 12 years as theologian-in-residence at Georgetown University—these rich experiences have combined to lead me to a final apostolic focus. Elected a senior fellow of the Woodstock Theological Center—a research institute established in 1974 by the Maryland and New York Provinces of the Society of Jesus, to put theology to work on social issues—I had a dream. Not quite as powerful a dream as Martin Luther King's, but in its own way profoundly significant for our church and our nation.

The purpose of the Center fits admirably the mandate given Jesuits by their general congregation in 1974: "The mission of the Society of Jesus today is the service of faith, of which the promotion of justice is an absolute requirement." My project complements the theological activity of the Center. It is an effort to move the *preaching* of social-justice issues more effectively into all the Catholic pulpits and congregations of the country. What social issues? Abortion, business ethics, children, ecology, education, healthcare, human rights in the Church, poverty, prisons, racism, substance abuse, war and peace, women's concerns, and a good deal more.

How do we go about it? By retreat/workshops across the country, of five days' duration, directed by a team of eight, men and women competent in spirituality, the Spiritual Exercises of St. Ignatius, social-justice theory and activity, Scripture, homiletics, and liturgy. For we are convinced that if the project is to succeed, it cannot be merely a communication of ideas, principles, and skills, important as these are. It calls for a spirituality, a conversion process that turns the preacher inside out, shapes a new person, puts "fire in the belly." That is why "Preaching the Just Word" is centered at a Jesuit retreat house, Manresa-on-Severn, outside of Annapolis, Maryland.

When this volume appears, we shall have conducted at least six of these retreats: two here at Manresa-on-Severn, four others in California, Michigan, New York, and Florida. Twenty more are being negotiated. The reactions to the project and to the retreats have been highly enthusiastic; it seems clear to ever so many, laity and ordained, that here is an idea whose time has come. Nor are the retreats limited to ordained priests; we have gradually incorporated permanent deacons, religious, laymen and laywomen engaged in preaching.

The project is vast indeed; I am not aware of anything similar in scope in our country's history. But the situation, social and homiletic, is little short of desperate, and desperate situations call for imaginative measures. As wise Gamaliel put it to his fellows in the council, "If it is of God," it will not fail (Acts 5:39). So be it.[14]

Walter J. Burghardt, S.J.
July 31, 1992

from
Advent
to
Easter

1
WHEN CHRIST MEETS CHRIST
First Sunday of Advent (B)

- Isaiah 63:16–17, 19; 64:2–7
- 1 Corinthians 1:3–9
- Mark 13:33–37

Good friends: This is my 50th Advent as a priest. My experience of Advent? Usually these four weeks have been exciting. But not for the best of reasons. Students are harassed by semester exams; business folk are badgered by end-of-year inventories; parents spend hours on what to give and to whom; last-minute shopping is a must; and all the while our ears are blasted by "Jingle Bells," "White Christmas," and "Rudolph the Red-Nose Reindeer." It does complicate Christian contemplation. But I refuse to waste homily time on the secularization of Advent. I shall accent the positive, highlight a preparation for Christmas that combines good theology, practical action, and Christian excitement.

To make my case, I shall not focus on the past, Christ's coming in Bethlehem, central as this is to Christmas. Nor shall I focus on the future, Christ's return in glory at a time we know not, important though this is for the full Christian vision. I shall urge you to prepare for Christmas by bringing Christ to life again. I shall say that Advent is rich preparation for Christmas if you can sear into your souls three truths crucial for your Christian living: (1) Christ is alive; (2) Christ is here; (3) Christ wants other Christs.

I

First, Christ is alive. Why a whole point on this? Because all too many Christians do not really believe it. Oh yes, they might have the

15

"notional" knowledge Cardinal Newman distinguished from "real" knowledge. They recite each Sunday, "He is seated at the right hand of the Father," and "He will come to judge the living and the dead." But is he actually more to them than a unique Jew who lived and died in a corner of the world two millennia ago, a shadowy figure who will return Star-Wars-style trailing clouds of glory long after you and I die? Is he more alive than Elvis Presley?

Advent is a fine time to bring Christ to real life. The child who came from Mary's flesh in a stable; the grown man who walked the roads of Palestine teaching and touching, caring and curing; the "criminal" who left this life with nails in his hands and feet—that same person lives. He is alive with the life of God's only Son, alive with the life of a human being who has reached the perfection of humanity, who is everything God wanted the human to be when God fashioned the first man and woman in God's image. Not a statue, not a photo in a frame. A God-man, yes, and therefore difficult to picture; but still a man, vibrant, as real as he was when after his resurrection he appeared to his mother,[1] surprised Mary Magdalene, asked Thomas to put his hands in the place of the nails, prepared breakfast for seven disciples on the shore of the Sea of Tiberias.

I admit, the Christmas crib does well to remind us that the God-man who borrowed our flesh was actually a baby, what someone once called "omnipotence in bonds." But Christmas will be somewhat deceptive if it fails to tell you that Christ is no longer a child, that Bethlehem was a prelude to Calvary and Easter, that the only real Christ at this moment is Christ risen from the dead, Christ more alive than you and I, more alive than Kevin Costner or Donald Trump, Gorbachev or George Bush—yes, more energetic, more electric than Madonna or Roseanne.

II

Second, Christ is here. This Christ who is alive is not just a historical personage like Napoleon, is not a recluse in outer space, is not twiddling his thumbs at the right hand of his Father. He is active, incredibly active, involved in just about every facet of human activity. In various ways he is present even though your eyes do not see him. Concretely how?

1. What we call the Real Presence. When a priest murmurs "This is my body," Christ is present, and his presence is real. Theologians of all stripes have argued endlessly over those four precious Gospel

words, but after the mind has had its say, we had best fall on our knees and sing with theologian Thomas Aquinas:

> Godhead here in hiding, whom I do adore
> Masked by these bare shadows, shape and nothing more,
> See, Lord, at thy service low lies here a heart
> Lost, all lost in wonder at the God thou art.[2]

Godhead here in hiding. . . . Here.

2. For all too long "real presence" was a term limited to the Eucharist. But that can be deceptive. Vatican II has a simple but striking sentence: "[Christ] is present in his Word, since it is he himself who speaks when the holy Scriptures are read in the Church."[3] Sunday after Sunday a lector proclaims, "This is the Word of the Lord." Do you actually believe that? Take today's readings. When Isaiah, speaking for his people, confessed their sin and their hopelessness—"We have all become like one who is unclean. . . . You have hidden your face from us" (Isa 64:6a, 7b)—were your ears open to what God might be saying to you? When Jesus warned, "Watch, for you do not know when the master of the house will come" (Mk 13:35), did you hear him speaking to you? Only if you listen to the Word as the two discouraged disciples listened on the road to Emmaus after the crucifixion will you say to one another, as they did, "Did not our hearts burn within us while he talked to us on the road, while he opened to us the Scriptures?" (Lk 24:32). "While he talked to us. . . ." He does, you know.

3. Christ is here in love. This is not some Jesuit pop artist moaning "love . . . love . . . love." I mean what Jesus promised at the Last Supper, the eve of his dying for us: "If [you] love me, [you] will keep my word, and my Father will love [you], and we will come to [you] and make our home with [you]" (Jn 14:23). If you can murmur sincerely, "Dear Christ, I really do love you," you are a shrine of the Holy Spirit, a living tabernacle housing God as truly as the tabernacle here in Holy Trinity. How know whether you can honestly murmur those three monosyllables, "I love you"? Thumb the Scriptures to discover what he asks of you. Commandments that forbid false gods, robbery and violence, sexual sin and character assassination. Beatitudes that praise the compassionate, the single-minded, those who work to make peace. A hilltop sermon that warns against anger and lustful looks, tells you to pray for those who persecute you, warns you against laying up treasures on earth and judging others, insists that you will not reach God by mouthing "Lord, Lord," but only by doing the will of his Father.

You may indeed fall short of all this, but granted that you are serious about what Christ wants, this is a proof of love. And what corresponds to your love for Christ is Christ's love for you. Not something vague. Christ's love for you is his presence within you.

4. Christ is alive in people. From the newborn baby to the care-worn aged, each was fashioned in the likeness of Christ. Mull over Matthew 25 till you find Christ in the hungry and the thirsty, in the naked and the homeless, on beds of pain and behind bars.

5. Christ is alive in every corner of his creation, in every single work of his creative hand. How is it that 200 billion billion stars (yes, 200 billion billion) can light the universe? Because Christ gives them mass and energy—not once for all, but ceaselessly. How is it that giant sequoias can grow more than 200 feet high? Because Christ continuously gives them life. How is it that the skylark can sing, the panther prowl the earth, the shad ascend the rivers? Because Christ gives them voice that delights, senses sensitive beyond our imagining, instinct we do well to envy. This is not science fiction; this is theology on a realistic "high."

III

My third Advent point: This Christ who is alive, this Christ who is here, wants other Christs. This is not just another pious Christian axiom. This is why the Son of God became like us: to make us like him. But there are obstacles. Not only the sin in our lives; not only the distractions that take us away from Christ; not only the indifference that plagues our religious lives. Right now, in our fair country, we have a fresh crisis that makes for an agonizing Advent.

The villain is our economic slump. In consequence, *Time* magazine claims in its current issue, "more and more Americans find themselves clinically depressed." Where is business booming? In psychiatric referrals. Where are sales brisk? In drugstores: Tagamet (for ulcers), Prozac (for depression), Halcion (for insomnia). The slump threatens to divide our people more than ever because the gap between the haves and the have-nots is widening. Six decades ago it was different. A depression indeed, but in the 30s "everyone was in the same boat"; today's "problems affect people so unevenly that they don't pull together." Some turn to alcohol, some to chocolate bars; for "When things are lousy anyway [says a Columbia University psychiatrist], "who cares about cholesterol?"[4] In this context racial crimes are rising; white males are vying for jobs they never had to compete for. "People who have lost their jobs experience anger, denial and a need to grieve, just as they would if they had lost a loved one."[5] Link economic anxiety to fear of war in the Middle East, on Muslim turf, and we have an Advent not experienced since Vietnam, a Christmas without promise of peace.

My sisters and brothers in Christ: You and I do not live on islands of isolation. All around me I find people who are afraid, depressed. And yes, I confess it: I too am afraid. Not yet depressed, but frighteningly fearful. Therefore what? Advent in these circumstances calls for Christians who care, who are open to the hurts of others even when they themselves are hurting, open to the fears of others even though they themselves are afraid. It calls for other Christs. I mean Christians who are genuine disciples of the Jesus who thought only of others despite his own paralyzing pain—prayed forgiveness on the barbarians who had crucified him, promised paradise to a repentant robber, willed his own mother to his beloved disciple John. All from a cross.

No, this Advent cannot be "business as usual." Not even religion as usual. Definitely not Catholicism as usual. Each of us has three and a half weeks to discover at least one Christ who is afraid, one Christ who is depressed, one Christ who wonders why God has forsaken him. No need to imitate the Cynic Diogenes, moving about at midday with a lighted lantern in search of an honest man. The fearful Christ, the depressed Christ may be so close we do not see him or her—in your workplace, on your dorm floor, within your family, in my Jesuit community. What will you say, what do, when you discover the depressed, when you find the frightened? I don't know; I have no push-button solution. This I do know: The Christ who is alive, the Christ who is here, the Christ who is in you, will speak through you.

But, reverend sir, we didn't expect so gloomy an Advent. In response, I promise you a paradox. You will rarely experience a more profound joy than when your own hurt gives fresh courage to a crucified Christ. It's not at all surprising. That is what happens when Christ meets Christ.

Holy Trinity Church
Washington, D.C.
December 2, 1990

2
THERE WILL BE SIGNS. . . .
First Sunday of Advent (C)

- Jeremiah 33:14–16
- 1 Thessalonians 3:12–4:2
- Luke 21:25–28, 34–36

This is the *"good* news" of our Lord Jesus Christ? "Distress among nations"? "People will stop breathing out of fear and foreboding"? "The forces of heaven will be shaken loose"? (Lk 21:25–26). On this note we begin preparing for Christmas? If the Gospel that opens Advent did not puzzle you, you weren't really listening. This is what a dear black friend of mine used to call "deep stuff." Not only deep, but complex, complicated. To unpack the Gospel, suppose we focus on three realities: (1) Luke's Jesus; (2) today's Jesus; (3) you and me.[1]

I

First, Luke's Jesus. Whenever you snip seven verses from a Gospel chapter, you've lost the context. It's like making sense of *Hamlet* from his charge to Ophelia, "Get thee to a nunnery."[2] Or isolating the single sentence of a homily that began, "In the 200 years of this parish the Jesuit Fathers have had but one idea." Today's Gospel is part and parcel of a whole chapter in Luke. That chapter deals with two weighty events: the end of Jerusalem and the end of the world. It is not at all clear that Jesus delivered this discourse at one sitting; it is more probable that Luke has put together in a single discourse sayings Jesus uttered at different times.

No matter. What Advent's opening liturgy highlights is a fascinating wedding of two "days": tomorrow and today. Tomorrow has two acts: one soon, the other in the distance. Luke's Jesus has just foretold the "end" of Jerusalem. Jerusalem's Jews "will fall by the edge of the

20

sword [or] be carried off captive" and scattered among the nations; the city itself "will be trampled upon by pagans" (v. 24). Now he moves on to another "end," "what is coming upon the world," "the Son of Man coming on a cloud with power and great glory" (vv. 26–27). Luke, unlike a good number of Christians, did not see this happening soon, right after the destruction of Jerusalem. He put a goodly distance between the two acts.

Then, if you recall, Jesus shifts the stress from tomorrow to today. How do you prepare for the Lord's coming? "Be on your guard!" (v. 34). Don't let anything dull your mind, so that you fail to recognize the signs that announce his coming. Jesus mentions several ways our sensibilities can be dulled: "indulgence and drunkenness and worldly cares" (v. 34); concretely, a grade-A hangover and excessive anxiety over the worries of life. Not that these exhaust the obstacles; but in point of fact Jesus and/or Luke apparently found them strikingly present in their communities.

II

Luke's Jesus is a lead-in to my second focus: today's Jesus. Luke's Jesus spoke of "signs" that would herald the coming of Christ "with power and great glory" (Lk 21:27). Let's move on to our own "signs of the times." What does that phrase mean, "signs of the times"? I mean "the main characteristics and events, including secular ones, of each age and place, which reveal the actions and will of God in history, and in peoples."[3] Now different people see different signs. Much depends on who you are, where you are, your background, your interests, your hurts, your way of reading Scripture. Here, with you, I stress one significant characteristic of our age explicitly exploited by the Second Vatican Council: the "split between the faith which many profess and their daily lives." That split, the Council declared,

> deserves to be counted among the more serious errors of our age. Long since, in the Old Testament, the prophets struggled strenuously against this scandal; and far more so did Jesus Christ himself in the New Testament threaten it with heavy punishments.[4]

Now that split is rarely proclaimed more thunderously than in the way Christians fall under the challenge hurled in the First Letter of John: "If anyone has the world's goods and sees his brother [or sister] in need, yet closes his heart against him [or her], how does God's love abide in him?" (1 Jn 3:17). It is simply a concrete application of what Jesus called the "second great commandment": You shall love your sisters and brothers—every human being—at least as much as you love yourself (cf. Mt 22:39). The Lord demanded much the same of Israel, demanded that Israelites love not only fellow Israelites but the stranger as well: "You shall love [them] as you love yourself" (Lev 19:18, 34).

For Christians and Jews, I suggest strongly, our most significant signs (not the only ones) have to do with justice. Not simply ethical justice: giving to each man and woman what they deserve because they have rights which can be proven by philosophy or have been written into law. Ethical justice is indeed important: Simply as a human person, I must respect the rights of others. But for a Christian that is only a beginning. The justice of which Scripture speaks—the Old Testament prophets and the Gospels—makes a stronger demand, a richer demand. When Micah thundered, "What does the Lord require of you but to act justly, love steadfastly?" (Mic 6:8), what did he have in mind?

The just man, the just woman, have a covenant with God, a pact with their Lord. This covenant demands that we treat other humans as *God* wants them treated, as our brothers and sisters, as images of God. The Jews were to father the fatherless and feed the stranger, not because the orphan and the outsider deserved it, but because this was the way *God* had acted with *them*. A text in Deuteronomy is telling: "Love the sojourner [the stranger, the resident alien], for you were sojourners [strangers] in the land of Egypt" (Deut 10:19). Their justice was to image not the justice of man and woman, but the justice of God, was to be an expression of love. Not to execute justice was not to worship God.

This is the tradition that sparked the ministry of Jesus. Take Jesus' proclamation of his mission in the synagogue at Nazareth: "The Spirit of the Lord is upon me, because [the Spirit] has anointed me to preach good news to the poor, to proclaim release to the captives, to set at liberty the oppressed" (Lk 4:18; Isa 61:1–2).

But to a dismaying degree we are not doing so. The issues are discouragingly many—AIDS and sexual abuse, inferior education and inaccessible healthcare, poverty and ecology, coke and crack, racism and women's issues, and so on into the night. But, with Christmas and the Christ Child close at hand once again, a sign of the times that agonizes me is America's children. In a 1990 message to the World

Summit for Children, John Paul II struck us squarely between the eyes: ". . . in the Christian view, our treatment of children becomes a measure of our fidelity to the Lord himself."[5]

And yet, each day in our fair land 110 babies die before their first birthday; each day nine children die from guns; each day almost 2000 teen-agers drop out of school. Among industrial nations the United States ranks 19th in keeping babies alive, 28th if you look only at black-infant mortality. In 1990 13 million children lived below the poverty line. Half of all divorced fathers never see their children; two thirds fail to pay child support.[6] And if you cast your eyes beyond our shores, do you know how many children are likely to die in this decade alone, most from diseases we know how to prevent? 150 million. One hundred and fifty . . . million!

Each of these children is the Christ Child. Not indeed physically, but in a sense deeper still. Each is a human shaped of love by a creator God, for whom the Son of God died of love on a bloody cross. Each is one of the innocents over whom Rachel wept, refused to be comforted "because they are not" (Jer 31:15; Mt 2:18). Oh yes, you can argue, debate, complain, rage: Why does God allow what God can prevent? But while we are struggling with that question, with the problem of evil, we have a more pressing problem: Why do *we* allow what *we* can prevent? Not everything—an earthquake in Guatemala, a landslide in the Philippines, brother bloodying brother in Yugoslavia. But so much, so very much.

Luke's Jesus rages against "dissipation," against literal "drunkenness" (Lk 21:34), Christians of his time soused out of their socks. But implicit in this is a broader warning to disciples of Christ: Don't get so intoxicated by the attractions of this world that your mind is dulled and you cannot read the signs of the times. Be aware with the eyes of the spirit, so that you can see Christ however he comes— Christ riding high on the clouds of heaven at the end of time, Christ crossing your way each day.

III

This summons up my third point: you and me. What intoxications can blur our vision? Their name is legion. Still, experts highlight today a big word: consumerism. In simple language, all too many Americans are bitten by the consumer bug: We like it, we buy it; we no longer like it, we throw it away. What does it do to others? We overconsume and someone does not have enough—all too often the utterly dependent, our children.

Simply from my own experience—not from irrefutable statistics —I suggest that few of us who live fairly comfortably have nothing to confess in this regard. What does it do to us? John Paul II put it bluntly: It makes us slaves, "slaves of 'possession' and of immediate gratification—no other horizon than multiplying or continually re-placing what we already own with what is better."[7] It is the cult of "having"—not evil in itself, evil only if having does not serve "being," does not serve caring. Only if Imelda Marcos' 3000 pairs of shoes never warm a bare foot other than her own, if a youngster is ready to kill for a Reebok, if I never listen to Christ chiding me: "I was hungry, and you ordered reindeer with lingenberry sauce. I was thirsty, and you hoisted your fifth Bud Lite. I was naked, and you bought the best in clergy gray. I was a beggar, and you passed me by like a leper. I was sick in a lonely hospital, and you were 'overcommitted.' I was in prison, and you debated capital punishment."

The Christ of the first Christmas is no longer a child; he has grown up; he has risen from the dead. But his place is taken, the manger is filled, by other Christs. What will I see when I kneel before the Christmas crib? It is no longer a cherubic little Christ that is enfolded in Mary's warm arms. It is an infant born with AIDS; a child with Down's syndrome who will never really grow up; a wee one rid-dled with bullets from a passing car; a black Christ abandoned by her father; a brown Christ bloated from hunger, eyes empty of hope. Perhaps the crib is empty, because a fetus was not allowed to reach it.

Am I spoiling your Christmas? Only if Christmas is a refuge from reality. Only if Advent casts off its violet hue, its summons to repent, to change our way of looking at people and things. Only if you and I ceaselessly see the Baptist's whiplash hurled exclusively at first-century Jews, not at 20th-century Christians: "You brood of vipers! Who has warned you to flee from the wrath that is coming? Produce fruits worthy of repentance" (Lk 3:7–8)—that is, show by your ac-tions, by your conduct, that new life, God's life, has sprung up in you. Only if you fail to realize that the most Christian of gifts, the most human of gifts, is to bring hope into the eyes of the hopeless. There is no joy comparable to that.

After all, isn't this why the Son of God took our flesh, shivered in Mary's arms, had no place whereon to rest his head? He took what is ours, our flesh and blood, only to give us what is his, a share in his

Godlife. Advent is a strong reminder, in the rhetoric of the Baptist, that Christmas calls for conversion, a fresh turning to God not simply from the age-old litany of sins that stamp us as children of Eve and Adam, but from the blindness and unawareness that keep us from seeing the image of God in each human crucified.

Good friends and former colleagues: A sympathetic Jew once told us Christians gently but firmly:

> We [Jews] must . . . question, in the light of the Bible, whether the message of the Old Testament which the New Testament claims has been fulfilled, has in fact been fulfilled in history, in the history lived and suffered by us and our ancestors. And here, my dear Christian readers, we give a negative reply. We can see no kingdom and no peace and no redemption.[8]

Now my theology can counter such absolutes with defensible distinctions. The Church on earth is not identical with the full-fledged kingdom; peace is not primarily the absence of war but "God's love poured into our hearts through the Holy Spirit who has been given to us" (Rom 5:5); redemption is an ongoing process only initiated, not consummated, on Calvary. Still, the agonies that assail crucified hearts across the world are not allayed by distinctions. When the Jew, the Muslim, the atheist, the agnostic look at us, is their instinctive reaction "See how these Christians love one another—see how they love us"?

Which brings me back to the children—in Iraq, in the Sudan, in Yugoslavia, in Cambodia, on our city streets. Where is the kingdom, where the peace, where the redemption for the 150 million children who will perish needlessly this decade? Frankly, I don't know. But I do know that the Advents from 1991 to 2000 will hardly prove a prelude to Christmas unless we initiate a massive effort to "save the children." If the numbers stagger you, dispirit you, remember Mother Teresa descending on D.C. some years ago. Announcing her intention to feed the District's hungry and house its homeless, she was confronted by a cynical politician: "Mother Teresa, there are thousands of these! How are you going to feed and house thousands?" Her answer was classic Teresa: "One by one."

Rarely has the Gospel injunction of Jesus been more appropriate for you and me: "Go and do likewise." Is it sheer fantasy, "off the wall," to take as our patron, our example, the Bethlehem Jew who gave a segment of his stable to the first of countless Christs, and unwittingly helped initiate a kingdom not of this world, a peace that passes understanding, and our redemption from sin and Satan and, especially, self?

Dahlgren Chapel
Georgetown University
Washington, D.C.
December 2, 1991

3

TO *US* A CHILD IS BORN?
Feast of the Epiphany (B)

- Isaiah 60:1–6
- Ephesians 3:2–3, 5–6
- Matthew 2:1–12

A hidden danger lurks in today's readings. We have grown so familiar with three wise men guided by a star to Bethlehem's stable that we pass lightly over the first two readings. Granted, for an exceptional feast like Epiphany Rome insists on three passages from Scripture. And so we suffer through seven verses from Isaiah, verses utterly out of context, not knowing why the prophet tells Jerusalem to "shine," to "glow," in what sense Jerusalem's "light has come" and "the glory of the Lord has risen upon" the center of Jewish religion. Is this a prophecy about Christ? We do a bit better with St. Paul, but we still wonder what it means for Christians to be "coheirs" with the Jews. Thank God, the Gospel returns us to the Christmas crib, to three "kings" bent low in adoration.

Today, good friends, to forget Isaiah would be a disservice to you.[1] If you are to grasp why, I must dwell on three characters or sets of characters: (1) the Old Testament prophet; (2) Christ and the three strangers from the East; (3) you and me.

I

First, the prophet. The passage from Isaiah introduces poems on the glory of Jerusalem, the glory of God's people. Glory in what sense? Salvation has come to the Jewish people. I mean, the exile of the Jews in Babylon is over. This people of God's predilection, once terribly discouraged, depressed, almost despairing of ever casting off their

27

chains—this people whose holy city lay in ruins, whose temple had been destroyed, whose power was emasculated—light has now come to them and the glory of the Lord has been revealed. Jerusalem welcomes her children home; the dispersed of Israel have returned to risen Zion. The prophet sees Jerusalem as the single point of light in a world flooded with darkness. Not only will God reign in a sacred city regenerated by God's power, illuminated by God's presence. The nations will come to Jerusalem, not simply to be taught in the temple but to reshape the city; Arabia's riches will be brought by caravan; tribes will come from the East. The new Jerusalem will surpass Solomon's city in beauty and tranquility.

But what you did *not* hear today was the gloom before the glory.[2] Just before the passage read to you, the prophet had summoned the people to a national repentance. Why? Because lies, injustice, violence, and slaughter of the innocent had added up to a denial of God, so much so that the prophet could proclaim:

> Your iniquities have made a separation
>   between you and your God,
> and your sins have hid His face from you
>   so that He does not hear.
>
> (Isa 59:2)

What shall we make of Isaiah 60? How ought we to react? Before all else, a grateful recognition that Jewish life and worship, from the faith of Abraham through ceaseless diasporas to the unique Holocaust, have been and continue to be "a light for revelation to [us] Gentiles" (cf. Lk 2:32). Plus a realization that, however dear to God, God's people are ceaselessly in need of repentance. The Jewish experience of gloom and glory should impress on us a twin truth: The Lord God continues to "come to Zion as Redeemer" (Isa 59:20), but redemption, salvation, involves a change of heart, a conversion, a repentant people.

II

Isaiah brings me to Christ and the three strangers from the East. You see, for Christians Isaiah's "Arise! Glow!" speaks to a still wider world than Jerusalem. Not in its literal sense: I dare not read the New Testament into the Old. Rather because in the story of salvation

Isaiah's resounding poem must be supplemented by the early Christian hymn quoted by St. Paul to the Christians of Ephesus:

> "Awake, O sleeper, and arise from the dead,
>   and Christ shall give you light."
>
> (Eph 5:14)

"Christ shall give you light." For the Christian, God's glory is perfectly present in him who, the Letter to the Hebrews declares, "reflects the glory of God" (Heb 1:3). The evangelist John was convinced that it was Jesus' glory Isaiah saw, of him Isaiah spoke (Jn 12:41). Jesus not only radiates this glory in his risen state: transcendent purity, holiness, light, power, life. It energized his matchless miracles on earth, pervaded even his passion, which is the cross transfigured, Calvary revealing the mystery of the divine "I AM."

Christianity is constructed on a conviction enshrined in the Prologue of John's Gospel: "The true light that enlightens every man and woman was coming into the world. . . . And the Word became flesh and dwelt among us, full of grace and truth; we have beheld his glory, glory as of the only Son from the Father" (Jn 1:9, 14). *Every* man and woman. Our Christmas is not a private birthday party; it is an epiphany, a manifestation, a revelation that overleaps the boundaries of Bethlehem. It is "joy to *the world*."

That is why the Church this day borrows Isaiah's vision of worldwide belief, the colorful picture he drew of people from the Arabian peninsula associated with Abraham and the earliest ancestors, and welcomes it into her liturgy for the Epiphany, touches it to Jesus, God's self-revealing to the world:

> A multitude of camels shall cover you,
>   the young camels of Midian and Ephah;
>   all those from Sheba shall come.
> They shall bring gold and frankincense,
>   and shall proclaim the praise of the Lord.
>
> (Isa 60:6)

That is why Epiphany is of such crucial importance. The three strangers from the East—in all probability, astrologers—do not *add* anything to the basic Christmas story. But they do serve to *remind* us of something the "little town of Bethlehem" might possibly obscure. Jesus was indeed born of a Jewish maiden; he did indeed come first to "the house of Israel"; but it is "every man and woman" he came to enlighten, to live for and die for and rise for.

III

Every man and woman. This summons up my third point: you and me. It brings us from Babylon and Bethlehem to today's world. Yes, Epiphany celebrates God manifesting, revealing Godself to the world in Christ. But how did God manifest Godself, reveal Godself in Christ? As a child. Whom did the astrologers from the East adore on their knees? A child. The Son of God was born as we are, came from a mother's body, became what each of us grownups once was. That is basically why Christmas is so special for children, why we delight in toys for children, in Santa Claus with a child on each knee, in baby Jesus clothed like a king, in the Vienna Boys Choir, in pyjama-clad children opening gifts around a tree, children on sleighs, children enveloped in love.

But the Christ child raises a problem. Pope John Paul II put it bluntly: ". . . in the Christian view, our treatment of children becomes a measure of our fidelity to the Lord himself,"[3] the Lord who asserted, "Whoever receives one such child in my name receives me" (Mt 18:5). For all too many of the world's children, there is "no room in the inn" (cf. Lk 2:7). In the next 60 seconds 27 children under five will die in developing countries—almost 40,000 each day. And they will die mostly from diseases we know how to prevent—measles, diarrhea, respiratory infections. In this decade, the 90s, at present rates, do you know how many children will die needlessly? 150 million. The United Nations Children's Fund (UNICEF) phrased the pertinent moral principle with devastating clarity:

> . . . whether a child survives or not, whether a child is well-nourished or not, whether a child is immunized or not, whether a child has a school to go to or not, should not have to depend on whether interest rates rise or fall, on whether commodity prices go up or down, on whether a particular political party is in power, on whether the economy has been well managed or not, on whether a country is at war or not, or on any other trough or crest in the endless and inevitable undulations [of] political and economic life in the modern nation state.[4]

More tragically for you and me, we need not fly to Ethiopia, to Cambodia, to the sub-Sahara to find "no room in the inn" for children. If you take the latest available data in six categories—infant mortality, child abuse, children in poverty, teen-age suicide, teen-age drug abuse, and high-school dropouts—in our own land of power and prosperity their social well-being reached a new low in 1987, "the worst year for children in two decades."[5]

We treat them like statistics, these children for whom the Child was born, for whom he bled. In a recent Gallup survey, 55% of those questioned were satisfied with the way things are going in the United States, 83% were content with the way things are going in their own lives. While minds are blunted and bodies stunted, most Americans can eat and drink, play and pray, as if "God's in His heaven and all's right with the world." We forget what the Second Vatican Council saw so clearly: "The future of humanity lies in the hands of those who are strong enough to provide coming generations with reasons for living and hoping"[6]—our hands.

Have I forgotten Isaiah, forgotten the adoring Magi? Not at all. The prophet continues to protest that "justice is far from us" (Isa 59:9). He might even suggest that we "walk in gloom" as long as "25 percent of America's children under six live in poverty," as long as hundreds are born with AIDS or addicted to cocaine or crack, as long as on our own streets "a child is injured or killed by a gun every 36 minutes."[7] There is no point in offering the Christ child "gold and frankincense and myrrh" (Mt. 2:11) if D.C.'s children for whom he was born are hollow-eyed from hunger, if black children have to beg for the crumbs that fall from white tables. Before we can bask in God's glory, we must scatter some of the gloom that envelops our world, repent of the injustice to children that challenges our life style, take as spoken to us the ageless question Yahweh addressed through Isaiah to the Jews:

> Is not this the fast that I choose:
>   to loose the bonds of wickedness,
>   to undo the thongs of the yoke,
> to let the oppressed go free,
>   and to break every yoke?
> Is it not to share your bread with the hungry,
>   and bring the homeless poor into your
>   house;
> when you see the naked, to cover him,
>   and not to hide yourself from your own
>   flesh?
> Then shall your light break forth like the dawn,
>   and your healing shall spring forth speedily;
> your righteousness shall go before you,
>   the glory of the Lord shall be your rear
>   guard.

> Then you shall call, and the Lord will answer;
> you shall cry, and He will say, Here I am.
>
> (Isa 58:6–9)

Only if we love our sisters and brothers at least as much as we love ourselves can our native gloom be transfigured into graced glory. Only then can we really say that in Christ God has indeed manifested Godself to the *world*, to *us*. Reach out to just one of these little ones, and you can sing with sincerity, "Unto *us* a child is born." The Christ child.

St. Patrick's Church
Washington, D.C.
January 6, 1991

4
LOVE, GIVE, LIVE
Fourth Sunday of Lent (B)

- 2 Chronicles 36:14–17, 19–23
- Ephesians 2:4–10
- John 3:14–21

We humans are strange creatures. There is so much we marvel at: a rocket ship on the road to Mars; Michael Jordan soaring to the basket from the foul stripe; our military intercepting Scud missiles in the Middle East; Pavarotti reaching a high C with the greatest of ease; a heart transplant; the softest diaper in history.

What amazes me is how we Catholics can cease to marvel at, can take for granted, the most marvelous event ever to shake human history. It was summed up in the Gospel just proclaimed to you: "God so loved the world that He gave His only Son, that whoever believes in him should not perish but have eternal life" (Jn 3:16). Three words in that sentence are crucial: love, give, life. God loved . . . so God gave . . . that we might live. Each word is mystery-laden, but the mystery has been somewhat unveiled. A word on each word.

I

First, "God so loved the world." It's awesome. Many of us—perhaps most of us—have a fearsome idea of God. For whatever reason —childhood experience, grade-school religion, Jesuit homilist— many a Catholic sees God only as Judge. I mean the God who "answered [Moses] in thunder" (Exod 19:19). The God who refused to let Moses enter the Promised Land "because you broke faith with me" (Deut 32:51). The God who punished David's offspring for David's adultery: "The child that is born to you shall die" (2 Sam 12:14). The God who declared to a faithless people:

33

> I sent among you a pestilence after the manner of Egypt;
> I slew your young men with the sword;
> I carried away your horses;
> and I made the stench of your camp
> go up into your nostrils;
> yet you did not return to me.
>
> (Amos 4:10)

The God who threatened, "Behold, the day comes, burning like an oven, when all the arrogant and all evildoers will be stubble; the day comes that shall burn them up, . . . so that it will leave them neither root nor branch" (Mal 4:1). In consequence, we grow up to see in the Old Testament a pitiless God, a God waiting to pounce on the sinner, a God of sheer justice.

A caricature, a travesty. It fails to recognize the God who heard Israel's cry of despair, "The Lord has forsaken me, my Lord has forgotten me," and responded in unforgettable phrases that spell love:

> Can a woman forget her sucking child,
> that she should have no compassion
> on the son of her womb?
> Even these may forget,
> yet I will not forget you.
> Behold, I have graven you on the palms of my hands.
>
> (Isa 49:14–16a)

This is the God of whom the Psalmist sings:

> The Lord is merciful and gracious,
> slow to anger and abounding in steadfast love. . . .
> He does not deal with us according to our sins,
> nor requite us according to our iniquities.
> For as the heavens are high above the earth,
> so great is His steadfast love toward those who fear Him;
> as far as the east is from the west,
> so far does He remove our transgressions from us. . . .
> For He knows our frame;
> He remembers that we are dust.
>
> (Ps 103:8–14)

This is the same God to whom the New Testament bears witness from beginning to end, the God of whom the First Letter of John declares: "Beloved, let us love one another; for love is of God, and he who loves is born of God and knows God. He who does not love does not know

God; for *God is love*. . . . In this is love, not that we loved God but that God loved us . . ." (1 Jn 4:7–10).

II

God . . . is . . . love. You can have all sorts of philosophical "fun and games" with that three-syllable sentence. Of no one else can you say, "He or she is love." You can be uniquely loving and lovable, love everybody from the depths of your heart, always, everywhere, with no respect of persons; and still we can never say of you, "You are love." You're *a* love, perhaps; but you *are* love? Sorry. Only God exhausts the total meaning of love.

But that is so abstract. "Little children," the First Letter of John urges us, "let us not love in word or speech but in deed and in truth" (1 Jn 3:18). It is Ignatius Loyola's insistence in his Contemplation for Learning to Love Like God: "Love ought to manifest itself in deeds rather than in words." All of you have at least heard of, if not met, the smoothie whose rhetoric or blarney can charm you out of your wallet, out of your virginity. I cannot remember my immigrant father ever saying to my brother and me, "I love you"; but his whole life of labor for us thundered more loudly than syllables.

And so it is with God. The God who *is* love gave us a gift. Not a lifeless thing, silver or gold; a person. Not an angel; not another patriarch like Abraham, another prophet like Jeremiah. God gave us God's only Son. Sweat, if you can, to make that come alive for you, understandable, believable. God gave you and me the very Son of God.

Gave? How paltry a monosyllable! The gift was a baby shivering in straw—at once the Son of the Most High and the child of a Jewish teen-ager. The gift was an adolescent who called God his Father and Mary his mother, did everything an all-powerful Father in heaven commanded and a carpenter father on earth demanded. The gift was a man of 30 who scuffed the dust of Palestine from one end to the other because "The Spirit of the Lord is upon me: He has anointed me to preach good news to the poor, has sent me to proclaim release to the captives and . . . sight to the blind, to set at liberty the oppressed" (Lk 4:18). The gift was a God-man sold for silver by one of his intimate friends, delivered to his enemies by a cowardly Roman, whipped like a dog, crowned with thorns, pinned to twin beams of wood, and left to die between two criminals. The gift was a Christ raised from the rock by the power of God.

A gift—the whole package. A gift because we had no claim on Christ, did not deserve him. A gift because he was born for you and me, lived for you and me, died and rose for you and me—as if you and I were the only men and women in the world.

III

For you and me. This leads into my third point. The gift, Jesus, is not something out there. Why did God give us Jesus? Jesus made it quite clear: "I came that they may have life, and have it abundantly" (Jn 10:10b). Life. Focus on that word—one of the most important four-letter words you'll ever experience. This is not pretty poetry. This, as an ancient TV show used to declare, "This is your life." What do I mean?

There are different levels to being alive. A squalling, teething baby is alive; mothers will swear to it. Patrick Ewing is alive; less-gifted centers deny it at their peril. So too Madonna and Kevin Costner, George Burns and George Bush, even Saddam Hussein. To be alive on a sheerly human level is to think and be free, to have purpose and passion. To that extent all of you are reasonably alive.

But in giving us Christ, God had much more life in mind than book knowledge or the Dow Jones, foaming mugs of Bud Light and Saturday Night Live. You heard it in St. Paul's upbeat proclamation to the Christians of Ephesus, capital of the Roman province of Asia:

> God, who is rich in mercy, out of the great love with which He loved us, even when we were dead through our trespasses, made us alive together with Christ . . . and raised us up with him. . . . For by grace you have been saved through faith; and this is not your own doing, it is the gift of God. . . . For we are [God's] workmanship, created in Christ Jesus for good works. . . .
>
> (Eph 2:4–10)

Alive with Christ? What can that mean in plain English? Paul put it simply yet profoundly: You are "a new creation" (2 Cor 5:17). You are radically different from what you would have been if Christ had not come, had not carried a cross to Calvary. But precisely how? You know what it means, what it feels like, to be humanly alive. You can think, shape an idea, argue a point, listen to Mozart or Michael Jackson. You can do things: work and play, walk and sing, love and laugh, "pump iron" or sway to aerobics.

To be alive with Christ means that in the power of his passion you can think and act, live and love, more fantastically than in your wildest grass-induced dreams. You can believe what passes belief: accept God's word for the incredible Creed you repeat so facilely each Sunday. You can hope for what seems hopeless: confidently expect that God will be with you wherever you are in this life, with you days without end in the next. You can love as you've never loved before, as Christ has loved you: love without looking for what you can get out of it, love those you don't like, love the outcasts of your world, love when it costs you, even unto crucifixion.

All this you *can* do in the power of the passion. But not wearing out the seat of your slacks waiting for God or Godot. God is here, the risen Christ is here: because you have gathered together in Jesus' name; when you cry "This is the word of the Lord"; when the celebrant murmurs in Christ's person, "This is my body which will be given for you"; when you cradle in your hands or on your tongue not bare bread but a living Lord. Your reaction? A Lent alive, your passionate participation in the passion of Christ. I mean a realistic Lent, a Lent for our season. The rugged individualism sociologist Robert Bellah finds resurgent in our culture calls for men and women who repent of their smallness, fast from their selfishness, abstain from isolation.

Good friends: The passion of Christ did not end on the first Good Friday. The passion of Christ surrounds you, chokes you: every human wasted in the womb; every third black child languishing below the poverty line; the thousands of women savaged by men vowed to love and honor; the homeless on your streets rummaging for food in garbage cans; the racism that lurks just below our civilized surface. The death that envelops us, from the apartheid of South Africa through the bloody sands of Kuwait to our barricaded cities, lays a heavy demand on us who share a risen life given us freely from a cross.

You and I have been graced indeed, gifted by God beyond our deserving. But, as Protestant martyr Dietrich Bonhoeffer saw in World War II, grace that comes cheap, grace that keeps us ever so comfortable, will never redeem this sin-scarred earth. Only costly grace can do that; only men and women like yourselves who find in this Eucharist the power to repeat in their own persons, "This is *my* body . . . given for you." Given for Christ, given for the crucified images of Christ. It's a great way to come alive . . . alive in Christ.

University of Scranton
Scranton, Pa.
March 10, 1991

5
UNLESS YOU SEE SIGNS
AND WONDERS. . . .
Fourth Week of Lent, Monday (B)

- Isaiah 65:17–21
- John 4:43–54

"Unless you see signs and wonders you will not believe" (Jn 4:48). The rebuke of Jesus[1] poses a problem; the problem calls us back to God's Word; and God's Word leads us into the present, to you and me. With your time at a premium,[2] a brief word on each.

I

First, the problem. What is so terrible about believing because you have seen signs and wonders? Isn't that what happens all the time, all through history, to just about everybody who believes? Didn't doubting apostle Thomas exclaim "My Lord and my God!" when the risen Jesus showed him his pierced hands and side (Jn 20:28)? Doesn't the New Testament tell us that the Lord supported the words of Paul and Barnabas by "granting signs and wonders to be done by their hands" (Acts 14:3)? Didn't Peter tell the people of Israel about "Jesus of Nazareth, a man attested to you by God with mighty works and wonders and signs which God did through him" (Acts 2:22)? Of those many signs and wonders, recall simply the water changed to wine during the marriage feast at Cana: "This, the first of his signs, Jesus did at Cana in Galilee, and manifested his glory; and his disciples believed in him" (Jn 2:11).

In our own culture, what is it that makes believers out of us? If you can credit the commercials, isn't it signs and wonders? A Bud that is the lightest of them all, "clean, crisp, and cold"; Pearl Drops that would draw the opposite sex like flies; a credit card so lifesaving that you dare not "leave home without it"; the softest diaper in history. How do you accept anything on the say-so of another without supporting signs? No, I'm afraid we are so constituted that the sheer word of another is not enough. We're all doubting Thomases: "Unless I see in his hands the print of the nails, and place my finger in the mark of the nails, and place my hand in his side, I will not believe" (Jn 20:25). What is so reprehensible in that? Without it, how do you separate the honest guys and dolls from the charlatans, the quacks?

II

The problem forces us back to Scripture.[3] Characteristic of the evangelist John is sign as miracle. What do these miraculous signs have to do with faith, with believing? John suggests four ways in which men and women actually reacted to Jesus' signs, to his miracles.

First, some refused to see the signs with any faith, refused to come to the light, were wilfully, deliberately, blamably blind. Such was the high priest Caiaphas. He knew from the Pharisees that Jesus was performing "many signs" (Jn 11:47), and still he counseled the Pharisees, "It is expedient for you that one man should die for the people, and that the whole nation should not perish" (v. 50). Such folk, Jesus declared, "have no excuse for their sin" (15:22).

Second, some seeing Jesus' signs and wonders believed in him—but only as a wonder-worker sent by God. With such men and women Jesus was regularly unhappy. But why? Recall Jesus in Jerusalem for a Passover feast. "Many believed in his name, for they could see the signs he was performing; but Jesus did not trust himself to them, because he knew them all. He needed no one to testify about human nature, for he was aware of what was in man's heart" (2:23–25).[4] The point is, it was not enough for Jesus if you were impressed by his miracles as wonders wrought by the power of God; they should be seen as revealing who Jesus is, his oneness with the Father.

Third, some saw the signs for what they actually were, and so came to believe in Jesus, came to recognize who he is, his relation to his Father. Such was the official in today's Gospel. When he found out that the hour his son's fever left him was the hour Jesus had said, "Your son will live," John tells us that the official "himself believed, and all his household" (4:53). Jesus could and did challenge men and women to put faith in his works, to believe in him because of his signs and wonders. About to cry out to a Lazarus dead four days, "Lazarus, come out!," Jesus lifted up his eyes and spoke to his Father: "I thank you because you heard me. Of course, I knew that you always hear me, but I say it because of the crowd standing around, that they may believe that you sent me" (11:43, 41–42).[5]

Fourth, some believed in Jesus without ever having seen his signs and wonders, his miracles. Recall his words to Thomas, "Happy those who have not seen and yet have believed" (20:29). You may speculate through the night, ask if those who saw and believed were inferior to those who believed without seeing; it will get you nowhere. But it does lead us to my third point, to you and me.

III

We are living at a time when we no longer see the human Jesus working miracles. Yes, miracles still take place. You have to be terribly blind to write off Mary's shrine at Lourdes as one grand hallucination. But ever since Jesus returned to his Father, what has largely replaced the miracle in revealing a living Christ is . . . sacrament. Here for us is the supreme sign that should reveal the face of Christ. The faith of the Church today begins with water bathing the brow of an unsuspecting infant. That faith is reinforced when the oil of the Holy Spirit pours strength into youthful flesh and spirit. That faith is reconciled with God and the faithful when the sinner confesses his or her sin. But more than anywhere else your faith has to be nourished by the Eucharist. Here, if anywhere, the Church Catholic comes together, gathers as one.

It did not begin yesterday. It began one enchanted evening when Jesus told his special friends, "Do this in remembrance of me" (Lk 22:20). A remarkable liturgical scholar, Dom Gregory Dix, has described the effect of that command in rapturous phrases:

> Was ever a command so obeyed? For century after century, spreading slowly to every continent and country and among every race on earth, this action has been done, in every conceivable human circumstance, for every conceivable human need from infancy and before it to extreme old age and after it, from the pinnacles of earthly greatness to the refuge of fugitives in the caves and dens of the earth. Men have found no better thing than this to do for kings in their crowning and for criminals going to the scaffold; for armies in triumph or for a bride and bridegroom in a little country church; for the proclamation of a dogma or for a good crop of wheat; for the wisdom of the Parliament of a mighty nation or for a sick old

woman afraid to die; for a schoolboy sitting an examination or for Columbus setting out to discover America; . . . because the Turk was at the gates of Vienna . . . [and] on the beach at Dunkirk; . . . tremulously, by an old monk on the fiftieth anniversary of his vows; furtively, by an exiled bishop who had hewn timber all day in a prison camp near Murmansk; gloriously, for the canonisation of S. Joan of Arc. . . . And best of all, week by week and month by month, on a hundred thousand successive Sundays, faithfully, un-failingly, across all the parishes of christendom, the pastors have done this just to *make* the holy common people of God.[6]

Good friends in Christ: If you would feed your faith, bring mind and body here, and with the simplest of the faith-full sing full-throated to a hidden God as theologian Thomas Aquinas did (I quote the mas-terly version of Gerard Manley Hopkins):

> Godhead here in hiding, whom I do adore
> Masked by these bare shadows, shape and nothing more.
> See, Lord, at thy service low lies here a heart
> Lost, all lost in wonder at the God thou art.[7]

Marywood College
Scranton, Pa.
March 11, 1991

6

WITNESSES TO HIS RESURRECTION
Seventh Sunday of Easter (B)

- Acts 1:15–17, 20–26
- 1 John 4:11–16
- John 17:11–19

Easter, right now, is something of a dead issue. The cherry blossoms have withered, spring break is a memory, the Ultra Slim diet has worked (or it hasn't); even the pollen has grown sluggish. Still, the Easter liturgy carries on. Week by week it reveals aspects of Christian living triggered by the resurrection of Jesus. Several facets we have experienced these six weeks: *joy* in Jesus risen from the rock, "a living *hope*" for our own resurrection (1 Pet 1:3), *belief* in a Jesus alive now, with us now, our good shepherd.

Today a fresh Easter facet focuses our attention. It does so through the three texts proclaimed to you. They speak of a Christian witness, a witness that takes place in love, a love that challenges the world. I want to muse over those three words—witness, love, challenge—in the context of the readings. Its centerpiece is . . . apostles. And so I shall speak of (1) the original apostles, (2) apostles down the ages, (3) apostles here and now.

I

First, the original apostles. The fascinating story we call the Acts of the Apostles, Luke's continuation of his Gospel, begins with Jesus' ascension, his return to the Father with our flesh, the flesh he fixed to a cross for our redemption. The departure of Jesus is followed by a summit meeting: the apostles of course, but surrounded by more than a hundred fellow believers. Peter stands up to announce a neuralgic

42

need. The original Twelve are now the Eleven, for one of the Twelve has proved unfaithful. He has not simply denied Jesus, as Peter did; he has not simply run away, as all save John did. This one has sold his Master for silver, and in despair has hanged himself. It is time to replace him, time to replace . . . Judas.[1]

To qualify, the new apostle had to satisfy several criteria: He had to be a male (sorry about that); he must have "accompanied" the Eleven "during the whole time that the Lord Jesus moved in and out among" them (Acts 1:21); and he must have been "a witness to [Jesus'] resurrection" (v. 22)—not seen him actually rising, but able to say he had seen the risen Jesus, could testify that, yes, he is the very one we knew before Calvary.

The apostle could testify, bear witness. . . . There's the crucial word. Remember what Jesus said to his disciples[2] just before return-ing to his Father: "You shall receive power when the Holy Spirit has come upon you; and you shall be my witnesses in Jerusalem and in all Judea and Samaria and to the end of the earth" (Acts 1:8).

The apostles were to witness in ever so many ways. They were to teach, to baptize, to found communities, to do what Jesus did at the Last Supper. But indispensable to each of these activities was the inner drive, the motivating force, the Christian stimulus. And that was proclaimed to you from the First Letter of John: "If God so loved us [loved us enough to give us God's only Son as expiation for our sins], we also ought to love one another." For "if we love one another, God abides in us and [God's] love is perfected in us" (1 Jn 4:11–12).

And love is indispensable because it is only through love that the task of the apostles could be persuasively accomplished—the purpose Christ had in mind when he sent them out (the basic meaning of "apostle"). Why were they sent? To challenge the world—the world as John understands it in today's Gospel, the world as representing those who have turned away from Jesus, are under the power of Satan. That world has to be proved wrong, has to be conquered.[3]

II

Second, apostles down the ages. If you insist on the criteria Luke sets down, the apostles ceased to exist when the last of those who had moved about Palestine with Jesus died. But elsewhere in the New Testament we find an understanding of apostle we can adapt to the centuries that followed. An apostle is a person who has seen Jesus the Lord and has been commissioned by him to proclaim the Christ-event.[4] Put another way, an apostle is a man or woman who has experienced Jesus and has for mission to proclaim him to others.

By an experience of Jesus I do not mean necessarily a vision, such as, say, St. Margaret Mary had of the Sacred Heart. I mean that a man or woman has encountered God, the living and true God, and in consequence is driven to proclaim God to others. Down the centuries men and women have done this in ever so many different ways, have borne their varied witnessings so as to challenge their world, conquer it through love.

The ways are endless. There is Mary Magdalene, long called in Western Christianity "the apostle to the apostles" because she was sent to the disciples by the risen Jesus himself, to proclaim the standard apostolic announcement of his resurrection, "I have seen the Lord" (Jn 20:17–18).[5] There is teen-age Agnes, done to death under Diocletian for her faith and her chastity. There is Monica, mother of Augustine, preaching Christ to her unfaithful husband "by her character,"[6] winning her son to Christ by her prayers. There is Thomas Aquinas, bearing the witness of his high intelligence and piety in theological tomes and moving verse. There is Thomas More, the "man for all seasons," bearing bloody witness to Christ in the Tower of London, decapitated because he would not give Henry VIII jurisdiction over the Church: "the king's good servant, but God's first." There is the black Dominican Martin de Porres, serving all Peruvians with utter unconcern for color, asking his superior to sell him into slavery if it will help his less fortunate sisters and brothers.

There is the Jewish Carmelite nun, contemplative philosopher Edith Stein, who tried to synthesize Thomas Aquinas with modern thought and died in a gas chamber in Auschwitz. There is short-story writer Flannery O'Connor, dead of lupus at 39, with her mature acceptance of limitation, with her God never far away, quietly loved, with so much Christlife in her frail frame—what I can best describe as grace on crutches. There is Thomas Merton, moving from contemplation to passionate protest—against Vietnam and violence, against pollution, against racial injustice and nuclear war. There is Dorothy Day, who moved from Communism to Christ, from Union Square to Rome; started houses of hospitality that spread across the country, bread lines in Depression days to feed the hungry, clothe the naked, shelter the homeless; walked picket lines, struggled against segregation in Georgia, was jailed for supporting Mexican itinerant workers, squared off against a New York cardinal in defense of cemetery strikers; argued passionately that "the poor do *not* have the Gospel preached to them";[7] lived "with the criminal, the unbalanced, the drunken, the degraded . . . with rats, with vermin, bedbugs, roaches, lice. . . ."[8] There is El Salvador's archbishop, six Jesuits, two laywomen cruelly slain for witnessing to the faith that does justice.

There are the countless unsung Christians who ever since Calvary have preached Christ quietly by their lives. Not only prelates and priests, but the whole vast concourse of the laity, single or married it matters not. And today, Mother's Day, it is singularly appropriate to remember gratefully those apostles whose apostolic task it has been, in imitation of Mary, to give a Christ to the next generation.

III

This leads into my third point: apostles here and now. I said above that an apostle is characterized by two qualifications: An apostle is sent and has seen: sent on mission, seen Jesus.

An apostle is sent—sent on mission. But how and when? Apostles are not created by ordination. It happens very early on. It happens when water flows over your brow. For, as Belgian Cardinal Léon-Joseph Suenens phrased it dramatically in the late 60s, the greatest day in the life of a pope is not his coronation but his baptism, the day of his mission "to live the Christian life in obedience to the gospel."[9] That mission was splendidly proclaimed by the Second Vatican Council:

> The mission of the Church is not only to bring to men and women the message of Christ and his grace, but also to penetrate and perfect the temporal sphere with the spirit of the gospel. . . . It is the laity who must take on the renewal of the temporal order as their own proper function. It is they who . . . must act directly and definitively in the temporal sphere. . . .[10]

This mission complements the council's strong warning, to be scotch-taped to every rectory refrigerator: "Let the laity not imagine that their pastors are always such experts that to every problem which arises, however complex, they can readily supply a concrete solution, or even that such is their mission. . . ."[11]

There is simply no one of you who is not an apostle, who is not sent. You have no choice, save to refuse to be a Christian. A burden, yes; for it forces on you a way of life that is genuinely "out of this world." But even more importantly, a privilege; for it rejects the dreadful, widespread conviction that the laity are passive subjects of an autocratic hierarchy, a priest-ridden society whose task is to shut up and do what you are told.

The reality is, the world's redemption for which the Son of God died is impossible without you. Not just difficult; impossible. Popes may write encyclicals till the cows come home, bishops confirm and ordain and produce pastorals on peace and the economy till the computer's bytes give out, priests offer the Sacrifice of the Mass from the rising of the sun to its setting, theologians compose the most brilliant of treatises; but unless the Word is preached to the billions who know not Christ or know him but do not love him, redemption is in its infancy. And only you can reach out day after day to the Trumps and the slums, to Wall Street and the insider traders, to "L.A. Law" and the imprisoned, to the racist and the enslaved, to the child tormented and the spouse abused, to the raped and the dispossessed, to the homeless and the jobless, to the politician and the demagogue, to the economist and the ecologist, to the Kurds[12] and Bangladesh,[13] yes to the AIDS-afflicted who have somehow become the latest outcasts of American society.

I cannot define any particular role for any of you. That is not my purpose today. I do know, from more than a decade of contact with you, that yours is a singular Catholic community. You are known throughout the District for your openness to the other, to the disadvantaged. What I want to impress on you, if it needs impressing, is that you are not doing social work, good as that can be. You are acting as apostles. You are challenging your world because the Holy Spirit has come upon you, has designated you to carry on the work of Christ, the function he described so eloquently in the synagogue at Nazareth: "The Spirit of the Lord is upon me, for He has anointed me; He has sent me to preach good news to the poor, to proclaim release for prisoners and sight for the blind, to set at liberty those who are oppressed" (Lk 4:18).

The Spirit of the Lord is upon you. You are gifted indeed—gifted with the Gift beyond all others. But, strangely enough, that is not enough. It is not enough to know that you have the Holy Spirit within you. It was philosopher Jacques Maritain who insisted that the height, the acme, the perfection of knowledge is not conceptual—a brilliant idea, an encyclopedia of theology. The perfection of knowledge is experiential: Man/woman *feels* God.

That was what happened to the Twelve at Pentecost. They were "filled with the Holy Spirit" (Acts 2:4). Not just intellectually convinced that God dwelt in them, as Jesus had promised to those who love. No. They felt different; they talked differently; they looked different—so different that people thought they were drunk at 9 a.m. Not out of their minds, bereft of their senses, the kind of irrational "ecstasy" the Church has had to condemn from its infancy. Simply so possessed by the Spirit, so aware of God within them, that not only cold intellect but strong feelings were involved. The Twelve felt God.

Such is the Easter experience, the experience that rivals the encounter of Magdalene at Jesus' tomb. Such was the experience of St. Ignatius Loyola. Even apart from his mystical experiences, Ignatius was convinced that he had encountered the living God. Not visions or voices. Not simply human words describing God. Not images pointing to God. Rather, the true and living God, "nameless and unfathomable, silent and yet near." God was a living, dynamic, ceaseless presence to him. And he was convinced that this experience of grace God refuses to no one.[14] Such is the experience today's apostle needs if you are to challenge a world that, for all the presence of the risen Christ, has much in common with the world Jesus warned against. You must experience the risen Christ, see Jesus.

How realize that experience? I know no better way than to walk with him every day. In your prayer: Let him unfold the Scriptures to you, somewhat as he revealed them to the two discouraged disciples on the road to Emmaus, so that you too can cry out, "Did not our hearts burn within us while he talked to us on the road, while he opened to us the Scriptures?" (Lk 24:32). Walk with him in your work: Sear into your soul the profound insight of Ignatius that you do not labor alone, that Christ is at work for you, with you, in every created reality you handle. Walk with him in the other you touch or pass each day: Try your level best to see in each an image of Christ crucified or risen.

Finally, in this month of Mary it would not hurt to approach the mother of Jesus with the touching request some Greeks addressed to the apostle Philip, "We would like to see Jesus" (Jn 12:21). Jewish mother that she still is, she'd love to show her Son to you.

Dahlgren Chapel
Georgetown University
and
Holy Trinity Church
Washington, D.C.
May 12, 1991

Ordinary
Time

7

SO THAT THESE PEOPLE MAY EAT
Seventeenth Sunday of the Year (B)

- 2 Kings 4:42–44
- Ephesians 4:1–6
- John 6:1–15

Today St. Luke's parish opens a series of sermons on social justice. By "social justice" I do not mean some sheerly secular activity—turning this congregation into unpaid social workers, admirable as such work is. I mean how we live out the second great commandment of the Mosaic law and our Lord's gospel, "You shall love your neighbor [at least as much] as you love yourself" (Lev 19:18; Mt 22:39). Why now? Because 1991 celebrates a century of ceaseless social teaching—letters from popes, pastorals from bishops, research by theologians and social theorists.

Now a homily is not a lecture; it is an effort to evoke from the faithful, from men and women who believe, a response to God's call at a specific moment in the story of salvation. How evoke this response? I begin this series by pulling together three basic Catholic realities: (1) what has been called the Church's "best-kept secret," her social teaching, (2) a liturgy that on this day stresses the breaking of bread and points to the Eucharist, and (3) your social apostolate and mine. Social teaching . . . liturgy . . . you and I.

I

First, the Church's best-kept secret. Over my 50 years as a priest, many sins have engaged the Church's attention—and my own. Those sins centered around the Ten Commandments. What we had to confess was a Catholic version of the tablets Moses brought down from God's mountain: false gods and cuss words, missing Mass and disobey-

51

ing parents, anger and petty thievery, idle gossip and gouging another's reputation. And it seemed to many of us—certainly to outsiders—as if the Catholic Church abominated above all one type of transgression: sexual sins. On these she came down hard—in the box, from the pulpit, in parish missions.

In the process, in stressing so-called "private" sins, in focusing narrowly on the Ten Commandments, we rarely heard another facet of Catholic teaching. We never listened to Leo XIII declaring the right of workers to dignity, to a living wage, to labor unions. We never heard Pius XI recommend that workers share in ownership, in profits. We never heard Pius XII insist on the strict right all humans have to whatever material goods they need to develop as persons, as images of God. We never heard John XXIII declare that farmers should share in the rewards of industrialized societies, that developing countries should share in the benefits of more highly developed nations. We heard, and forgot, Paul VI telling the United Nations, "War, never again!" We have not heard John Paul II denounce both Marxist socialism and unbridled capitalism, castigate an all-consuming desire for profit and a destructive thirst for power, his warning on the danger of "having" over "being." How many Catholics can mention another encyclical besides the one on contraception?

Very simply, our best-kept secret is a rich storehouse of social tradition, a tradition that teases out the implications of God's revelation: In God's creative love, in Christ's redeeming love, all of us are brothers and sisters. It also tells us that in reality there are no such things as purely private sins. What "two consenting adults" do "in private" triggers a human spider web: "if you touch it anywhere, you set the whole thing trembling."[1]

II

Second, what has all this to do with today's Gospel? The miracle just read to you conceals rich resources for your Catholic existence. Why did Jesus multiply "five barley loaves and a couple of dried fish" (Jn 6:8) for more than five thousand? Mark tells us explicitly what John does not. When Jesus saw the "great throng, he had compassion on them" (Mk 6:34). And indeed Jesus did. That expression the Gospels echo all through Jesus' life: He had compassion. On whom? On the sick, a leper, two blind men, a father and his epileptic boy, a mother who had lost her only son, crowds that were "helpless, like sheep without a shepherd" (Mt 9:36).

No doubt then: Jesus fed the thousands out of compassion, the compassion that brought him to our earth in the first place. That is an important part of the story. But not the whole story—not even the most important part. You see, the Gospel tells us that the disciples "did not understand about the loaves" (Mk 6:52).[2] Surely they had no trouble understanding Jesus' compassion. What, then, did they fail to understand? Let me explain.

As you know, the miracles of Jesus were handed down by word of mouth in the Christian communities; they were retold in the Sunday assemblies, meditated, mused over, pondered, long before the Gospels were written as you have them. As the story of the loaves and fishes was passed along, the Christian people were increasingly struck by a startling resemblance. They grasped more and more clearly the connection of this miracle with a central Christian mystery. I mean the Eucharist. They began to see "the close parallels in gesture and wording" between the multiplication of the loaves and the Last Supper. Fix your memory on what the priest says and does when he re-enacts the Last Supper, consecrates the bread and feeds you with the body of Christ. Now listen to what the Gospels say about the multiplication. Jesus "took the loaves and, looking up to heaven, he gave thanks and blessed them; he broke them, gave them to the disciples to set before the crowd. And they all ate and were satisfied. And he told the disciples to gather up the fragments left over by those who had been fed" (cf. Jn 6:1–15; Mk 6:30–44, 8:14–21).

Now that multiplication was not the Eucharist. But the Gospels see the multiplication as a sign: It fulfilled the Old Testament promises that in the days to come God would feed God's people with plenty. For example, in promising the exiles from Babylon a new exodus, Isaiah echoes the words of the Lord:

> They shall feed along the ways,
> on all bare heights shall be their pasture;
> they shall not hunger or thirst. . . .
> (Isa 49:9–10)

And it looked forward to the Last Supper and all subsequent Suppers, when Christ would feed his sisters and brothers with the food that gives everlasting life, the food that is his own flesh and blood. I mean the Eucharist which a century ago Pope Leo XIII called

> the soul of the Church. . . . From the Eucharist the Church draws and possesses all its vigor and glory, all the gifts with which God has embellished it, all the blessings it has. That is why the high point of

the Church's solicitude lies in this, that the Church prepare and lead the souls of the faithful to an intimate union with Christ through the sacrament of his body and blood.[3]

III

Now, as my third point, let me draw all that together: compassion, Eucharist, social justice. You see, the Eucharist is not primarily a personal, individualistic thing, a solitary supper, your private party. Its function is to form a community, a body of men and women strikingly one in what they believe, in how they worship, in the way they act. St. Paul phrased it beautifully: "Because the Bread is one, we, though many, are one body; for we all partake of the one Bread" (1 Cor 10:17). But our oneness is only a beginning. The Eucharist must move us from church to world, thrust us out to the hungers of the human family. Let me explain.

What has liturgy to do with social justice? From the gathering song to the recessional, how does this affect the way we react to social, economic, and political injustice? One thing it does *not* do. Our gathering together does not of itself change oppressive structures, speak directly to complex issues—poverty and ecology, racism and date rape, the war abroad and the war on the womb, child abuse and euthanasia. The liturgy does not make liberal senators or conservative representatives, does not tell you how to vote on the confirmation of Clarence Thomas.[4] It is not a substitute for sociology, economics, or political science.

What, then, does the liturgy do? It effects change by effecting conversion. The temporal order, the sins in our society, can be changed only if men and women turn from sin and selfishness. And for Catholics the primary source of conversion is the Mass. The sacrifice of Christ re-enacted on our altars, the Word of the Lord proclaimed and preached, should free us from our inherited concentration on ourselves, fashion us into sisters and brothers agonizing not only for a church of charity but for a world of justice. Good liturgy should make us aware of our addictions and illusions, cast a pitiless light on our nearsighted self-interest, detach us from narrow selfishness. If we let God speak to us in the liturgy, we shall emerge from this church new people.

What does this mean, "new people"? What should the presence of Christ within you do to you? It should do what Pope Pius XII claimed: "If you have received worthily, you are what you have received." This is one food that is not changed into you; you are changed into Christ. Oh, not physically; you are not a clone of Christ. But you are reshaped. As St. Paul exclaimed, "It is no longer I who live, Christ lives in me; the life I now live in the flesh I live by faith in the Son of God, who loved me and gave himself for me" (Gal 2:20). You have a new way of living. You are linked to the risen Christ more intimately than to husband or wife, sister or brother. Concretely, you can believe what passes belief, hope for life without end, love as Jesus loved.

Love as Jesus loved. Here is your new life above all else. "This is my commandment"—not my suggestion, but my commandment—"love one another as I have loved you" (Jn 15:12). But to love as Jesus loved is to be a woman or man for others, even unto crucifixion. There is no such Christian thing as a me-and-Jesus spirituality. Our life is to give life, human and divine.

A few days before his assassination, Martin Luther King Jr. called his mother to tell her the title of his next sermon: "Why America May Go to Hell." Twenty-three years later that title is still a reality. We do not celebrate Eucharist to get away from the rest of the week. We celebrate Eucharist to deepen our oneness with the Bread of Life, and in so doing to get courage from Christ to be Christs to our acre of God's world, to lessen the hungers of the human family. Each time you leave this house of God, you re-enter a paradoxical world: unbelief lives side by side with faith, fear with hope, hate with love, death with life. When one American child out of five grows up below the poverty line, dare we still say that the fault lies with the poor themselves? When perhaps three million are homeless, can we forget that the main cause is that the poor are being squeezed out of the housing market?[5] When more blacks are in jail than in college, can we disclaim all responsibility, call these descendants of slaves lazy or inferior? When this day alone 4000 unborn American children will die—some call them "parasites" or "tenants" or "air-borne spores" or "property"[6]—we need not only to weep with Rachel "because they are no more" (Jer 31:15; Mt 2:18); we need compassion rather than condemnation, alternative programs, outreach to women in crisis.

I am not "beating on" you. You are a generous people. I look with admiration on St. Luke's outreach: to your sister black parishes in Washington and Kingston; to the hungry who must beg for bread from SOME and Zacchaeus[7]; to the homeless and the hungry and the naked in Fairfax County. I know of your involvement in SHARE and in the Community for Hope. I joy in your young fixing homes as far away as South Carolina and Michigan.

And still it is not enough. If we are to play Christ to our world, we cannot rest satisfied with the way things are. Sociologists claim that in the States today we are witnessing a resurgence of late-19th-century rugged individualism, where "I" am ultimately the only one who matters; the race is to the swift, the shrewd, the savage. The same sociologists find that in this respect Catholics on the whole are no different from their non-Catholic neighbors—much the same values, much the same style of life, much the same attitude to the disadvantaged.

Good friends: After 50 years of priesting, after a half century of preaching from Georgetown to Guam, my heart is terribly torn: by the countless calvaries I see all around me; by the realization that in this decade alone 150 million children will die who need not die; because of the times without number when, like the priest in Jesus' parable, I have passed the half-dead on the other side. And I am ceaselessly struck by the resources, intellectual, material, spiritual, so much of them untapped, that lie within our Catholic communities for changing the face of our world. I cannot tell you what God expects of any of you; that you have to hear from the Master, from Christ. But this much I dare say. All of you are people of faith; many of you are people with power, are movers and shakers. Each of you must ask yourself what I have to ask myself: Where I work, where I spend my day, is that place different, better, more human and Christian, more "for others" because I am there?

When you receive Christ today in hand or on tongue, simply repeat the words of Paul knocked to the ground on the road to Damascus. Simply ask the Christ within you, "What shall I do, Lord?" (Acts 22:10). What . . . shall . . . I . . . do?

Saint Luke's Church
McLean, Virginia
July 28, 1991

8
PROPHET OF THE MOST HIGH
Solemnity of the Birth of St. John the Baptist

- Isaiah 49:1–6
- Acts 13:22–26
- Luke 1:57–66, 80

Lest today's Gospel weary the faithful, the powers-that-be in Rome have skipped 13 verses on the birth of the Baptist. I mean the re-sounding Benedictus, Zechariah's canticle at the birth of his son. A regrettable omission, for that song of joy tells us precisely why John was born.

> And you, child, will be called prophet of the Most High;
> for you will go before the Lord[1] to prepare his ways,
> to give knowledge of salvation to his people
> in the forgiveness of their sins,
> through the tender mercy of our God. . . .
> (Lk 1:76–78a)

It is in this context that I want to address today's feast and its significance for you and me.[2] I shall do this in three stages. I shall speak of three "preachers of the just word": (1) John the Baptist, (2) the Old Testament prophet, and (3) today's prophet.

I

First, John the Baptist—John the Baptizer.[3] John is a figure of transition, "the caesura between the Period of Israel and the Period of Jesus."[4] He belongs to both: to the Period of Israel by circumcision and incorporation into the Israel of God; to the Period of Jesus because he inaugurates the age when salvation was to be accomplished.

57

Gabriel had told Zechariah to give his promised son the name John
(Lk 1:13). An appropriate name, for in Hebrew it means "Yahweh is
gracious." This child would be "filled with the Holy Spirit, even from
his mother's womb," would become an ascetic of Israel, would walk
"in the power and spirit of Elijah," would turn many Israelites to their
Lord (1:15–17).

In his canticle Zechariah sings of his son as Yahweh's "prophet"
(1:76), a mouthpiece of God, a man who utters God's word with authority to human beings. In preparation, John spent his youth in the
wilderness of Judea, "possibly the Jordan valley."[5] It may be that he
was adopted by the Essenes of Qumran, to be molded in their ways.[6]

When John appeared in the region of the Jordan, what the Jews
saw was not a priest like his father, but a preacher clothed in camel's
hair, the traditional garb of the prophets. He was Isaiah's "voice crying in the wilderness" (Isa 40:3). His message was as stern as his garb
and his diet: Repent! With him the kingdom of God was beginning to
unfold. He preached a moral reform designed to prepare the Jews for
the coming of the Messiah. Abraham your father will not save you;
unless you bear good fruit, you will be cut down like a barren tree and
cast into the fire. Interior conversion indeed, but visibly proclaimed
by baptism with water and a confession of sin.

Stern yes, but humane as well. No profession is denied salvation
—not the tax collector, not the soldier. What is demanded is that they
act justly, reveal love. And always, everywhere, "he who is mightier
than I is coming" (Lk 3:16); always "He must increase, but I must
decrease" (Jn 3:30). It is a thesis inscribed in liturgical stone; for "Just
as the birthday of Jesus was fixed at December 25, the time of the
winter solstice after which the days *grow longer* . . . , so John the Baptist's birthday was fixed at June 24, the time of the summer solstice
after which the days *grow shorter.* . . ."[7]

And, like so many preachers of justice throughout history, John
paid a price: imprisonment and death. This man whom Jesus declared
Elias-come-to-life-again, the one about whom Malachi wrote, "I am
sending my messenger ahead of you, to prepare the way before you"
(Lk 7:27; cf. Mal 3:1), had frightened tetrarch Herod Antipas: This
persuasive reformer might instigate a popular rebellion.[8] More than
that, he had denounced Herod to his face for his sinful marriage with
his brother's wife (Mk 6:18), had reproved him "for all the evil things
that Herod had done" (Lk 3:19). And one more courageous head fell
victim to injustice for justice' sake.

II

Second, this man whom Jesus lauded as "a prophet and more than a prophet" (Lk 7:26) does not exist in splendid isolation. Irresistibly he recalls his predecessors. What manner of men were the Old Testament prophets? How did they address the people? Five significant facets.[9]

First, the Hebrew prophet is extraordinarily sensitive to evil, to injustice—so much so that at times he seems to pay excessive attention to trivialities, to what we might deplore but have learned to live with. "To us a single act of injustice . . . is slight; to the prophet, a disaster. To us injustice is injurious to the welfare of the people; to the prophets it is a deathblow to existence; to us, an episode; to them, a catastrophe, a threat to the world."[10]

Second, and in consequence, this "man who feels fiercely,"[11] who is stunned by human greed, whose prophecy is the voice God has lent to the silent agony of the plundered poor, this man in whose voice God rages, this man rarely sings; he shocks. Listen to Isaiah:

> Tremble, you women who are at ease,
>   shudder, you complacent ones;
> strip, and make yourselves bare,
>   and gird sackcloth upon your loins.
>   (Isa 32:11)

Third, the Hebrew prophet is an iconoclast. He challenges sacred institutions, sacred beliefs, sacred persons. To those who keep mouthing "This is the temple of the Lord" Jeremiah insists that the temple will not save; they must amend their ways, execute justice (7:4–5). As long as faithfulness is far from the people, frankincense from Sheba makes no sense, sacrifice is unacceptable (Jer 6:20). To the kings anointed to shepherd Israel Ezekiel cries: "The weak you have not strengthened, the sick you have not healed, the crippled you have not bound up, the strayed you have not brought back, the lost you have not sought, and with force and harshness you have ruled them" (34:4–5).

Fourth, the prophet is a man embarrassed, lonely, frustrated. Embarrassed because, while others are predicting peace and prosperity, he threatens disaster and destruction. Lonely because he alienates simply everyone: not only the wicked but the pious, not only cynics but believers, not only princes but priests, not only false prophets but judges. Frustrated like Jeremiah: "For 23 years . . . I have spoken persistently to you, but you have not listened" (25:3). "To the patriots they seemed pernicious; to the pious multitude, blasphemous; to the men in authority, seditious."[12]

Fifth, the prophet's words are charged with divine power because he has experienced God's own pathos.[13] He is not interested in God's essence; his God is not the Wholly Other. He has encountered the God of the covenant, involved in history, with a stake in the human situation, intimately affected by events. He has experienced God "as living care."[14] He has seen sin not only as human failure but as divine frustration—a God not only loving and compassionate but disappointed, indignant, angry. He not only hears God's voice; he feels God's heart. How, then, can he ever speak dispassionately, serene and unruffled? How can his words be ever other than aflame, afire with a God whose living is caring?

III

The Hebrew prophets, like the Baptist, compel my third point: today's prophet. Not one who predicts the future; rather, the primary sense of scriptural prophecy: the word of one inspired by God to speak in God's name. How do John and his predecessors help us to uncover the qualities demanded of the prophetic priest in our time? Mull for a moment on each of the five qualities.

First, many of us have lost, or have never had, the neuralgic sensitivity to evil and injustice that should mark every prophet. Some surely share that sensitivity; but it is usually those who have experienced firsthand the sorry existence of the poor and the imprisoned, the hungry and the downtrodden. More of us simply deplore injustice; we are against sin; we take up collections for the refugee Kurds. Like the priest and Levite who passed by the half-dead victim of robbers, we are perfectly at home in our temple; we can handle the water of baptism and the bread of sacrifice, the words that reprove and the words that forgive and the words that unite for life. What we find difficult to handle is what a black pastor called in inimitable accents "the évent on the Jericho road." How often have I "passed by on the other side" (Lk 10:31, 32)? And how has it affected my prophetic word, my preaching?

Moreover, there is so much evil and injustice over the globe that we grow used to it. We were shocked when TV first brought war into our living rooms; now we can wolf our pizzas and slurp our Schlitz to the roar of rockets and the gusts of gore. It no longer grabs our guts—no more than shattered knees in the Sugar Bowl or the blows that dethrone a Mike Tyson.

When that happens, our preaching will not reflect a second significant facet of Hebrew prophecy: We will not "feel fiercely." When I began to preach five decades ago, the Catholic stress was on the clear and distinct idea. From seminary on, we were dispassionate searchers for truth, cool critics of error and heresy: beetle-browed, lynx-eyed, hard-nosed, square-jawed. Imagination was for poets. We did not show our emotions. Emotions were for women, and women could not be ordained.

For effective preaching the analytic mind is not enough by half. I do not mean ranting and raving. I do mean that our people should sense from our words and our faces, from our gestures and our whole posture, that we love this sinning, struggling community with a crucifying passion; that we agonize over our own sinfulness, our failure to be holier than we are; that we weep with the refugees whose tears water the ways of Kurdistan; that we too are awfully vulnerable, must at times cry out, "Lord, help my unbelief"; that our celibacy has not turned us into crotchety old bachelors but opens us warmly to all who need the touch of our hand; in a word, that we too share the dread-full human condition.

Third, the Christian preacher, like the Hebrew prophet, must prove a ceaseless challenge to the community. It may sound unseemly that I speak of us as iconoclasts. I mean that our task, in part, is to shatter false images, destroy idols. That these parade in the cloak of the sacred—institutions, beliefs, persons—only makes our task more delicate; it does not remove responsibility.

Not that the pulpit is for Savonarola, that we preach to castigate, condemn, flay the faithful before us. But must we not insist to them, with Jeremiah, that the temple of stone in which they worship does not save; that only Jesus saves; that the more important temple is this living temple of the Spirit? Must we not constantly preach that the faith which is a firm acceptance of revealed propositions is sterile without the faith which is a total self-giving to the revealing God? Should it not leap forth from our preaching that the shepherds, whether pope or pastor, are servants; that we see ourselves in our shepherding as all too "unprofitable servants"; that it is not only the laity but we ourselves who are ceaselessly summoned to conversion; that our homilies are directed in the first instance to our own lives?

But the sacred institutions that call for challenge are not only those solemnly blessed in a religious rite. They include those attitudes, life styles, and ways of acting that mark our culture as less than Christian. I mean, for example, the rugged individualism that Robert Bellah and others see conquering our culture, pervading our Catholicism —the conviction that the race is to the swift, the shrewd, and the savage. Is it impertinent for the modern prophet to apprise his people of this peril, this Baal, in their midst, even to challenge them on their fidelity to the Pauline doctrine of a single body in which no one can say to any other, "I have no need of you" (1 Cor 12:21)? I mean, too, the conviction of unnumbered Catholics that issues of social justice do not belong in the pulpit, the Catholic ears that go deaf when the preacher dares pollute the sacred air with the pastorals on peace and the economy.

Fourth, it is the rare preacher who is rarely lonely and frustrated. I doubt that we echo Jeremiah's plaint "Cursed be the day on which I was born!" But the loneliness that is built into our priesthood presses upon our preaching. For the genuine prophet must listen. I have to hear what God says to me: in the word I read on the sacred page, in the word that is Christian reflection on God's revelation, in the word God speaks to me in the depths of my heart, in the voices of the world around me. I must struggle with that word, at times wrestle with God, lay hold of the word not only with cold intellect but with my rebellious emotions. Most taxing task of all, I must live, be shaped by, the word I preach.

That, my friends, is a lonely toil. Not without joy, satisfaction, moments of ecstasy. But if you have not experienced how lonely, almost unbearably lonely, the modern prophet's task can be, either you are uncommonly graced by God or . . . you're not really working at it!

Hand in hand with loneliness runs the prophet's frustration. Not necessarily Jeremiah's 23 years without anyone listening. More frequently we are discouraged by our prophetic inadequacy, by the low level of so much of "Christian" existence, by our inability to see the increase God alone can give to the seed we sow.

Fifth, our words should be charged with divine power, not primarily because we have been ordained to preach, but because we have experienced God. A God intimately involved in history—in our history. A God who transpires not only in a burning bush millennia ago, but in today's passionate cry for freedom. A God whose pulsing image is every one of us. A God who *became* one of us.

Here a rigid scholasticism can get in the way. It is difficult to experience as "living care" a God whom we conceive as Immovable

Mover, a kind of Christian Buddha staring unblinkingly into space. Whatever intellectual contortions we must suffer to reconcile "living care" with "single Pure Act," we shall be effective preachers in the prophetic mold to the extent that we experience and preach not a God who dwells only in light inaccessible but a God who is personally involved in, somehow stirred by, what happens to you and me.

A final word. Like John, we too are called to "go before the Lord to prepare his ways." Two thoughts pertinent for that privilege, pertinent for our preaching, refuse to ebb away: the incredible intimacy of prophets like Isaiah and John with their Lord, and their passionate concern for their people. To hear the word, we must love the Lord who speaks it—love with all our strength and spirit. And to speak that word ourselves, to inflame the hearts of the faithful, we must love the Lord's paradoxical people with a crucifying passion. Only if we love dare we address to them the word that sears as it heals. Only if we love dare we proclaim "Hear, O new Israel! The word of the Lord has come unto me."

Manresa-on-Severn
Annapolis, Maryland
June 24, 1991

9
THE WISDOM OF THIS WORLD
IS FOLLY WITH GOD
Twenty-second Week of the year, Thursday (A)

- 1 Corinthians 3:18–23
- Luke 5:1–11

It is a piece of irony to say farewell to you when I shall remove all of 45 minutes from you.[1] So, to keep this homily within the limits of what in philosophy we called "moderate realism," let me focus on today's readings. Since fewer or more than three points might disappoint you, I shall move swiftly from Paul up to Jesus, then down to me.

I

First, Paul. This snippet, proclaimed to you utterly out of context, goes back to a lack of unity in Corinth: "It has been reported to me . . . that there is quarreling among you" (1 Cor 1:11). A generation after Golgotha, perhaps four factions had formed within the Corinthian community. The majority, poor freedmen and slaves, rested their faith on their founding father, Paul. Others preferred Peter, prince of the apostles. Still others were entranced by Apollos, "an eloquent man [Acts tells us], well versed in the Scriptures" (Acts 18:24). A fourth faction said in effect, "A plague on all your houses," claimed an elite relationship with Christ, not the low-level Christianity of the masses.

Paul is unhappy with all four factions. All four have fallen prey to "the wisdom of this world" (1 Cor 3:19). Such wisdom, Paul thunders, must yield to the folly of the cross, to a crucified Christ. You do not belong to Paul, to Apollos, to Peter; these leaders belong to you; they are your servants. In fact, "all things are yours, whether Paul or Apollos or Cephas or the world or life or death or the present or the future, all are yours" (3:22), everything belongs to you. But . . . only if you belong to Christ, who himself belongs to God. It is "Christ Jesus whom God made our wisdom . . ." (1:30). "What have you that you did not receive? If then you received it, why do you boast as if it were not a gift?" (4:7).

II

Second, Jesus. On the face of it, the Gospel sounds like a moving miracle story: an unexpected catch of fish that brings Peter to his knees; an application to Peter, who will catch in his Christian net not aquatic animals but men and women; a happy ending, when Peter, James, and John leave everything to follow Jesus.

But there is far more to this than meets the unsuspecting eye. Peter is indeed center stage. But the episode makes gospel sense only in the context of what has gone before. Luke makes several major points closely knit.[2] (1) The response of Peter, James, and John to Jesus is the first such response in the Gospel. It is worlds apart from the response of his townsfolk. Increasingly hostile as they grasped the meaning of his "The Lord has anointed me" (Lk 4:18), they had "led him to the brow of the hill on which [Nazareth] was built, that they might throw him down headlong" (Lk 4:29). (2) The fish story is Luke's way of telling how Jesus engages Peter for the work of his kingdom, "calls Peter, James, and John to follow his kingdom life-style."[3] They surrender all for Jesus. (3) Peter's success in the apostolate, like the catch of fish, will not be his own doing; it is the Lord's.

III

Third, myself. I leave you with regret—frankly, with an occasional tear. A psychologist friend recently reminded me that leaving what you love, leaving whom you love, is a kind of dying. And yet Jesus insisted that only through dying does new life arise. "Unless a grain of wheat falls into the earth and dies, it remains alone [a solitary grain of wheat]; but if it dies, it bears much fruit" (Jn 12:24). I learned this painfully when I left rural Woodstock reluctantly; I learned this even more painfully when urban Woodstock closed on my hopes.[4] Each time fruitful living sprang from painful dying.

Today's age-old readings promise new life on a new scale. I have agreed to galvanize an imaginative project: a large-scale effort to move the preaching of social issues more effectively into the Catholic pulpits of the country. Not simply to provide information and skills; rather, to integrate all that into a spirituality, a conversion experience, to inject what someone called "fire in the belly," in large measure through the Ignatian Exercises. It is part and parcel of the apostolic thrust proclaimed by our 32nd General Congregation: "The mission of the Society of Jesus today is the service of faith, of which the promotion of justice is an absolute requirement."[5] Put perhaps more attractively, I shall try, in the years that remain to me, to fill our Catholic pulpits with priests of contemplation and compassion.

Luke's Jesus makes it pellucidly clear that if the project "Preaching the Just Word" is to bear fruit, the increase must come from the Lord, that however gifted the human instrument, each apostle must be "astonished" at the lavishness of the Lord, has reason to fall down at Jesus' knees with a ceaseless prayer, "Depart from me, for I am a sinful man, O Lord" (Lk 5:8). And Paul, echoing his Master, warns me that a wisdom which is not ultimately grounded in Golgotha, in the folly of crucifixion, will come to naught.

That said, I ask that in your orisons not only "be all my sins remembered" but a "mission impossible" unless our gracious Lord graces this grain of wheat with new life. In return, paradoxically, I promise primarily to keep plaguing you for the kind of inspiration and information, the humor and the wild ideas, that have endeared you to me through 12 years and made me more priestly, yes more human. For all that and a great deal more, much thanks in Christ.

Jesuit Community Chapel
Georgetown University
September 6, 1990

10

OWE NO ONE ANYTHING EXCEPT LOVE
Twenty-third Sunday of the Year (A)

- Ezekiel 33:7–9
- Romans 13:8–10
- Matthew 18:15–20

Through most of the 80s it has been my privilege to share a monthly liturgy with you—to celebrate with you and to preach to you. Because through those exciting years you have been a source of incredible grace to me, I want to speak very frankly to you. Since you expect three points of me, I shall focus on (1) St. Paul, (2) you, (3) me.

I

First, St. Paul. My springboard is the absolutely basic Christian affirmation you have just heard Paul proclaim:

> Owe no one anything, except to love one another; for whoever loves the other has fulfilled the law. The commandments, "You shall not commit adultery, You shall not kill, You shall not steal, You shall not covet," and any other commandment, are summed up in this sentence, "You shall love your neighbor as you love yourself." . . . Love is the fulfilling of the law.
>
> (Rom 13:8–10)

Now Paul knew that there were *two* great commandments in the Mosaic law. And he must have known that "the" great commandment was the one Jesus plucked from the book of Deuteronomy in response to a lawyer: "You shall love the Lord your God with all your heart, and with all your soul, and with all your mind" (Mt 22:37; Deut 6:5). Paul is not saying it doesn't matter whether you love God or not, just love

67

your neighbor and you've got it made. Just before the passage on loving one another he has assured the Christians of Rome, "We know that in everything God works for good with those who love Him" (Rom 8:28).[1] With those who love *God*. And if he had lived till the close of the century, Paul would have agreed with the First Letter of John: "Beloved, let us love one another; for love is of God, and whoever loves is born of God and knows God" (1 Jn 4:7).

But Paul is not content to mouth the word "love." He does indeed repeat the word, hammer away at it, "socks it to" his churches the way a rock star might: "Love, love, love, love, love." But he goes further; he makes it concrete: "You were called to freedom, my brothers and sisters; only do not use your freedom as an opportunity for the flesh, but through love be servants of one another" (Gal 5:13). Servants. It is demanded by the reproof Jesus gave to his disciples: "You know that those who are supposed to rule over the Gentiles lord it over them. . . . Not so among you: Whoever would be great among you must be your servant, and whoever would be first among you must be slave of all. For the Son of man, too, came not to be served but to serve, and to give his life as a ransom . . . " (Mk 11:42–45).

The primary thrust of the Church, and therefore of every Christian, is summed up in the impassioned confession of Paul to the Christians of Corinth, "I will most gladly spend and be spent for you" (2 Cor 12:15).

II

Second, Paul sends me on to you, to God's people at worship. The servant role is not easy to play. For your service, your love, must go out to at least three communities: to the men and women who gather here, to the unfortunates who surround you in the District, and to the wider world that includes Iraqi and Iranians.

Each of these communities raises problems for love. Inevitably, as in just about every human family, so here, divisions can arise. Without taking sides, I can at least repeat what St. Paul wrote to his beloved Christians in Corinth: "It has been reported to me, my brothers and sisters, that there is quarreling among you" (1 Cor 1:11). When you lift your eyes above this worshiping family, you find wounds that call for compassion while they fuel your anger: blacks and whites in a tension-filled truce, coke and crack crippling our children, real-estate speculators defrauding thousands of Washingtonians of their homes, teen-age pregnancies, the rape of the poor. And when you see a

hundred thousand Americans preparing to war, perhaps to die, on
the hot sands of the Middle East, and hostages are selectively housed
where American bombs might kill them, love for Saddam Hussein
must flow sluggishly along your veins.

And yet, the Christian, everyone who carries the name Christian
with pride, must echo the prayer the priest says in the Canon of the
Mass, "Make us grow in love." Of course love is tough—perhaps the
toughest four-letter word in your vocabulary. But you dear people are
known in Washington as a singular community of love—of love in the
sense of service. I have seen you in action—your hands and your
hearts, your minds and your money, open to so many who share far
more of Christ's crucifixion than of his resurrection.

Back in the fourth century a remarkable bishop and splendid
apostle to the poor, John Chrysostom, preached passionately to his
people:

> Do you want to honor Christ's body? Then do not scorn him
> in his nakedness, nor honor him here in the church with silken
> garments while neglecting him outside where he is cold and naked.
> . . . I am not forbidding you to [give golden vessels]; I am only
> demanding that along with such gifts and before them you give
> alms. . . .
>
> Of what use is it to weigh down Christ's table with golden
> cups, when he himself is dying of hunger? First, fill him when he is
> hungry; then use the means you have left to adorn his table. . . . Do
> not adorn the church and ignore your afflicted brother [and sis-
> ter], for [they are] the most precious temple of all.[2]

III

All of which drives me to my third point: me. You see, a week
from now I shall be leaving Georgetown. Why? Frankly, fire in my
belly. After three quarters of a century, I am deeply disturbed at the
poverty of our preaching. Not just in general; specifically, on the love
that dots the pages of Scripture, the love that fired Isaiah and Jesus,
the love St. Paul thrust at you in the second reading, "Love your
sisters and brothers as you love yourself."

I agonize because in this land of milk and honey one of every five
children grows up beneath the poverty line—and our pulpits are silent. I agonize because in this land of the free blacks and Hispanics are
still shackled as second-class citizens, are leaving our church in record

numbers—and we preachers have nothing to say to their hungers. I agonize because thousands upon thousands of women are battered by the men who vowed to respect them, untold children abused by the barbarians who brought them into being—and we mouth mealy platitudes about a God who cares for everyone. I agonize because devout Catholics claim the Church has no right to intrude into social, economic, and political issues—and so we ban the bishops' economic pastoral from the pulpit. I agonize when I see how Americans rape the earth in the name of progress or simply because they do not care— and we still preach simplistically from Genesis that God gave us "dominion over all the earth" (Gen 1:26). I agonize when sociologists tell me that we are experiencing a resurgence of late-19th-century rugged individualism, where the race is to the shrewd, the swift, and the savage, where your ultimate responsibility is to yourself, that Catholics in this regard are little different from their fellow Americans—and we heralds of God's word dare not raise our voices in protest. I agonize because our young Catholics find God's word on our tongues an endless bore, when it should strike fire even in green wood. I agonize because I see how difficult it is for our educated Catholics to endure the pap, the unsubstantial gruel we dole out to them as God's message to a computerized world.

I am resigning as editor of the scholarly journal *Theological Studies* (45 years on a magazine is service sufficient) and as theologian-in-residence at the university, to become a Senior Fellow within the Woodstock Theological Center, a research institute putting theology to work on social issues: human rights, nuclear strategy, business ethics, the environment. I have sold the Center on an apostolate dear to my heart: "Preaching the Just Word." It is an effort to move the preaching of social issues more effectively into the Catholic pulpits of our country. Not to solve complex social, economic, or political problems; this is not possible even within the very best of homilies. Rather to raise the issues, to raise the Christian conscience, to get our graced faithful thinking, talking, acting.

We at the Center are persuaded that such preaching will always be less persuasive than it should be unless sheer skills are integrated with a spirituality. So, time and again we shall bring preachers of promise and compassion to a retreat house, where spirituality is the heart and soul of the enterprise, fill not only their minds with information but their bellies with fire, and send them forth to spread the flame in their acre of God's world.

In consequence, next week I shall remove to Manresa, the Jesuit retreat house in Annapolis, on the shores of the Severn. I shall miss

Georgetown dreadfully: faculty and students, 80 Jesuits and dear laity in the District, the Dahlgren community and Holy Trinity. It is, psychologists tell me and I experience it, it is a little bit like dying. But for all the pain, for all the grief, I am convinced that in the Christian vision it is only by dying—to self, to the past, to where I am—that new life can be born. "Unless a grain of wheat falls into the earth and dies, it remains alone; but if it dies, it bears much fruit" (Jn 12:24).

For this work to succeed, to give glory to God and grace to earth, I shall need your support. Pray, then, good friends, that the Lord who has inspired this enterprise may favor its aging director with uncommon strength to pursue it. The cause is noble, the excitement contagious, the prospects promising.

With the 80s in my fond memory, I can say no more sincere a farewell to you than to steal from St. Paul—this time the inspired syllables that open his letter to the Christians of Philippi in Macedonia:

> I thank my God in all my remembrance of you, always in every prayer of mine for all of you making my prayer with joy, thankful for your partnership in the gospel from the first day until now. And I am sure that [the God] who began a good work in you will bring it to completion on the day [when Jesus Christ will return]. It is right for me to feel this way about all of you, because I hold you in my heart, for all of you share in the grace that is mine. . . . For God is my witness, how I yearn for all of you with the affection of Christ Jesus. And it is my prayer that your love may abound more and more, with knowledge and all discernment, so that you may approve what is excellent, and may be pure and blameless down to the day of Christ, filled with the fruits of righteousness which come through Jesus Christ, to the glory and praise of God.
>
> (Phil 1:3–11)

Dahlgren Chapel
Georgetown University
and
Holy Trinity Church
Washington, D.C.
September 9, 1990

11
WHAT THINK YOU . . . ?
Twenty-fourth Sunday of the Year (B)

- Isaiah 50:4–9
- James 2:14–18
- Mark 8:27–35

Today's readings—Isaiah, James, and Mark—are a powerful challenge. Not only to this jubilarian[1] but to each of you at worship with me. For they force us to face three questions—interrogations intimately interconnected: (1) What think you of Christ? (2) What think you of your sisters and brothers? (3) What think you of suffering, of pain?

I

First, what think you of Christ? It is the question posed by Jesus to his disciples as they move toward the settlements around Caesarea Philippi, "Caesar-town." To begin with, a kind of Gallup poll: "The people you meet, who do they say I am?" The disciples report fair confusion: Some, believe it or not, think you're John the Baptist raised from the dead; others see you as Elijah returned to earth after nine centuries; still others, a prophet of some sort. Then comes Jesus' pointed question: "But you—who do you say I am?" And Peter answers for all: "You are the Messiah," you are the Christ, "the anointed king of the House of David expected to come and deliver Israel from its enemies and to establish a world empire, marked with justice and peace."[2] It is not perfect recognition, but it is a giant step on the way.

What think you of Christ? The question has been central, has been crucial, to the civilized world since Calvary. On our answer depends in large measure the way we order our lives. Indeed, Roman Catholic faith and theology echo the cry of apostle Thomas faced with

72

the risen Christ: "My Lord and my God!" (Jn 20:28). But the response Christ awaits is not a sheerly intellectual act.

Creed, cult, code—what we believe, how we worship, the way we live—these three facets of Catholicism have to be acts of love. Creed is not simply words we repeat each Sunday: "I believe in one Lord Jesus Christ, the only Son of God, eternally begotten of the Father, God from God, Light from Light, true God from true God, begotten, not made, one in Being with the Father." Important of course, lest Christ become just another god in a pantheon. But not enough for my Christianity to come alive. I don't reach Christ by an act of the intellect— only if my whole person reaches out to him. Faith saves only if it is an act of love. Only if "I believe" surges from "I love."

Cult—the way we worship—is not in the first instance a Sunday obligation under pain of serious sin. Eucharist is the matchless, peerless, supreme act of Catholic worship, should be my love-laden response to the love that moved Christ to murmur at the Last Supper, "This is my body, which is given for you" (Lk 22:19). The response is less than adequate if I ask, "Do I have to?"

Code—the way we live—is not legalism, sheer conformity to a set of rules invented arbitrarily by hierarchical humans. Law and morality are human efforts to define, specify, particularize what the two great commandments demand: Love God, love your sisters and brothers. Like all human laws, church laws can be "off the wall," become outmoded, call for revision, raise conflict with conscience. One thousand seven hundred and fifty-two "canons" in the 1983 Code do not instantly trigger a love light in our eyes; but behind it all is a gigantic effort to spell out what love demands in practice.

Who, then, do I say Christ is? He is the center of my universe. Literally. I believe him when he says, "Apart from me you can do nothing" (Jn 15:5). Human living ceases to be senseless only because God's own Son took my flesh, nailed it to a cross out of love to save me from sin, from Satan, from myself. Apart from him, playing priest is a mockery, liturgy is play-acting, Communion is sheer ceremony. My whole life should echo the response Peter gave to the risen Jesus after breakfast on the beach. Remember how Jesus asked Peter, "Do you love me?" Hurt that Jesus had put the question three times, Peter responded with all his heart, "Lord, you know everything; you know that I love you" (Jn 21:15–17).

What do I think of Christ? I don't "think" as much as I used to. Theology, rich as it is, has moved into love. My prayer is the moving song in *Godspell:* "These three I pray: to see you more clearly, love you more dearly, follow you more nearly."

II

Second, what think you of your sisters and brothers? Here the powerful passage from James is inseparable from genuine love for Christ. "What good is it if [you] say [you] have faith but have not works? Can [your] faith save [you]? If a brother or sister has nothing to wear and no food for the day, and you say to them, 'Good-bye and good luck, keep warm and well-fed,' but do not meet their bodily needs, what good is that? So it is with the faith that does nothing in practice; it is thoroughly lifeless" (Jas 2:14–17).

Increasingly, with the passage of the years, I have been challenged by the "just word" in Scripture. By the words of the Lord through the mouth of Micah: "What does the Lord require of you? Do justice and love steadfastly . . . " (Mic 6:8). On the lips of Isaiah: "Bring no more vain offerings. . . . Seek justice, correct oppression; defend the fatherless, plead for the widow" (Isa 1:13, 17). God's trumpet call in Amos: "I hate, I despise your feasts. . . . Let justice roll down like waters" (Amos 5: 21, 24). Especially Jesus' declaration of his mission in the Nazareth synagogue: "The Spirit of the Lord . . . has anointed me to preach good news to the poor . . . , to set at liberty the oppressed" (Lk 4:18). So powerfully have these "words of God" impacted on me that after 50 years as priest, 60 as Jesuit, I am devoting my remaining years to a national project of my own conceiving —"Preaching the Just Word"—an effort to move social-justice issues more effectively into the pulpits and congregations of our country.

Social justice is not a secular offshoot of Christianity. For the justice God asks of us is not a sheerly ethical affair. It does not merely mean: Give to each what is due to each, what each person has a strict right to demand, because he or she is a human being, has rights which can be proven by philosophy or have been written into law. As with Israel, so with us: Justice is a whole web of relationships that stem from our covenant with God. We are to "set at liberty the oppressed" not because they deserve it but because this is the way *God* has acted with *us*. Because we have experienced God's love, "This is my body given for you," "This is the cup of my blood, the blood of the new and everlasting covenant, shed for you," we have to live the second great commandment of the law and the gospel, "You shall love your neighbor [at least as much] as you love yourself" (Mt 22:39). Not only that; we are commanded by Jesus to love one another as he has loved us (Jn 15:12)—even therefore unto crucifixion. And the incredible result? That startling sentence of Jesus about the way he will welcome us at the end: "I was hungry and you gave me food, I was thirsty and you gave me drink, I was a stranger and you welcomed me, I was naked and you clothed me, I was sick and you visited me, I was in prison and you came to me. Truly, I say to you, as you did it to one of the least of these my sisters and brothers, you did it to me" (Mt 25:35–36, 40).

And who are these least of our sisters and brothers today? The Jesus who described our neighbor as the man who fell among robbers would have a field day for parables in our culture. My sister is the black child born into slum poverty; my brother, the fetus never allowed to be born. My sister is the date raped and the wife battered; my brother, the youngster sexually abused. My neighbors are the adolescents in inner-city high schools "with as many security checkpoints as a Third World airport,"[3] the reforming alcoholic and the teen-ager dehumanized by crack or coke, the convict imprisoned in Lorton or Jessup, the elderly imprisoned in a lonely home unloved. My sisters and brothers are the nine million who look for work but cannot find it, the six million who cannot find full-time jobs, the million too discouraged to look for work.[4]

What think you of these your brothers and sisters? Impressive to me is how large is writ over your community the realization that each of these is Jesus crucified again. Ever since I have been privileged to share Word and Eucharist with you, I have found in you men and women for others. Liturgy moves you to life, from church to world, from Christ to the crucified.

III

From Christ to the crucified. This triggers my third point, my third question: What think you of suffering? Immediately after Peter confessed him as Messiah, Jesus "began to teach [the disciples] that [he] must suffer much, be rejected . . . , be killed." And when Peter protested, Jesus turned on him, rebuked him in uncommonly strong language: "Out of my sight, you satan," you tempter; "you are judging not by God's standards but by humans' " (Mk 8:31–33). Peter was turning Jesus aside from his God-given mission to suffer for humankind, tempting him to discard the divine plan of salvation.

You don't need 50 or 60 years to discover that suffering, pain, death are inescapable, are built into human living. But it can easily take a lifetime to see suffering with the eyes of Christ. In itself, suffering is neither good nor bad. The all-important question is, why? I have no persuasive answer to the bad things that happen to good people.

After three quarters of a century, I remain as puzzled as was dear Job protesting to the God he loved and served:

> I cry to you and you do not answer me;
>   I stand and you do not heed me.
> You have turned cruel to me;
>   with the might of your hand you persecute me.
>
> (Job 30:20–21)

This much I do know. A God who loved me enough to walk in my flesh, loved me enough to experience what I experience as I experience it, to die shamefully and willingly for me on a cross between two robbers—this God does not delight in earthquakes and war, in cancer and Parkinson's disease, in crib deaths and prolonged comas. We cannot unravel the mystery: why my father and only brother died painfully within three weeks of each other; why a dear friend disintegrated in a plunging plane last month; why millions of Russians perished in Siberia; why a child in D.C. was killed by a random bullet. We do not yet understand why, as poet Francis Thompson sang, "nothing begins and nothing ends, that is not paid with moan," why "we are born in others' pain, and perish in our own."[5] What you and I can do is keep our suffering from becoming sheer waste.

How? By transmuting suffering into sacrifice. There is a difference. Sacrifice is suffering with a purpose. Our world has long since learned a painful lesson: Perfect oneness with someone or something beloved—man, woman, or child, music or medicine, knowledge or art—can be achieved only in terms of self-giving, only in terms of love. It is the truth chiseled in deathless language by the Son of God when he said: "A woman about to give birth has pain. . . . But when she has brought forth her child, she no longer remembers the distress for her joy that a child is born . . . " (Jn 16:21).

In the Christian mystery the self-giving, the love, was summed up by Jesus in today's Gospel: "If you want to come after me, deny yourself, take up your cross, and follow in my steps" (Mk 8:34). A giant if: if you want to come after him, if you want to be his disciple, if you love him enough to suffer for him as willingly as he was crucified for you.

Decades ago I watched a film called *Claudia*. The character who plays the title role is a gay, carefree, utterly unsophisticated, supremely happy young wife. But Claudia has just been told that her mother, the mother she loves so dearly, on whom she depends so terribly, is about to die. Pain sears Claudia's breast like a knife thrust. David, her husband, murmurs to her: "Make friends with pain, Claudia, and it'll stop hurting you." A lovely thought, but not quite true. Pain, as long as it remains pain, will never quite stop hurting. The solution is more profound: "Make friends with God—make friends with Christ—and you will find a purpose to pain."

Good friends all: Several weeks ago a remarkable film director died at 94. The movie that epitomizes Frank Capra's inspirational films is his 1946 *It's a Wonderful Life*. That film is a "fantasy about a man who falls into suicidal despair because he thinks he has accomplished nothing of value." He "is rescued by a guardian angel who shows him, in a gloriously realized dream sequence, how miserable the lives of his town, his friends, his family would have been had he never existed to touch them with his goodness."[6]

I leave you—temporarily, I trust—with that Capra reminder. If I have to dredge up, from 50 years of priesting and more than a decade in your midst, one experience to share with you for your encouragement and consolation, it is this. Whoever you are, however difficult, discouraging, perhaps desperate your experience of human living, one thing is certain. Your acre of God's world would be less human, less divine, had you never existed to touch it with your goodness. Your self-giving to Christ, the cup of cold water to a sister or brother, and your suffering turned into sacrifice—this is what renews the face of the earth even if you rarely experience the renewal, never live to see it.

One correction: You have indeed lived to see it. In large measure because of you, *I* am a more committed Christian, a more priestly minister, a more Ignatian Jesuit, a more human man. For that, I expect to be, in a very literal sense, *eternally* grateful to you.

Dahlgren Chapel
Georgetown University
and
Holy Trinity Church
Washington, D.C.
September 15, 1991

Wedding Homilies

12
ONE HAND, ONE HEART, ONE LIFE
Wedding Homily 1

- Genesis 2:18–24
- 1 Corinthians 12:31–13:8
- John 15:12–16

Dear Jean and Rob: This afternoon you lay on me a privilege and a burden. The privilege? To receive, in the name of Christ's Church, your promise of deathless love. The burden? To shape words that match the matchless reality of your love. For all my affection for you, the love you vow to each other this day is not for me to analyze, to dissect. Not my task, from my celibate experience, to apprise you of pitfalls, to signalize roadblocks, to urge you to be good parents. Much better to move out from what God has revealed to us—three ideas that tell us something about marriage and something about you.

Concretely, let me set before you three sets of paradoxes. A paradox, you know, is a seeming contradiction. On the face of it, at first sight, two things don't fit, don't go together, but in point of fact they are both quite true, they actually do fit.

I

Paradox number 1: In your married life you must be at once *one and two*. You must be one. Jesus insisted on that when the Pharisees were testing him about divorce. Going back to the creation story just read to you, the story Jean and Rob plucked from Genesis, he declared: "From the beginning of creation God made them male and female. 'For this reason a man shall leave his father and mother and be joined to his wife, and the two shall become one' [Gen 2:24]. So they are no longer two but one" (Mk 10:7–8).

It is not only Scripture that proclaims this, not only religions that

81

preach it. Poets sing of it; pop music raises the decibels on it. It's Adam murmuring to Eve in John Milton's *Paradise Lost:*

>   . . . we are one,
> One flesh; to lose thee were to lose myself.[1]

Or, if you prefer *West Side Story* and Stephen Sondheim:

> Make of our hands one hand,
> Make of our hearts one heart,
> Make of our vows one last vow,
> Only death will part us now.
>
> Make of our lives one life,
> Day after day one life.
> Now it begins,
> Now we start;
> One hand, one heart.
> Even death won't part us now.[2]

A man and a woman take what is most intimately theirs, what makes them this man and this woman, what makes each an unrepeatable person, what makes each so gloriously free and independent, and each says to the other, "All this I share with you. Not by dividing it with you: You get half and I keep half. No. No longer is there 'mine and thine.' All is ours."

So incomparably one will you be, so close to each other, that St. Paul says your wedded love symbolizes, signifies, represents, typifies the incredible oneness that links Christ our Lord and the Christian people, Christ and the Church Paul calls the body of Christ. "Even so," Paul declares, "husbands should love their wives as their own bodies," nourish and cherish their wives "as Christ does the Church" (Eph 5:28, 29).

Yes, you must be one. But, strange as it sounds, while incredibly one, you still remain two. Indeed no "mine and thine," but still and always "I and thou." Rob does not become Jean; Jean does not fade into Rob. When St. Paul exclaimed, "It is no longer I who live, but Christ who lives in me" (Gal 2:20), he did not lose his own personality, did not actually become the God-man. Why, even the most startling sayings of the mystics, like "My *me* is God,"[3] are an effort to put into inadequate words an intense experience of loving union, a sense of fusing, of merging with God. For all their wondrous oneness, the most passionate of lovers never cease to be two. That is why the modern prophet from Lebanon Kahlil Gibran, who wrote so eloquently of the oneness of the wedded, could urge them, "Let there be spaces in your togetherness."[4]

One miracle you will discover as the years fly by: The more you give of yourself to each other, the more fully will you become yourself, your own person fulfilled. Such is the experience that encircles the earth, the experience of all who love with all their heart and soul—Catholic and Protestant, Hindu and Jew.

II

Paradox number 2: In your new-found oneness, you are at once *divine and human*. Exaggerated though it sounds, each of you is divine. Not God; still, divine. Never forget the opening chapter of Scripture: "God created the human in God's own image; . . . male and female God created them" (Gen 1:27). Created like God, how can you not be in some genuine sense divine?

What does this mean in the concrete? It means that what makes you genuinely human is that you share in the divine life of God. Like God, you can know; and, like God, you can love. Most amazingly, you can know and love not only the God who shaped you out of love; you can know and love each other. And as the years go on, as you grow in knowledge and love, as you see ever more deeply the fulness of each other, as you share ever more completely who you are and what you have, you become more and more like God—the God whose very name is Love, who no matter how much love He lavishes on you has always more to give. And so, through a lifetime of loving you will, by God's grace, be living examples of the text you have lifted from St. Paul and proclaimed to us: "Love is patient and kind, not jealous or boastful, not arrogant or rude. Love does not insist on its own way, is not irritable or resentful, rejoices not at wrong but [only] in the right. Love bears all things, believes all things, hopes all things, endures all things" (1 Cor 13:4–7).

Yes, love is all of this and more—if it is the love that St. Paul had in mind, "God's love poured into [your] hearts through the Holy Spirit who has been given to [you]" (Rom 5:5). The problem is, this divine life has to be lived on earth, amid tensions and crosses, by a man and a woman who never cease to wear the skins of humans. And so Paul could have added: "However, lovers can be impossibly impatient: 'What in God's name took you so long?' Lovers can be unbearably unkind: 'Don't bother me now: The Brewers have the bases loaded.' Lovers can be jarringly jealous: 'That smile is reserved for me.' Lovers can be maddeningly rude: 'How can you possibly be so clumsy?' Lovers can and do insist on their own way, take their irritations out on the nearest and the dearest, believe only what they can see, hope for what is satisfying to them individually, endure only as much as they must.''

For this there is no instant prescription, no miracle drug. There is only God's gift to both of you together: God all round you, God within you, within the other. And there is that power the Holy Spirit instils in you, the readiness to forgive. It is the antithesis of the sentimental drivel that once captured America, "Love is never having to say you're sorry."

III

Paradox number 3: You are at once *for each other and for the others*. For each other, of course; otherwise marriage is not "one hand, one heart, one life," but lust or a business deal, a poker game or a battle of wits, the survival of the fitter.

But granted you are for each other, a complementary truth has come down to us from a rich Christian tradition—a tradition confirmed by the best of modern psychology: "A love that is not for more than itself will die. . . . Over the long haul an intimate relationship . . . which doesn't reach outward will stagnate."[5]

You see, turning together to others, turning as one to others, should have two splendid effects. First, it might well make the difference between a marriage that is ceaselessly exciting and a marriage that the years turn into a rut, routine, dull as dishwater, "b o r i n g." You need others. Not as a distraction, a diversion, an escape from your housemate, marriage as an endless cocktail party. Rather, to strengthen your love, to fill it out, to people it with men and women who are part and parcel of your love. I mean men and women such as surround you at this moment, who have played some part (bit parts and star roles) in your coming together, without whom the years that lie ahead could be lonely indeed, a terrible risk. And I mean untold men and women you have not yet met, who will touch your lives in ways not yet known. Reach out—if only to deepen your love for each other. Remember that insightful sentence, "Over the long haul an intimate relationship . . . which doesn't reach outward will stagnate."

Second effect: If you turn your love to others, you will change the acre of God's world on which you dance so lightly. You deliberately chose as your wedding Gospel the solemn command of Jesus, "Love one another as I have loved you" (Jn 15:12). The other you are ordered to love has many faces—contrasting faces: ruddy with health or wasted with hunger, hearty with hope or bowed in despair, comfortable in condos or shivering in shelters, basking on beaches or bound behind bars, living lavishly or existing below the poverty line, greeting each day with song in shower or dreading each inhuman dawn. All of these you are commanded to love—not invited, commanded; and to love each and all as Jesus loved them, as Jesus loves them. And how does he love them? Even unto crucifixion. Recall your Gospel: "Greater love no one has than to lay down life itself" for another (Jn 15:13).

I have no crystal ball, no crystal vision, no special insight into the years that lie ahead. But after seven decades of wedding watching, I can promise you this: The more your love reaches out to others, the greater will be your growth in your love for each other. I have seen it time and again. And it makes perfect sense; for the grace to grow in love comes ultimately from the same Lord who the night before he died for love declared, "This I command you, to love one another" (Jn 15:17).

That mission is impossible only if you try it alone: a Rambo and a Wonder Woman conquering "hell and high water" by muscle and wit, by superbrains and technology. No. Your presence here, your vows in so sacred a spot, your communion in the blood of Christ—this whispers to the world that your hope for happiness rests not so much in what you have made of yourselves, rests far more in a God who wore your flesh to experience your pain, who died that you might live life to the full.

Yes, God will be with you—the God who invented marriage so imaginatively. But not only God. This congregation gathers here today because in varied ways our love has touched you, has helped bring you to this moment. But there is more. Our presence is a promise. A promise that, however many the miles that part us, we shall never be far from you. Even when our eyes meet not, you will be alive in us: in our hearts ever warm to you, in our hands ever outstretched to you, in our prayers that wing to heaven for you.

We ask but one rich grace in return: that your love for each other will shed its warmth over us as well. For we too need what is so obviously yours to give: the example of young lovers who are about to live a threefold paradox. You will be wondrously one, yet have space in your togetherness. You will be like the Lord of love in your love for each other, yet have to struggle like all humans to keep your love aflame. You will turn to each other only to turn outward together to share your love with others, especially the loveless and the unloved.

Come now, dear Jean and Rob, and before God and God's people murmur the sacred promise that keeps this aging world young, weds earth to heaven, gives endless delight to angels: "I will love you and honor you all the days of my life."

Old St. Mary's Church
Milwaukee, Wisconsin
June 30, 1990

13
THIS IS A GREAT MYSTERY
Wedding Homily 2

- Song of Songs 2:8–16a; 8:6–7a
- Ephesians 5:22, 25–32
- Mark 10:6–9

Ann and Kevin: Your choice of Scripture readings delights me. It will not surprise you that, being a priest, I resonate to the Gospel from Mark, "What God has joined together, let not any human put asunder" (Mk 10:9). You might be surprised that, being a priest, I take delight in the Song of Songs, "My beloved is like a gazelle or a young stag" (Cant 2:9). But even more than those two readings, it is your selection from St. Paul's Letter to the Ephesians[1] that intrigues me, and so I shall focus on that passage. I want to spell out in some detail why this passage is so important for two who marry in Christ—so important for you.

You see, Paul proclaims marriage "a great mystery." Some of you husbands and wives, I see, agree that it is. But the mystery *you* experience is not the mystery Paul had in mind. By "mystery" he means a secret "hidden for ages" in God "but now made manifest" to those who believe (Col 1:26), to you and me. He unveils some of the mystery. He implies that the oneness of Christ with our humanity—God's Son become man—helps mightily to understand what human marriage is all about; and he declares that the marriage of Christ and his Church is the model for the union between husbands and wives. This, I admit, is "deep stuff," but unless you grasp to some extent what Paul is saying, you will miss the deeper meaning of today's event. Christian marriage will seem no different than the union of unbelievers, save that our ceremony takes place in a church.

Three stages spell out my development: (1) the marriage of Christ and the Church; (2) the marriage of Christians; (3) the marriage of Kevin and Ann.

I

First, the marriage of Christ and the Church. In St. Paul's inspired insight, Christ is the bridegroom, the Church is his bride. It is a
give-and-take, a breath-taking exchange. It began when the Son of
God became a man. What happened? He took what was ours and gave
us what was his. He took our skin, our bones and blood, our nerves
and arteries. He took our emotions and passions, the way we feel, our
anger and our love, our fear and our grief, our joy and our sorrow. He
took our pain, our anguish of flesh and of spirit. These he took because he wanted to experience what we experience, as we experience
it. These he took because he wanted to shape men and women into a
community so closely joined to him that St. Paul would call us the
Body of Christ.

Run through Jesus' life, see in living color how he took to himself
all we are, except for our sin. He was born in poverty, knew what
hunger tastes like, had no place whereon to rest his head. His fellow
townsfolk tried to toss him from a cliff, his relatives said he was mad,
his enemies claimed he had a devil, the powerful hated him, plotted
his death. All day long the unfortunates of Palestine surrounded him:
the poor and the prostitutes, the possessed and the paralyzed, the
lepers and the hemophiliacs. He grew angry enough to whip buyers
and sellers from the temple, wept over Jerusalem and Lazarus, over
his city and his friend. He learned what it means to be afraid, begged
his Father not to let him die. He experienced what it's like to feel
abandoned: by a Judas who sold him for silver, by a Peter who denied
he ever knew him, yes by a Father to whom he cried, "My God, my
God, why have you forsaken me?" (Mt 27:46). He climaxed all this by
taking to himself our very dying.

But Jesus not only took; he gave. He gave us what you and I could
never have anticipated. It is splendidly summarized in the prayer a
priest murmurs as he mingles wine and water in the chalice at the
Offertory: "By the mystery of this water and wine may we come to
share in the divinity of Christ, who humbled himself to share in our
humanity." He took what was ours: our human frame. He gave us a
share in what is peculiarly his: his divinity. If that sounds extravagant,
read the priestly prayer of Jesus to his Father at the Last Supper for all
who believe in him: "I in them and thou in me" (Jn 17:23). Through
grace God lives in us—Father, Son, and Holy Spirit. It is Jesus' promise the eve of his crucifixion: "If [you] love me . . . my Father will love

[you], and we will come to [you] and make our home with [you]"
(Jn 14:23).

All this, the give-and-take, had one purpose above all others: to
fashion a community that would be like a bride to Jesus, wed to him in
mutual love, a oneness born in baptism and nourished by his own
Eucharistic flesh and blood, a union that is kept alive and grows because his Holy Spirit is ours as well.

II

My second point: the marriage of Christians. You see, Christ as
bridegroom, the Church as his bride—these are not abstract ideas
that theologians can jaw about if they have nothing more practical to
do. The oneness between Christ and us his people sets the ideal for
your life together. The marriage of Christians is not some vague contract that somehow keeps you together through the bittersweet of
human living, that keeps the human race alive, that peoples heaven
with more and more souls. Your wedded oneness should increasingly
reflect, reproduce, mirror the unique society we call the Church. And
the Church, in its deepest reality, is not pope and people, Rome and
rebellion, Sunday obligation and antiabortion. The Church is Christ
and we—linked together by God's life pervading us like another
bloodstream. In marriage you take another's self to yourself—flesh
and spirit—and you give to each other what is most intimately yours.
You take to yourself the other's joy and sorrow, pleasure and pain,
success and failure, hopes and fears, achievements and frustrations;
and you give to that other all that makes you . . . you. There still
remain "I and thou"; what ceases to be is "mine and thine."

Only in this way will love make Christian sense. "Love" is a monosyllable that used to express something sacred, something profound,
something very special. Now it literally covers a multitude of sins. It
covers lust at first sight, one-night stands, the new dirty pop.

St. Paul put it admirably: "Husbands, love your wives, as Christ
loved the Church and gave himself up for her, that he might sanctify
her" (Eph 5:25–26). If you want to grasp what your wedded love
should be like, listen long and lovingly to the Christ who commanded
his disciples the eve of his death, "Love one another as I have loved
you" (Jn 15:12). Not just "Love one another"; that opens the flood-
gates to every TV romance. No: "as I have loved you." And how did

Jesus love us? Remember how John's account of the Last Supper begins: "Now before the feast of the Passover, when Jesus knew that his hour had come to depart out of this world to the Father, having loved his own who were in the world, he loved them to the end, loved them to the uttermost" (Jn 13:1).[2] He literally loved us "to death."

Here is the model for the counsel in the First Letter of John, "Little children, let us not love in word or speech but in deed and in truth" (1 Jn 3:18). To say "I love you" is awfully important; many a marriage has foundered because the language of love died with the honeymoon. But those three monosyllables must be translated into "deed and truth." Into deed and truth that mirror the life and love of Jesus, that frequently confront husband and wife with the Last Supper declaration of Jesus: No greater love can you possibly have than to give your very life for your friend (cf. Jn 15:13). Such is Christian marriage, even when the cross is bloodless.

III

This brings me to Kevin and Ann. For it is you two who are immediately touched today by St. Paul's insight into wedded love. It is you two who are to reflect in your life together the remarkable love that links Christ our Lord and his people. From seven decades of wedding watching let me suggest several facets of marriage that can be splendidly creative.

First, wedded life demands routine but need not be a rut. One danger in living together from ten to 50 years? You can easily take each other for granted. The love you symbolize, the wedding of Christ and his people, faces that danger day after day. Not because Christ takes us for granted; he never does. The New Testament Letter to the Hebrews declares that "he always lives to make intercession" for us (Heb 7:25), to plead for us to his Father. "Always." But we his people often take Christ for granted. We pay him a courtesy call once a week (40% don't even do that), yawn when his Word is proclaimed to us, pass him by on the street when he is naked and hungry, come running to him when all else fails.

A similar peril hangs over your marriage. The romance of the engaged is over; the honeymoon will soon be a memory; after it you must live life "in the raw." And that means the day-to-day grind, the selfsame motions over and over again, the same eggs once over lightly, the nine-to-five workaday, yes the selfsame "act of love." How keep routine from stagnating into rut? Recapture, time and again, the wonder of the other. Routine brings out the ever so human flaws, from the socks on the bathroom floor to the mechanical kiss, from paranoia for punctuality to rage over a limited menu—even different interests: "*My* thing is ballet"; "*I'm* for rock-'em-and-sock-'em pro football." Every so often you must look more deeply, somewhat the way Jesus could see through the sin and the leprosy, the hemorrhage and the paralysis, the blindness and the lameness, to the dear person within. Flawed yes, but so are you—save that *your* flaws are clearly minor! Recapture the wonder that brought you together, that saw in each other someone special, someone shaped not in your image but in the image of Christ.

Second, if your wedded love is to mirror the love between Christ and his Church, you cannot do it simply with high IQs and engaging personalities, blue eyes and a sense of humor. It can only be done with God's grace, through God's own gracious giving. That grace will be *promised* you when you exchange your vows, exchange yourselves. But it will be *effective* only if you mold your love, mold your lives, on the love our Lord has for us, a total love, nothing held back, that led to Calvary.

Such love is a gift—not from Lord & Taylor, but from the Lord of your life, from the Holy Spirit of his love. Once again St. Paul summed it up in a single striking sentence: "Hope does not disappoint us, because God's love has been poured into our hearts through the Holy Spirit who has been given to us" (Rom 5:5). *God's* love. Not our love for God, but God's love of us[3]—this is what has been poured into your hearts; this is what makes possible a marriage that mirrors the oneness of Christ and his people. Right now you two are precious persons, for your total selves are pervaded, penetrated, by God's love for you, by God alive in you.

But God's love alive in you demands a response, a return of love: your love for God. You begin it beautifully this morning, for this Eucharist is your root response, the Church's radical reply, to the command of Christ at the Last Supper, "Do this in remembrance of me" (Lk 22:20). Here you stand together, bride and groom, and here around you is the Church, Christ and his people, the bridegroom and bride you symbolize. Let it never become rote, mindless repetition, something you have to do under peril of hell. Let it always be what the word "Eucharist" means: your thanksgiving together, your united gratitude to God, for the gift of each other, for the gift of God within you, for the gift of the Church which, for all its spots and wrinkles, is the focus of your faith, the locus of your love.

Third, from today's recessional on, let this Eucharist lead you

from church to world, from the serenity of Christ's peace to a
wounded world. For you go out hand in hand to a land where love of
children lives side by side with war on the womb: casualties, 1.5 million
each year. A land where unbelievable wealth and natural resources
coexist with unrelievable hunger and thirst: casualties, 20 percent of
our children below the poverty line. A land that we sing as "land of the
free," and yet uncounted women and blacks stay shackled in second-
class citizenship. There is so much beauty out there, the touch of
God's green and gentle hand on an earth of God's own craftsmanship;
but still more beauty yet to be seeded by such as you, by the young and
the restless, by men and women who, like Christ, love this world
enough to live for it, perhaps to die for it.

Kevin and Ann, I have set before you a Christian vision of
marriage you rarely hear, a challenge which my younger friends would
call "awesome"—something that inspires dread, veneration, and
wonder. I do so because to ask less of you would be to undervalue two
exceptional humans; because to preach mawkishly about "Love is
never having to say you're sorry" would not address the profound
depths of marriage in Christ; and because only the kind of wedded
love I have set before you is calculated to bring you the joy Christ
promised "no one will take from you" (Jn 16:22).

St. Ambrose Church
Annandale, Virginia
August 11, 1990

14
THIS DAY I MARRY MY BEST FRIEND
Wedding Homily 3

- Genesis 2:18–24
- 1 Corinthians 12:31–13:8
- John 15:9–17

The wedding invitation that brings us together this afternoon carried a unique introduction. It was a single sentence from Ana and Thomas, and it reads: "This day I will marry my best friend, the one I laugh with, live for, love." When I received it seven weeks ago, it triggered the three points I want to develop here: Christian marriage at its best is a special kind of friendship—a friendship that involves laughter, life, and love. A word on each.

I

First, "This day I will marry my best friend, the one I laugh with." To marry is to laugh. Not that marriage is a laughing matter, to be taken and treated lightly. But neither is laughter at its best a belly explosion over a raunchy joke. To laugh is to enjoy. And laughter reaches a peak of enjoyment when laughter is shared, when you can grab a friend and shout, "Hey, look at this! Isn't it hilarious?"

It is in marriage that laughter is most intimately shared. Not always, of course. You do not laugh over the croup of your child, over the mortgage on your home, over infidelity that defiles your bed. But by and large, spouses with a sense of humor start wedded life with an advantage. Married laughter means that you take *yourself* seriously but never too seriously. You can look in the mirror and smile. Why? Because you see behind your workaday face a theater of the absurd. You are a creature of contradiction. Today you believe and tomorrow you doubt, today you hope and tomorrow you despair, today you love and tomorrow you hate. You are exciting and boring, enchanted and disillusioned, manic and depressive. You are "cool" on the outside and you hurt within. You feel bad about feeling good, are afraid of your joy, feel guilty if you don't feel guilty. You are trusting and suspicious, selfless and selfish, wide-open and locked in. You know so much and so little. You are honest and you still play games. Aristotle said you are a rational animal; I say you are an angel with an incredible capacity for beer!

Married laughter means you can look at the *other* and enjoy the foibles, the human frailties, that irritate the ultraserious. I know, life together is made up of thousands of little things: individual toothbrushes, a bathtub without dirt rings, stop-watch schedules, kisses without passion, friends I like and you loathe, TV football versus PBS, fashion plate or Levis-lover. Not that the little things are unimportant; rather that to laugh is to have a sense of proportion—recognizing what is more important or less important, agreeing to disagree when cold logic is on your side, refusing to make the other over into your own image. It is not that you do not care; you simply sense that humor, as the English novelist Thackeray put it, is "a mixture of love and wit."

Married laughter means you can look out at the *world* together and see what God saw in the beginning: how good it is. Oh yes, Iraq may lay waste our courage, coke desecrate the flower of our youth, poverty rape one of every five U.S. children, AIDS ravage 25% of New Yorkers by the year 2000. And still you can spy the goodness latent in innumerable human hearts; you know from your own experience and from a host of Augustines that even saints can sin; you realize from your Catholic theology that only God's grace can keep us weak mortals moral for any length of time. And so you extend your "mixture of love and wit" to all whose path you cross—even those who make us sweat to like them.

II

Second, "This day I will marry my best friend, the one I live for." Tom and I have been friends a long time—a friendship that in a sense began the day I baptized him over 28 years ago. But for all our closeness, I am not his "best" friend, Tom does not live for me the way he will live for Ana. When two people live without reserve for each other, you have what St. Augustine called "one soul in two bodies."[1] Here is perfect friendship, here the highest type of oneness to be found on earth. The "I and thou" never quite disappear; what does disappear is "mine and thine."

The most remarkable expression of such friendship is the unique union that obtains between husband and wife. Not every married couple can say they are friends; in fact, some separated couples are closer friends now than they ever were in bed. But the ideal God had in mind when shaping the first man and the first woman for each other was . . . perfect friendship.

In such friendship, in living for each other, Tom never ceases to be Tom, Ana is always and everywhere Ana; they are not submerged in each other, do not cease to be individual, free personalities. What disappears is not the ego but egoism, where the world revolves around me, my insightful ideas and my deep-seated desires, my gall bladder and my hiatal hernia, my sensitive skin and my hurt feelings, my gourmet tastes and my sense of what is true or beautiful or good; where your wants and your needs are never comparable to mine, are shrugged off with an impersonal "that's the way the ball bounces."

Not so, Ana and Tom, not so for you. The vows you will shortly exchange are a sacred promise: to live for each other. Not only to "be true to" each other "in good times and in bad," not only to "honor" each other "all the days of [your] life," but to make the other the center, the focus, the very meaning of your existence.

Obviously, it cannot mean that others do not share in that fresh focus. After all, the same Lord who blesses your yearning to live for each other tells you that the very first commandment obliges you to live for the Lord. For a Lord who *is* Life and lives for ever, from whom all life is born, who gifted you with life, who is your very life. And the same Lord told you that "a second" commandment is "like" the first: You are to live for your sisters and brothers (cf. Mt 22:39). Especially for those whose living is limited—by the color of their skin or the illness in their bones, by the hunger in their stomachs or their thirst for your affection. It is a marvelous mission: You are to live for each other, live for God, live for others. Not a "mission impossible." Impossible only if your life is not rooted in God, if something or someone God has made takes God's place in your life. But if, as your presence here suggests, God is *numero uno* to both of you, then your living for each other is drawn into your living for God; and your living for God and each other will draw you out into a world that desperately needs what you two have to offer. I mean your deep faith, your confident hope, your boundless love.

III

Your boundless love. This sets the stage for your third assertion, "This day I will marry my best friend, the one I love." What love means to you does not demand a definition; it is splendidly summarized in your promise to live for each other. It might help, however, to realize that, for all the centuries of romantic poetry that surround it, love is one of the toughest four-letter words in your dictionary.

Love is tough because time can turn into love's enemy. Unless you are careful, time can make for a rut. The wonder of the other disappears and you take each other for granted. What was a covenant symbolizing the love between Christ and his Church is swallowed up in the legal contract, in your rights and his or her obligations. Faults that earlier fell through the cracks or raised only a smile now become federal cases. The same person who offered a love note with long-stemmed roses now tells a secretary to order flowers delivered—any kind she thinks appropriate. Civilized conversation is replaced by shrewish scolding or icy silence. And the breakfast table that once held your hands together is divided in two by the *Washington Post* or the *Wall Street Journal*.

For love to grow, the love in your hearts is not enough. The love within has to express itself. "It is" indeed "the thought that counts," but the thought has to escape your head. Love has to be creative, imaginative. Diamonds may be for ever, but you cannot for ever be giving diamonds. And you need not. What is genuinely for ever is you: the you in each touch, the you in your voice, the you in your eyes.

Have you ever read a touching short story by O. Henry entitled "The Gift of the Magi"?[2] It is the story of a young married couple, almost penniless. There are two possessions in which both take a mighty pride: Jim's gold watch that has been his father's and his grand-father's, and Della's beautiful brown hair that cascades below her knees. Della has only $1.87 to buy a Christmas gift for Jim. So she sells her hair for 20 dollars; now her head is "covered with tiny, close-lying curls that made her look wonderfully like a truant schoolboy." Jim's present to Della? A set of expensive combs to be worn in her lovely, now vanished hair, combs she has worshiped in a Broadway window. But she hugs them and exclaims with dim eyes and a smile, "My hair grows so fast, Jim." Her present to him? A platinum pocket chain for his watch. He smiles: "I sold the watch to get the money to buy your combs. And now suppose you put the chops on." And O. Henry concludes: " . . . two foolish children who most unwisely sacrificed for each other the greatest treasures of their house. [But] Of all who give and receive gifts, such as they are wisest. Everywhere they are wisest. They are the magi."

Good friends all: The wedding invitation that stimulated this homily conceals a challenge. A challenge mainly to the married among you. Whether wed one year or ten years, 25 or 50, time may well have taken its toll, has surely exacted a price from you, if only by removing the original glow. Why not recapture some of that first day's excitement? How? When Tom and Ana vow themselves to each other, why not join your own hands, and in the secret places of your heart murmur as once before, perhaps as never before, "This day I marry my best friend, the friend with whom I laugh, the friend for whom I live, the friend I love above all else on earth"?

Holy Trinity Church
Washington, D.C.
September 8, 1990

15
CHRIST AND/OR BUDDHA?
Wedding Homily 4

- Genesis 1:26–28, 31
- 1 Corinthians 12:31–13:8
- John 15:9–12

Today we gather to celebrate. To celebrate love. The love of a man and a woman. There is always reason to celebrate such love. But today, I suggest, we have special, singular reason to rejoice, because today love unites a woman who is Roman Catholic and a man who is Buddhist. Cause for joy? I am acutely aware that to many of you this may sound strange; so let me expand on it in three stages. First, the differences that divide us. Second, the elements that unite us. Third, the role that Cathy and Dien will play in our lives. Let me speak very frankly to all of you here, because we are closer to one another than we think, but must come closer than we actually are.

I

First, the differences that divide us. However much we try, a certain uneasiness hovers over a Catholic-Buddhist marriage. The backgrounds are so different. To begin with, Christ and Buddha seem so far apart: the eternal Son of God who was born of a virgin, lived a celibate existence, spent three years preaching repentance and rebirth and a kingdom not of this earth, and died in agony on a bloody cross; and the Buddha who married, renounced wife and child to seek deliverance from pain and rebirth, reached the stage of emptiness through asceticism, and attained "Enlightenment" by understanding suffering and the way to conquer it.

Again, the Catholic is brought up on a system of beliefs. Not that dogma alone can save; it cannot. But the system is terribly important

98

for Catholics; untold thousands have died cruel deaths rather than forsake their faith. On the other hand, for all its reverence for sacred teachings, Buddhism is not a belief system in the Western sense. Buddhists "require of religion not that it be true rather than false, but that it be good rather than bad."[1] Buddhism is doing—living this moment.

Again, as we move about the world, there is a recognizable sameness about Catholicism, despite the cultural clothes that, for example, distinguish an African Mass from an American. But as we move from India to Sri Lanka, to Burma and Thailand, to Vietnam and Laos and Cambodia, to China and Tibet and Mongolia, to Korea and Japan, the variety of Buddhist beliefs and sects, monasteries and temples, traditions and worship, impressive though they are, understandably confuse us. As we must confuse you with our insistence on a body of doctrine significant for salvation: one God in three persons, a dying/rising Son of God; a worship that centers on the body of Christ made present on our altars and in our bodies; a moral code that guides our living from bedroom to board room.

Our total cultures are so different. We look different, talk a different language, eat different foods, have different values. In consequence, we often feel uneasy in one another's presence; all too often we do not know what to say. We are such different people. Let's admit it, and start from there.

II

But, second, where do we go from there? We start with an awareness: I mean, recognizing that we are closer than we think, have more in common than we realize. A Catholic, I resonate to the Eightfold Path the Buddha formulated to overcome the desire that for him was the root of suffering in human existence. (1) You know the truth. (2) You intend to resist evil. (3) You say nothing to hurt others. (4) You respect life, morality, and property. (5) You hold a job that does not injure others. (6) You struggle to free your mind of evil and to embrace what is good. (7) You control your feelings and your thoughts. (8) You practice contemplation, concentration. In this way good men and women enjoy a remarkable freedom and endless bliss.[2] Buddhists, for their part, can echo a strong amen to what Jesus called the two greatest commandments of the law: "You shall love the Lord your God with all your heart, and with all your soul, and with all your mind, and with all your strength. . . . You shall love your neighbor as yourself" (Mk 12:30–31).

A Catholic, I can relate to the Buddhist stress on monastic life, with its insistence on poverty, meditation, and study. At the same time, I am drawn to the Buddhist ability to link contemplation with action, meditating and doing, eternal bliss and the supreme importance of the present moment.[3]

On the other hand, I know that Buddhists can feel comfortable with much that triggers Catholic daily life. Our Ten Commandments warn us against worshiping false gods, insist on reverence for parents, prohibit killing and stealing, adultery and false witness. We foster a profound respect for life, from the youngest fetus to the oldest of the aging. We are deeply concerned over issues of social justice: unethical business practices, the enslaving poverty that afflicts one of every five U.S. children, the rape of the earth, substance abuse, 35 million Americans without access to healthcare, minorities with second-class citizenship.

III

So then, we are closer than we think; still, we are not as close as we ought to be. This leads to my third and final point: the role of Cathy and Dien in our lives. Very simply, their love is the high point in our gathering, not only because these two individuals are joining hands and hearts, but because their love is a living symbol. Dien and Cathy symbolize the oneness that should exist between Buddhists and Catholics; they suggest without words the way we ought to see one another. Oh yes, they themselves do not see eye to eye on ever so many religious issues. But they are willing to join their individual lives, even their individual religions, in the conviction that their love will enable them to understand each other more intimately.

They are not mouthing the absurd aphorism "Love conquers all." No, love simply cannot overcome all problems raised by cultures and beliefs. But without love no serious effort can be made to decrease the distance that separates—separates nations and peoples, Catholic and Protestant, atheist and Jew, yes Christian and Buddhist. Without love we will not take the trouble to understand one another. And without understanding we live dreadfully isolated lives, live on the edge of tragedy, personal, national, universal. I recall vividly how a thoughtful journalist, Meg Greenfield, many years ago added a new dimension to explain America's tragic failure in Vietnam: We did not really know who the Vietnamese were. If love increases understanding, conversely understanding deepens love. It is a constant movement back and forth, like a pendulum that never stops.

That is why this religious ceremony, what Catholics call the Eucharist, is so important, even if some of you do not relate to it. For the Eucharist re-enacts what Catholics see as the most remarkable love in human history, the love that brought God's Son down to earth to share our flesh, to walk our ways, to experience our pain, to die our death. And he did all this for reasons the original Buddha, Siddhartha Gautama, would understand: to free us from enslavement to worldly desires, to bring an enlightenment that would pierce through the unhappiness of human existence, to deal a deathblow to death, to make possible perfect peace and happiness.

Knowing all this, we shall still be different; for we understand in different ways, we search for an ultimate Truth, a final Love, that is a mystery, that neither Buddhist nor Catholic can comprehend in our present stage of light-with-darkness. But we will be ever so much closer, because we shall be searching together, in sympathy with one another.

Cathy and Dien: Although I have not addressed you directly, I trust you have sensed that you are central to all I have said. For in a few moments your exchange of vows will not only bind you together for life in a unique personal relationship of love; it will lay on you a singular privilege, an uncommon burden. You see, the love and understanding you bring to each other must leap out to us, to Buddhists and Catholics—in fact, to all whose lives you will touch. The way the two of you look at each other in love, this should rub off on the rest of us.

It is not a mission impossible. The proof? This homily. You two have compelled me to look deeply inside myself, to regret my own neglect of Buddhism, to discover some of its religious riches. Strangely—or not so strangely—I am the better Catholic for the experience, much richer, if only because I have seen the hand of God outstretched over all the earth, have found the love of the Lord in ways of thinking foreign to mine.

Finally, I urge all of you to open your minds and hearts to the three texts just read to you from the Christian Scriptures. Three memorable affirmations. (1) All of us have been shaped to God's image, are like God. Male and female, Christian and Buddhist, we are gifted with the power to know and to love; we share God's own understanding, God's own freedom.[4] (2) All of us are challenged by St. Paul's lyrical outburst to the Christians of Corinth: "If I . . . understand all mysteries and all knowledge, and if I have the fulness of faith, so as to remove mountains, but have not love, I am nothing. If I give away all I have, and if I deliver my body to be burned, but have not love, I gain nothing" (1 Cor 13:2–3). (3) All of us can resonate to the words of a man who died for every single one of us: "This is my commandment, that you love one another as I have loved you" (Jn 15:12).

Holy Trinity Church
Washington, D.C.
November 3, 1990

16
LIFE IS A MYSTERY, LOVE IS A DELIGHT
Wedding Homily 5

- Micah 6:6–8
- Romans 8:31–39
- John 17:20–26

I preach today in full awareness of a paradox. A paradox, you know, is an apparent contradiction. One of the countless paradoxes within Catholicism you see before you: The homily to a man and woman about to be married is delivered by an unmarried male. Still, seven decades of wedding watching, with love and concern, make for a certain experience of marriage, from the outside indeed but not negligible. More importantly, Lisa and Marin have simplified my task, lightened the burden. How? By the three texts they have plucked from God's own Book, the passages just proclaimed in your hearing. For these texts chosen with care tell me something about them, reveal their ideals, their insight into the awesome relationship we call marriage. Let me unpack those texts in orderly fashion. They speak (1) of Christ, (2) of oneness, (3) of response.

I

I begin with Christ. From Paul's letter to the Christians of Rome Lisa and Marin have extracted a highly rhetorical, emotional passage. Listen to some of it once again:

> He who did not spare His own Son but gave him up for us all, will He not also give us all things with him? . . . Who shall separate us from Christ's love [for us]? Tribulation, distress, persecution, famine, nakedness, peril, sword? No, in all these things we are more

than conquerors through him[1] who loved us. I am sure that not
death or life, not angels or principalities or powers, not things
present or to come, not height or depth or anything else in all
creation, will be able to separate us from God's love in Christ Jesus
our Lord.

An exceptionally eloquent expression of Christian faith, hope,
and love. Eloquence linked to common sense. Notice, Paul is speaking
of God's love for us, not our love for God. On this love of God for us
he asks rhetorical questions—I mean questions that for a Christian
are not really questions at all. The God who freely delivered His only
Son to a bloody cross out of love for us, can He possibly be stingy,
grudging, mean in dealing with us after Calvary? The Christ who
freely died for us on twin beams of bloody wood, can he possibly stop
loving us whether we live or die, stop loving us when we are troubled
by forces outside or our psyche within, by supernatural beings or
astrological powers? No, he cries. Never, never can anything created
stop God and His Christ from loving us. Paul knows Israel's history,
summed up in Hosea: ". . . the Lord loves the people of Israel, even
though they turn to other gods" (Hos 3:1). Paul knows how Jesus
consorted with sinners, with despised toll collectors and harlots. The
genuine Christian knows that Christ's love for us is endless, does not
change when we change.[2]

This Lisa and Marin know. This is the strength behind their
marriage. In Jesus' own figure, the rains will fall, the floods will come,
the winds will blow and beat upon their house; but it will not fall,
because it has been "founded upon *the* rock" (Mt 7:25). More concretely, difficulties will almost certainly crowd on their life together—
whether financial or familial, psychological or physiological. There is
no guarantee, human or divine, that they will escape hurt—pain of
flesh or spirit. No year's warranty against ague or argument, discouragement or dejection, the death of dear ones—all the ills that flesh is
heir to. For if marriage is made in heaven, it has to be lived on earth—
an earth that breeds peace and war, poverty and wealth, sickness and
health, love and hate, wine and blood.

Through all of this and more, their security rests not so much in
what earth can do for them—from dear friends to technology—useful though these may be. Ultimately, they rest their hopes for happiness in the conviction that, whatever befalls, however surprising, God
will be there; the risen Christ, at God's right hand, will, as Paul promised, intercede for them. With such conviction, such faith, they can
with confidence take the risk that surrounds all marriage, the risk that

imperils all that is human. As Paul put it, if God is for us, what matter who is against us?

When Marin ripped that reading from Romans, he said to Lisa: "This seems to say it all: God, man, the structure of existence. Aquinas would concur." I know Lisa does.

II

Second, oneness. To speak of Christ is to speak of oneness. That is why the text from John's Gospel is so pertinent today. Listen once more to the prayer of Christ at the Last Supper, just before he left for the garden of his agony:

> I do not pray for [these my disciples] only, but also for those who believe in me through their word, that they may all be one; even as you, Father, are in me, and I in you, that they also may be in us, so that the world may believe that you have sent me. The glory which you have given me I have given to them, that they may be one even as we are one. I in them and you in me, that they may become perfectly one, so that the world may know that you have sent me and have loved them even as you have loved me. . . . I made known to them your name, and I will make it known, that the love with which you have loved me may be in them, and I in them.

Sounds outrageous, doesn't it? We who claim to be followers of our Lord, companions of Christ, are expected to be one not in some vague, gossamer, poetic sense. Jesus prayed that in our relationships we would reflect the oneness that exists between Father and Son in God's secret life. We are to be "perfectly one." You may not like the idea; you may think it an impossible ideal; you may not want to be that close to your next-door neighbor, to prochoicers or prolifers, to Iraq's Saddam, to Republicans or Democrats. But unless you and I are struggling to reach that ideal, to break down the barriers that divide individuals and nations, we are dreadfully unchristian.

Now in this struggle of all Christians for perfect oneness the oneness of a man and a woman in marriage plays a critical role. Your oneness, Lisa and Marin, the way you live your love, should symbolize, express, re-present in a unique way the love of Christ our Lord for his Father, his love for the people shaped in his image and purchased through his passion, his love for the loveless, the unloved, the unlovable. What God expects of you two, expects of every married couple, is a love like the love God's Son in flesh lived during the three decades he walked our dust. What does this demand in the concrete circumstances of your life?

1) Like the love within the Trinity, like Christ's love for us, your love for each other must be *total*. I do not mean you cannot love anyone else. I do mean you cannot love any other human the way you love each other. Married love, the oneness of wife and husband, is unique. Unique in that it is a gift of yourself on every level—spirit and flesh, heart and soul, mind and will, passion and emotion. You remain indeed two persons: Lisa does not become Marin, Marin does not fade into Lisa; there is always "I and thou," but . . . never "mine and thine." Yes, there should be what Gibran calls "spaces in your togetherness,"[3] but only so that love may not be smothered, your oneness turn destructive.

2) Like love within the Trinity, like Christ's love, you dare to say that your love is *for ever*. That expression has just about dropped out of our vocabulary. Nothing is for ever—not TV serials or Broadway SROs, not football contracts or Hank Aaron's home-run record, not hair or health, not peace or prosperity, not Garfinckel's, not even diamonds. In this cultural context Marin and Lisa pledge a love that rivals Christ's love for them. Not "as long as it works out," not "till we are attracted to someone else," but those five unparalleled monosyllables, "till death do us part." Such words should not be spoken lightly, particularly in the context of a Eucharist where we celebrate a love that not even death on a cross could bring to an end.

3) Like Christ, your very human love must link up with *God's love*. This is not pious prattle expected of even a Jesuit's homily; this is Christian realism. It means a recognition on your part that to marry is to risk. Today's odds on success? In a burst of generosity, Jimmy the Greek might give you even money. It only proves, if further proof were needed, that high IQs cannot fashion fidelity, blue eyes and brown do not promise permanence, delight in Michael Jackson and Mozart does not guarantee that the music of love will never stop.[4] What is needed is what you two already possess: the hope that St. Paul claims "does not disappoint" you, because "God's love has been poured into [your] hearts through the Holy Spirit who has been given to [you]" (Rom 5:5).[5]

The point is, it takes three loves to keep a marriage on track: Lisa's love for Marin, Marin's love for Lisa, *and* God's love for both. But God's love is not a monosyllable in outer space; God's love is God's intimate presence to them, guaranteed by the Holy Spirit who lives within them. Marvel of marvels, when Lisa and Marin murmur their love-laden yes, they will channel God's love to each other. For of this single sacrament *they* are the ministers, not I; I am no more than the Church's official witness.

III

God's love for them demands a response. How they are to respond our third text reveals—from an Old Testament prophet of doom named Micah. Listen to it again, this time with ears and hearts open to what God might be saying not solely to Israel, not merely to Marin and Lisa, but to you and me:

> With what shall I come before the Lord,
>   and bow myself before God on high?
> Shall I come before Him with burnt offerings,
>   with calves a year old?
> Will the Lord be pleased with thousands of rams,
>   with ten thousands of rivers of oil?
> Shall I give my first-born for my transgression,
>   the fruit of my body for the sin of my soul?
> He has showed you, O man, what is good;
>   and what does the Lord require of you
> but to do justice, and to love steadfastly,
>   and to walk humbly with your God?

With what shall Lisa and Marin come before the Lord? What does God ask of them? What love always asks: to be loved in return. But specifically how?

1) "Do justice." But for you, Lisa and Marin, as for Israel, justice is not limited to the law or philosophy: Give each human what he or she has a strict right to demand. For you, as for Israel, to do justice is to act towards others as God has acted towards you, and precisely because God has acted that way. "Love the stranger," God told the Israelites, "for you were strangers in the land of Egypt" (Deut 10:19). Your recessional will be a burden and a privilege: You go forth *together* to a paradoxical world where millions live "high off the hog" and a billion fall asleep hungry, where men and women love one another and kill one another; to a "land of the free" where one child out of five grows up below the poverty line, minorities are still second-class citizens, black and white live a tenuous truce, and our city streets are captive to coke and crack. Here is the arena of your love. Not to touch this world with your love is not to worship God.

2) "Love steadfastly." Very simply, imitate a God whose synonym is fidelity, whose love never lapses however much we betray Him, who "does not deal with us according to our sins, nor requite us according to our iniquities" (Ps 103:10). It will not be easy—not in a culture where promises are made to be broken, contracts yield to power plays, one's word is rarely one's bond.

3) "Walk humbly with your God." To be humble is to recognize who you are: left to yourselves, on your own, terribly weak, all but impotent; with God, new creatures, alive with the life of the risen Christ, believing what passes belief, hoping against hope, loving as Christ loved.

A final word. On May 10 of this year a notable Catholic novelist died. Walker Percy (remember *Love in the Ruins?*) had a sacramental view of the world. I mean, for him even the most mundane, ordinary, unreligious objects or places could "be magic": a trunk in the attic, the ninth green of a golf course. With this vision he could make two affirmations in *Esquire*, affirmations I suggest as stimulants to keep married life from ever degenerating into a rut, into routine. "Life," he said, "is a mystery, love is a delight." That conviction he lived even through the indignities of a painful cancer. And together with delight in love, in reference to Jacob wrestling with God: "I don't see why anyone should settle for anything less than Jacob, who actually grabbed aholt of God and wouldn't let go until God identified himself and blessed him."[6]

Lisa and Marin: As you begin the first day of the rest of your life, I pray, first, that within the mystery of human and Christian living you may constantly experience the delight that is love: delight in each other, delight in God, delight in God's human images who surround you. I pray, second, that as you wrestle with God (and you shall), you will never let God go until He shows you His face and blesses you. . . . As God does today.

Holy Trinity Church
Washington, D.C.
November 24, 1990

17
FILLED WITH THE HOLY SPIRIT
Wedding Homily 6

- Acts 2:1–11
- 1 Corinthians 12:3–7, 12–13
- John 20:19–23

Bridget and Donald: Know it or not, by chance or design, you have chosen your wedding day wisely. For today is Pentecost. And Pentecost celebrates the breath-taking day when the Holy Spirit was poured forth on the first community of Christians, when these believers were sent out to begin something remarkably new, when Jews from every nation heard them telling the mighty works of God. Let me try to link those three happenings to your singular celebration. I mean (1) the power of the Spirit, (2) something new, and (3) the mighty works of God.

I

First, the power of the Spirit. Go back to the original community of Christians. There they were, gathered in one place. A small group, hard to say how many. It was a critical moment, crucially important for the new people of Christ. Surprise had followed on surprise. To their sorrow, their Master had been crucified; to their amazement, he had risen from the rock; to their disappointment, he had returned to his Father. As yet they had no specific plan for their Christian apostolate; they knew only that they were to bear witness to the risen Jesus. At this point they had no road map, were somewhat disorganized, not sure which way to go, not particularly confident about their ability to bear witness, perhaps afraid of their enemies in Jerusalem.

"Suddenly," Scripture tells us, life changed. "A sound like the rush of a mighty wind filled all the house." What seemed like "tongues

109

of fire" rested on each of the assembly. And "all were filled with the Holy Spirit" (Acts 2:2–4). It changed them. They felt different; they talked differently; they looked different—so much so that when they stepped outside, the people thought they were drunk—at nine in the morning! From that point on, they had no doubts; all their hesitations vanished away. Aflame with the power of the Spirit, they moved out into their new world. Not yet with a detailed scenario, but confident that in the power of the Spirit anything God might ask of them was possible.

So too, Bridget and Donald, so too for you. I announce no news when I say this is a critical moment in your lives—surely the most critical to date. By "critical" I mean that today is a turning point, an important juncture in your existence. The scenario for the years that lie ahead is not etched in stone. An older exhortation opening the Catholic wedding ceremony had a significant sentence: "Not knowing what lies before you, you take each other. . . ." Not knowing what lies before you. If marriage were just another business transaction, you could calculate the odds, follow the Dow Jones, buy or sell, plan what to do if the bottom drops out of the market. But in a contract "for better for worse, for richer for poorer, in sickness and in health, till death," your help has to come primarily not from below but from above.

What today's sacred rite, this sacrament, promises you is precisely this help from above, God's personal presence for the years that lie ahead. At the moment you murmur "I take you," when you give yourselves totally to each other, the Holy Spirit, the Spirit of Jesus, will descend on you—very much as the same Spirit descended like tongues of fire on the first community of Christians. What this does for you concretely brings me to my second point.

II

You see, the Spirit descended on the first Christians because through them God was about to do something new in the world. This small group of ordinary folk, already changed by the Christ with whom they had walked, were commissioned by him to change the world. How? In three ways. First, they were to enlighten the world's darkness, shed the revelation of Christ over the entire earth. Second, they were to move men and women from death to life, baptizing them into a whole new way of living, alive with the life of the risen Christ.

Third, they were to transform human living from hate to love, link men and women to "the other" all around them, to the Other above and within them. For such change, the Holy Spirit was indispensable. Why? Because the Holy Spirit is the Spirit of light, the Spirit of life, and the Spirit of love. It is the Holy Spirit who renews the face of the earth. As you heard in the reading from Paul, "There are different gifts but the same Spirit; there are different ministries but the same Lord; there are different works but the same God who accomplishes all of them in everyone. To each person is given the manifestation of the Spirit for the common good" (1 Cor 12:4–7).

Through you, too, Bridget and Donald, God is about to do something new. Not in the sense that it has never been done before; the number of successors to Adam and Eve is beyond our counting. But in each couple vowing total self-giving, God's plan for a new earth takes on fresh promise. Marriage, the unique union of two images of God similar but not the same, is God's ceaseless way not only of flooding the earth with people but of changing our earth increasingly into God's kingdom of peace, of justice, of love.

What God promises you today is the Holy Spirit as the dynamic force in the "something new" that is you two-in-one. To begin with, the dynamo that enables you to be light, life, and love to each other. *Light:* I mean the ability, the willingness, the urge to share with each other without reservation. Share knowledge and understanding, ideas and insights; share feelings—emotions and passions, hopes and fears, resentments and disappointments, ups and downs. *Life:* I mean the power you have to activate the gifts latent in each other, encourage, support, rejoice; the power to make each other's dreams come true; miraculously, the power to create, to bring to birth human images of yourselves, human images of God. *Love:* I mean not the pseudo love story that claims "Love is never having to say you're sorry," but the tough love that St. Paul commended to the Christians of Corinth: "Love is patient and kind, not jealous or boastful, not arrogant or rude; does not insist on its own way; is not irritable or resentful; rejoices not at wrong but only in the right; believes all things, hopes all things, endures all things" (1 Cor 13:4–7). Never to let the sun set on your anger. Easy enough the first two weeks, terribly difficult as the years move on, as you take those blue eyes more and more for granted.

The same dynamic Spirit enables you to be light, life, and love to "the other" outside you. The love that gives you totally to each other has a paradoxical aspect. Like the love within the Trinity, where the love of Father, Son, and Holy Spirit for one another overflows in the loving creation of a whole world, your love for each other dare not be imprisoned within your isolated selves. Somewhat as your love will constantly create something new in each other, so must it bring new-ness to the world around you—a world that is in ceaseless peril of growing stale—that strange world where men and women die for one another and kill one another.

Again, what you must bring to it, to the people whose lives you intersect, is light, life, and love. Now no longer individually; from now on, together. *Light.* You are uncommonly privileged, you know—able to touch so much of reality with your minds: the things of God, the people of God, God's very self. Cast that light lavishly abroad. As Jesus commanded you, "Let your light so shine before men and women that they may see your good works and give glory to your Father in heaven" (Mt 5:16). Share your minds, your understanding, with the brilliant and the stunted, with the powerful and the powerless, with the famous and the infamous. That is why today's liturgy opened with a thrilling prayer: "Father of light, send your Spirit into our lives with the power of a mighty wind, and by the flame of your wisdom open the horizons of our minds." *Life.* In the midst of so much life, we see death never taking a holiday: the senseless slayings on the savage streets of the District and the unnumbered deceased on the battlefield that was Iraq; the living dead done in by AIDS and crack; the wives abased and children abused; the hundred thousand cycloned in Bang-ladesh and the uncounted thousands destroyed by cholera in Latin America. No need to fly oceans; the dying are just a stone's throw away. *Love.* In your wedded life, there will hardly be a day when no one will call out for a word, a touch, a look. Your eyes and ears have simply to be opened—by the Holy Spirit. Otherwise you risk what Jesus told us the priest and Levite did when they spied the poor fellow beaten half to death by robbers: They "passed by on the other side" (Lk 10:31–32).

III

This leads into my third point: the mighty works of God. What struck Jerusalem's inhabitants with wonder the day of Pentecost was that the Christian community was telling them "in [their] own tongues the mighty works of God" (Acts 2:11). In the last analysis, that is what we should be praising this afternoon. There is a peril in marriage ceremonies. We see so many, hear of so many, read of so many that each one becomes a one-day marvel, remembered mostly for the sets and costumes, the buffet, a homily by a confirmed bachelor, and, as today, the beauty of a Bridget.

These I do not downgrade. I simply submit that what is of supreme significance today is that the union of Bridget and Donald fits neatly into "God's mighty works." Those works often take place quietly, in relative obscurity. Like the day an angel dropped into backwater Nazareth and, with no one to hear and no announcement in the Jerusalem *Post*, asked a Jewish teen-ager to mother God's Son. Like the day an alleged criminal was crucified in a corner of the world, with crowds jeering and no one aware that our planet was undergoing its redemption, its salvation. Like the day the Holy Spirit fired a small band of apostles to spread the gospel to every nook and cranny of the earth.

In this lovely little chapel, with hymns instead of hoop-la, with select dear ones as witnesses, Donald and Bridget take their place in God's story of salvation—the story that began back in Eden with "Be fruitful and multiply" (Gen 1:28), moved a gigantic step higher when Christ made marriage a privileged symbol of his union with the Church his bride, is gloriously expressed within this Eucharist which celebrates the most remarkable love in human history.

In this context, good friends, it would be singularly unsuitable for you to see yourselves as sheer spectators, ticket holders to a spectacle. You are here because each of you, in small measure or large, has played a part in this love story of God and two of God's images, a love story that reaches a certain high point today. No one of you lies outside this story. Equally important, your role does not end when Donald and Bridget murmur their eternal yes. In fact, your role intensifies. For they will live out their wedded oneness not on a fantasy island, a TV "Love Boat," but in a world where darkness, discord, and death will challenge daily their gifts of light, love, and life. The Holy Spirit has indeed been promised them, but they count on your presence as well. All of you, but one type of presence in particular: the example of men and women who, for one year or 50, have linked their lives in the kind of love that enfolds our dear couple this day.

And so, a few moments from now, when Bridget and Donald bind their hands and hearts for ever, I would ask the wedded among you to join your own hands and with them murmur quietly the solemn yet joy-filled words that make possible God's dream for all of humankind: "I take you to have and to hold, for better for worse, for richer for poorer, in sickness and in health, as long as life shall last." No more practical gift can you tender to these two you prize so dearly.

> Dahlgren Chapel
> Georgetown University
> Washington, D.C.
> May 19, 1991

18
THE MORE YOU SHARE,
THE MORE YOU HAVE
Wedding Homily 7

- Song of Songs 2:10–14; 8:6–7
- 1 Corinthians 12:31–13:8
- John 15:9–12

Mary Beth and Chris: Despite half a century of preaching at weddings, I still do so with a touch of guilt. This message to a man and woman linking their love for life might be delivered more meaningfully by two of you here before me—two who have lived your love for anywhere from ten years to 50, have experienced the highs and lows of wedded life, and can still testify, "It's tough, yet I wouldn't exchange it for the world." That said, let me confess that I delight in the privilege, and I feel I have something pertinent to say. I shall focus on one of the passages plucked by our dear couple from God's own Book, the four verses from John's Gospel. For they stress, dear Chris and Mary Beth, three truths of prime importance for your life together: (1) how incredibly Jesus loves you, (2) your singular love for each other, and (3) the responsibility such love lays on you to share your love with the world around you.

I

First, Jesus' love for you. His words are awesome: "As the Father has loved me, so have I loved you" (Jn 15:9). The kind of love God the Father has for Jesus, that kind of love Jesus has for you. This is not "Love Boat" stuff, the mindless passion that TV grinds into our living rooms. What is the Father's love for Jesus like? It is a total love, unconfined, without restriction, utterly selfless, a love that will never end. It is a love that pervaded Bethlehem when Jesus was born, fled with him before Herod to Egypt, hovered over him as he grew up in

115

Nazareth, thrilled him as he preached and prayed, strengthened him in the Garden of Gethsemane, never abandoned him even when he felt utterly forsaken on the cross, raised him from the dead. It is a love that never changes, yet is never dull. Jesus never tires of it, is warmed by it even now in his risen flesh.

With that kind of love the Lord Jesus loves you. Reflect for a moment on the simple yet profound sentence of St. Paul, "The Son of God loved me and gave himself for me" (Gal 2:20). God's own Son not only took your flesh but nailed that flesh to twin beams of wood for you. It's almost impossible to believe; in fact, without God's grace to help us we could not possibly believe it— the "for me" of Calvary. Paul himself was amazed: "God shows His love for us in that while we were yet sinners Christ died for us" (Rom 5:8).

It is that love which hovers over you today. For the sacrament that will shortly bind you for life was born on Calvary. From that dark Good Friday all that is Christian stems. Had not God's Son hung for three hours pinned to a cross, neither you nor I would be here: no church, no crucifix, no Eucharist, no sacrament to bless this marriage. And as preface to Calvary you have the opening chapter of the Hebrew Testament: an imaginative God fashioning two images of God, strikingly similar but never the same, commanding them, "Be fruitful and multiply" (Gen 1:28). You even have God's extraordinary love for the aged. I mean Abraham and Sarah—Abraham a hundred years old, Sarah pushing 91 and just told by an angel she will have a baby, and both laughing, as a creative Protestant preacher put it, "at the idea of a baby's being born in the geriatric ward and Medicare's picking up the tab."[1]

How much does our Lord love the wedded? He made marriage between Christians a singular symbol. In the divine dream, your love is, or should be, the kind of love that expresses best the love that exists between Christ and his people. "This," St. Paul told the Christians of Ephesus, "is a great mystery, and I take it to mean Christ and the Church" (Eph 5:32). The true meaning of the mystery of two becoming one flesh is the union between Christ the bridegroom and his people the Church. And our Lord's love for the wedded is wonderfully practical. He will be there for you whenever you need him. Not automatically, not compelling your love; but if you live for him, you will experience his promise, "If [you] love me, . . . my Father will love [you], and we will come to [you] and make our home with [you]" (Jn 14:23).

II

This brings me to my second point: your love for each other. You heard the words of Jesus, "This is my commandment, that you love one another as I have loved you" (Jn 15:12). Not an invitation; a command. And the command applies to all who claim to be Christian, but in a singular way it should speak to the married.

You have just heard how profoundly Jesus loves you. Now you are told to love each other as Jesus has loved you. What does it demand of you in the concrete? At least three responses. First, your love must be a *total* gift. Ideally, you hold nothing back. You share not only all you have, but all you are. It is easy enough to give a dozen roses, especially by phoning a florist; it means so much more if a single rose has a love letter attached. It is nonsense to echo Hollywood, "Love means never having to say you're sorry"; living together for decades calls for constant remembrance of St. Paul, "As the Lord has forgiven you, so you also must forgive" (Col 3:13). Rather, love means never taking your beloved for granted. Not easy when you are so close so long. It calls for a way of living and acting modeled on the earthly Jesus, who took no one for granted—not his 12 apostles, not his 70 disciples, not his mother. Each person he met, no matter how many times, it was as if it were the first time, the last time, the only time.

Second, to love as Jesus loved is to give *joy* to the other. It is a love such as Jesus had when he said to his special friends, "You have sorrow now, but I will see you again and your hearts will rejoice, and your joy no one will take from you" (Jn 16:22). For this there is no magical push button that actuates joy. Marital joy is born of mutual thoughtfulness: What is it that pleases the other, delights, surprises with joy? The paradox of such thoughtfulness? What begins by striking joy in the other ends with unexpected delight for you.

Third, to love as Jesus loved is to love the other even unto *crucifixion*. Harsh words? Perhaps. But you folk know more intimately than I how much of Christ's cross is erected over families. I do not mean that wedded life is a ceaseless Calvary. I do mean that in the human and Christian vision what a German theologian called "dying in installments"[2] is part and parcel of human living. As time moves on, God takes from us gradually or swiftly so much that gave joy to our youth: energy, lustiness, health, life itself. Rather than bore you with abstractions, let me tell you a story—a story told by a remarkable surgeon who experienced the episode he recounts.

I stand by the bed where a young woman lies, her face postopera-
tive, her mouth twisted in palsy, clownish. A tiny twig of the facial
nerve, the one to the muscles of her mouth, has been severed. She
will be thus from now on. The surgeon had followed with religious
fervor the curve of her flesh; I promise you that. Nevertheless, to
remove the tumor in her cheek, I had cut the little nerve.

Her young husband is in the room. He stands on the opposite
side of the bed, and together they seem to dwell in the evening
lamplight, isolated from me, private. Who are they, I ask myself, he
and this wry-mouth I have made, who gaze at and touch each other
so generously, greedily? The young woman speaks.

"Will my mouth always be like this?" she asks.

"Yes," I say, "it will. It is because the nerve was cut."

She nods, and is silent. But the young man smiles.

"I like it," he says. "It is kind of cute."

All at once I *know* who he is. I understand, and I lower my
gaze. One is not bold in an encounter with a god. Unmindful, he
bends to kiss her crooked mouth, and I so close I can see how he
twists his own lips to accommodate to hers, to show her that their
kiss still works. . . .[3]

"He twists his own lips to accommodate to hers, to show her that
their kiss still works."

III

This brings me to my third point: your responsibility to share
your love with the world around you. Jesus' command "Love one
another" is not limited to a love canoe for two. The "other" is the
"neighbor" in the second great commandment, "Love your neighbor
[at least as much] as you love yourself" (Mt 22:39). And if you ask,
with the lawyer in the Gospel, "Who is my neighbor?" (Lk 10:29),
Jesus repeats his parable of the Good Samaritan. Your neighbor is
every man, woman, or child who has in some way fallen "among robbers," has been stripped, beaten, and left half dead (v. 30). That
number is legion.

The joyous recessional that will usher you down the aisle will
carry you from church to world, from this safe sanctuary to sin-
scarred states where all too many cannot sing "America the Beautiful." Our victory parades have to be halfhearted as long as one American child in five grows up in poverty (one black in three); as long as
40,000 children under five die needlessly each day in developing

countries—27 in the next 60 seconds; as long as the number of children who die this decade alone may reach 150 million. As long as the war on the womb destroys more lives in a year than two world wars. As long as our cities are jungles of child abuse and teen-age suicides, of adolescent drug abuse and high-school dropouts. As long as 37 million Americans have no access to health care.

I mention this not to cast a pall over our justifiably rich joy in this moment. I mention it because you must grasp what the Second Vatican Council expressed so pungently: "The future of humanity lies in the hands of those who are strong enough to provide coming generations with reasons for living and hoping"[4]—your hands. I mention it because only people who love as selflessly and intensely as you do can change the face of the earth on which you tread so lightly. Imagine how beautiful America would actually be if every married couple brought a smile to the features of some loveless child, listened to one lonely aged, walked into a hospital ward once a week, pushed the wheel chair of a cripple along city streets, lobbied for legislation in one area of justice—spouse abuse, public housing, prison reform. Perhaps never quite the Garden of Eden, but surely less today's Garden of Gethsemane in which untold millions of other Christs sweat blood in agony.

Chris and Mary Beth: To love others as Jesus loves you—such is your Christian calling from the Lord who brought you to each other out of numberless possibilities, molded your love to the intensity of this moment, and now asks you to touch your united love to the dear disfigured images of himself for whom he died. Another paradox: The more you share your love with these others, the more you will have for each other. This I promise you, on my honor.

A final word—to all of you "out there." Clearly, you are here out of love—because each of you has touched Mary Beth and/or Chris in some way, has played a part, large or small, in the love story that reaches a new high today. Brace yourselves, for your task has only begun. To love as Jesus loved, this dear couple depends not only on God but on you. Not primarily for linens and layettes. More importantly, for the example of your own loving. It is not a desert isle they will inhabit, but a puzzling, contradictory world where love struggles with hate, hope with fear, faith in God with belief in nothing; where human images of God die for one another and kill one another.

What this couple's love needs to survive is the example of men and women who for one year or 50 have tried to love as Jesus loves. And so, when Chris and Mary Beth vow their love without end, I would ask the wedded among you to clasp each other's hand and softly murmur to each other and to the others in the world in which you move: "I promise to be true to you in good times and in bad, in sickness and in health. I will love you and honor you all the days of my life."

Of all wedding gifts, however expensive, none prove more precious, more lasting, than this. Why? Because in this gift you are giving them in love . . . your very selves.

Holy Trinity Church
Washington, D.C.
July 13, 1991

19
MEETING LOVE HEAD-ON
Wedding Homily 8

- Tobit 8:5–8
- Romans 12:9–21
- John 15:9–17

Good friends: We gather in a church that has rich resonances for the Ruether clan—birth and baptism, first Communion and marriage, death and Mass of Resurrection. And so it is wonderfully appropriate that we come together in so hospitable a house of God to celebrate Margy's love for a man the Ruethers have long since adopted and today lay legal claim to.

But what to say on an occasion so rich in its past, so striking in its present, so promising yet unpredictable for the future? Let me focus on the passage Jim and Margy have borrowed from St. Paul's letter to the Christians of Rome. For there Paul spells out what he means when he urges, "Let love be genuine" (Rom 12:9). Genuine: literally, without hypocrisy, without sham. What does this say to a man and woman about to give themselves to each other for the rest of their lives? I take three themes from Paul's challenge: (1) the relationship of Margy and Jim to each other; (2) their relationship to those around them; (3) their relationship to God.

I

First, "outdo one another in showing honor" (Rom 12:10). Let me phrase it in more contemporary language: Never love less than you are loved. I don't mean you make love a matter of competition, a two-person volleyball game in deep wet sand, a ceaseless neurosis, "You don't love me as much as I love you." That way madness lies. Simply, don't put limits on your loving. Genuine love does not parcel out its affection: I give as much as I get. No. Through my half century of priesting, the marriages that are most meaningful, the loves that last, are where the gift is total.

I know, that is terribly abstract. The concrete model for your loving, the supreme example of loving more than you are loved, is the God who took your flesh for love of you. St. Paul put it bluntly: "God shows His love for us in that while we were yet sinners Christ died for us" (Rom 5:8). For the Judas who betrayed him as well as for the John who rested on his heart at the Supper; for the Samaritan woman who had five husbands as well as for the Mary who gave him virginal birth. Love is not born because the other is perfect; nor should love die because the other is imperfect. Love does not begin with perfection. We grow in loving, and we grow *by* loving. It will not be easy. A spiritual writer, a Carmelite, put it forcefully when he insisted:

> [Love] is hard work. Each time we choose to love, we endanger our way of living. Ease, comfort, security, survival—a veritable routine of false gods—are wrecked when met head-on with love. When we who love offer our lives at full risk we shake the foundations of our way of living.[1]

Perhaps even more threatening to lifetime love is habit. Do the same thing day after day, month in and month out, and the wonder of it all disappears. A surgeon excising malignant tumors six hours a day: What happens to his sense of wonder over the human frame? How retain what one eloquent surgeon learned from "the inner geographies" of man and woman?[2]

> So, I have learned that man is not ugly, but that he is Beauty itself. There is no other his equal. . . . I have become receptive to the possibilities of love (for it is love, this thing that happens in the operating room), and each day I wait, trembling in the busy air. Perhaps today it will come. Perhaps today I will find it, take part in it, this love that blooms in the stoniest desert.[3]

So too for me. Through 50 years of daily Eucharist—how not to lose sight of the wonder of it all. How to take that lifeless host into my hands each day not casually but with reverence, how realize, breathlessly, that I am about to breathe into it the Bread of Life. Each day for 50 years.

So too for you, Jim and Margy. As with your legal practice and your artistic designing, so with your life together: Habit has to enter into it; some things you do automatically, without thinking. Only, don't let habit destroy the wonder of the other, the wonder you discovered the first time your eyes met in love, the touch that was magic, the voice that was music, pure Vivaldi.

II

Second, "Rejoice with those who rejoice, weep with those who weep" (v. 15). It sounds so simple and easy, but it is profound and difficult. It has to do with your love for others, the love that fans out from your love for each other. For your life together—you know it—will not be lived on a private fantasy island. Increasingly, as the years go on, you will develop networks of relationships. Together you will touch men, women, and children beyond your ability to imagine this sacred day, this day of beginnings. You know only that in your journeying together you will touch tears and laughter, hate and love, death and life.

How prepare for such mystery? Margy and Jim, you began the process when you asked Deb Johns to proclaim from this pulpit St. Paul's message to the faithful in Rome, the Christian law of love: "Bless those who persecute you; bless and do not curse them. . . . Live in harmony with one another; do not be haughty, but associate with the lowly; never be conceited. Repay no one evil for good. . . . So far as it depends upon you, live peaceably with all. . . . Leave [vengeance] to God. . . . If your enemy is thirsty, give him drink. . . . Do not be overcome by evil, but overcome evil with good" (Rom 12:14–21).

Behind all this lie two awesome commandments: what Jesus called the second great commandment of the Mosaic law and the Christian gospel, "You shall love your neighbor as yourself" (Mt 22:39), and what Jesus called his own commandment, "Love one another as I have loved you" (Jn 15:12). There is only one thing more difficult than loving someone as much as I love myself: loving someone the way our Lord Jesus loved us. For when Jesus delivered that commandment, he added instantly, "Greater love than this no one has, to lay down life itself" for another (v. 13). In this context a remarkably pertinent story comes to us Christians from the Sufi, Mohammedan mystics who possess nothing and desire nothing. It runs like this:

> Past the seeker on the prayer rug came the crippled and the beggar and the beaten. And seeing them, the holy one went down into deep prayer and cried: "Great God, how is it that a loving creator

can see such things and yet do nothing about them?" And out of the long, long silence God said: "I did do something about them. I made you."[4]

Margy and Jim, God has been fantastically good to you. You have experienced love from your infant days—a crescendo of love that reaches rare heights in your love for each other. Paradoxically, for that crescendo to continue, for your love to grow, you must give it away. Sociologists tell us that in the States today we are witnessing a resurgence of late-19th-century rugged individualism, where ultimately the one thing that matters is the almighty I. Not so for you— you whose Christian commitment compels you to love others as Jesus has loved you. Today's sacred rite should stimulate that commitment for two good reasons. You go forth from church to world no longer two but one, and you go forth from a Eucharist that re-enacts the world's most generous act of love: "This is my body given for you."

III

This leads into my third point, St. Paul's intoxicating counsel, "Be aglow with the Spirit, serve the Lord" (Rom 12:11). You see, marriage, like priesthood, is too delicate, too risky an affair to leave in the hands of sheer humans. After all, it was God who invented marriage in Eden; it was God's Son-in-flesh who raised the marriage of Christians to the dignity of a special sacrament; it is the Holy Spirit who, Paul tells us, is the source of Christian faith, Christian hope, Christian love.[5] Which is a powerful way of saying that if you try to operate your wedded life with only a Sunday nod to its creator, it may well go the way of Savings & Loan.

All very true, but quite negative. You ask, with the crowds questioning John the Baptist, "What then shall we do?" (Lk 3:10). Before all else, God has to be as intimately a part of your life as food and drink, as law and design, as parents and friends. About the year 200, a North African Christian tried to express what he called "the happiness of that marriage which the Church arranges, the Sacrifice strengthens, upon which the blessing sets a seal, at which angels are present as witnesses, and to which [God] the Father gives His consent." He went on:

> How beautiful, then, the marriage of two Christians, two who are one in hope, one in desire, one in the way of life they follow, one in the religion they practice. . . . Nothing divides them, either in flesh

or in spirit. . . . They pray together, they worship together, they fast together, instructing one another, encouraging one another, strengthening one another. Side by side they visit God's church and partake of God's Banquet; side by side they face difficulties and persecution, share their consolations. They have no secrets from one another; they never shun each other's company; they never bring sorrow to each other's hearts. Unembarrassed they visit the sick and assist the needy. They give alms without anxiety; they attend the Sacrifice without difficulty; they perform their daily exercises of piety without hindrance. They need not be furtive about making the Sign of the Cross, nor timorous in greeting the brethren, nor silent in asking a blessing from God. Psalms and hymns they sing to one another, striving to see which one of them will chant more beautifully the praises of their Lord. Hearing and seeing this, Christ rejoices. To such as these he gives his peace.[6]

I am not suggesting that you sing hymns to each other—"Onward, Christian Soldiers" or "Alleluia: The Strife Is O'er"; that may not be your "thing." What that 1800-year-old exhortation pictures for us is a man and woman sharing their love with God, expressing their love through God, thrusting their love out to others in God. It may call for quiet contemplation; a lawyer friend of mine in Arizona brews the coffee each morning, intercepts the phone, creates an atmosphere where his wife can meditate for half an hour. It does demand that God be as natural a topic of conversation as Donald Trump or quarterback Joe Montana. It means that books about growth in the spirit take their place alongside Jane Fonda's workout in the flesh. It calls for involvement in Eucharistic liturgy as the very heart of your oneness with each other in God, in a sense the glue that keeps your marriage together.

One final word, awfully important for all of us. There is someone here who had to send his regrets for not coming in the flesh. You see, we who celebrate Easter with faith, we who cried out with the cast of *Godspell* "He's alive, he's alive, he's alive!", are convinced that Jesus Christ was only the first of countless brothers and sisters to come alive after dying. In that belief we declare with St. Paul, "If the dead are not raised, then Christ has not been raised" (1 Cor 15:16). Yes, Margy's father is alive and well; with his Christ Gene Ruether is an unseen guest today. Believe it, he is aware of what is happening and our joy is very much his joy. So then, as we move into the wedding ceremony proper, let's be uncommonly conscious of a basic Christian reality: Gene's communion with us in what we call "the communion of saints," the oneness of all who are one in Christ—here and beyond.

And let us each, in our hearts, breathe a warm prayer of gratitude to this dear "father of the bride" without whose quiet fathering none of us would be here.

Sacred Heart Church
Columbia, Missouri
August 10, 1991

THROUGH LOVE MORE HUMAN
Wedding Homily 9

- Tobit 8:4–9
- Romans 12:1–2, 9–18
- Matthew 22:35–40

Good friends: I find it quite remarkable that today's wedding falls within the Christmas season. Remarkable because what happened on the first Christmas, what Christmas is all about, says a great deal about a man and a woman linking their lives for life in love. So, let me (1) speak a bit about Christmas, (2) turn to Nancy and Greg, and (3) address a brief word to all of you.

I

First, a word about Christmas. Recently a Catholic writer had a splendid insight. He wrote:

> It is a felicitous coincidence that during this Christmas season of 1991 the most popular movie in our land should be Walt Disney's "Beauty and the Beast." Felicitous in that the meaning of Christmas and the theme of the folk tale are exactly the same: Both are stories of loving transformation. Beauty does not love the Beast because he is beautiful; instead, she restores his humanity and makes him beautiful by loving him. And so, at Christmas.[1]

You see, God's Son wedded Himself to our flesh for one prime reason. He wanted to re-create, reshape, refashion, re-form our humanity. That humanity had fallen on evil times. One of these days you might read the beginning of Matthew's Gospel. Matthew traces Jesus' royal descent, his genealogy, through David the king back to Abraham the patriarch. At first glance it looks like a dull list of names—Perez and Boaz, Abijah and Uzziah, Ahaz and Hezekiah, Josiah and Jechoniah, and so on. But, "though there are a handful of heroes on [Matthew's] list, most are noted liars, thieves, adulterers, murderers, cheats—rotten apples on the family tree, caught up in the perennial passions of sex and politics."[2] Such is the family into which Jesus was born; such the humanity he came to transform, make genuinely human.

This humanity Jesus changed by the power of his love. As in "Beauty and the Beast," so at Christmas. Jesus did not love us humans, did not take our flesh, because we were beautiful; he restored our humanity, made us beautiful, by loving us. The First Letter of John squeezed it all into one unforgettable sentence: "In this is love, not that we loved God but that [God] loved us . . . " (1 Jn 4:10). The Son of God made it possible for us to be genuinely human. It is history's most powerful example of love's power. Love may not conquer all, but Christmas reveals its unparalleled ability to make us better than we are. The stable and the manger are signs of human weakness; yet they contain the power to overturn what the world finds most valuable: wealth, power, prestige.

Christmas tells us that the most powerful love is from above, the love St. Paul spoke of: "God's love has been poured into our hearts through the Holy Spirit who has been given to us" (Rom 5:5). During Advent the prophet Zephaniah proclaimed: "The Lord, your God, is in your midst . . . will rejoice over you with gladness, will renew you in [God's] love" (Zeph 3:17).

So, what is Christmas all about? Love . . . love from above . . . love that seems so powerless shivering in straw . . . love that nevertheless transforms. Christmas tells us that, even if it is now economics that makes the world go round, it is only love that can transform economic man/woman into someone genuinely human—human as Christ our Lord was and is human. So human that by God's grace we become sisters and brothers of Christ.

II

Now turn from December 25 to January 4, from Christ wedding to himself all that is human, to Greg and Nancy about to wed. Here be careful. Don't carry the parallels too far. I am not suggesting that the marriage we celebrate today is a process wherein Beauty from the West tames Beast from the East. Nor am I implying that, like Christ transforming us into an image of himself, in marriage Greg turns into Nancy, Nancy into Greg. What, then, is the real parallel? Simply the power of love, love within us from above, to transform the other, make the other better than he or she is.

You see, God's scenario for making us more human through love only *began* in Bethlehem; it was not even consummated on Calvary. God's plan includes a people—a people of God's own choosing, a people so linked to Christ that St. Paul could call us the Body of Christ. It is this people that is to play Christ to the world. And within this people the vast majority play Christ, carry Christ's love, by linking their lives in a sacred union called marriage—a union which, St. Paul argued, symbolizes more vividly than anything else the love that binds Christ and his people. More powerfully than priesthood.

What precisely is this love which Nancy and Greg are to carry together? The Gospel they chose to highlight this sacred rite says it all: You shall love the Lord your God above all else, and you shall love the other at least as much as you love yourself. In the light of this twin commandment which sums up the Old Testament and the New, let me sketch my dream for Greg and Nancy.

First, I dream that you will increasingly experience—experience together—the Christmas revelation: Love begins above, in the mind and heart of God. I do not simply decide I will love God. God always takes the initiative, the first step. That you already experience this is clear from this setting. The setting is Eucharist—literally, thanksgiving. This nuptial Mass is a prayer of gratitude to the God who brought you together against odds off the board; gratitude for the gift of God's crucified and risen Christ; gratitude to the Christ who in a few short moments will bind you for life; gratitude to the risen Lord who will rest in your hands, on your tongue, and in your heart "body and blood, soul and divinity."

But this divine initiative, God's love within you, demands a response. And so I dream that you will help each other not only to know *about* God but to know God, to realize what a famous French philosopher, Jacques Maritain, declared: The height of human knowing is not conceptual but experiential, not an idea but an experience: You *feel* God. Yes, feel God's love invading your whole being, as completely as you feel the love you have from each other. And I dream that you will respond to this experience. I mean, your quest for God, for deeper and deeper oneness with the Christ who died for you, will overshadow your life together. It is not a burden, no more than our Lady felt it a burden when the Holy Spirit overshadowed her and asked her to mother God's Son.

Second, love the other at least as much as you love yourself. That other has two dimensions. The other whom you must love in a special way is the other to whom you link your life today. Here I dream that you will never take each other for granted, never forget the miracle that is Nancy, the miracle that is Gregory—each a unique image of God who has captured your heart. I dream that you will ceaselessly see in the other what God sees, never lose a sense of wonder, surprise, rapture, awe, amazement that this product of God's artistry could love you totally. With such wonder your love will never cease to make the other more fully human because ever so much more Christlike.

I am not transforming marriage on earth to an idyllic paradise. The clouds will gather, the unexpected will stun you. I have no crystal ball; I simply know from a half century of priesting, from a hill called Calvary, that profound love rarely if ever escapes crucifixion. I dream that, whatever your calvary, your response will echo a true story told by a caring, articulate surgeon after a delicate operation:

> I stand by the bed where a young woman lies, her face postopera-
> tive, her mouth twisted in palsy, clownish. A tiny twig of the facial
> nerve, the one to the muscles of her mouth, has been severed. She
> will be thus from now on. The surgeon had followed with religious
> fervor the curve of her flesh, I promise you that. Nevertheless, to
> remove the tumor in her cheek, I had cut the little nerve.
>
> Her young husband is in the room. He stands on the opposite
> side of the bed, and together they seem to dwell in the evening
> lamplight, isolated from me, private. Who are they, I ask myself, he
> and this wry-mouth I have made, who gaze at and touch each other
> so generously, greedily. The young woman speaks.
>
> "Will my mouth always be like this?" she asks.
>
> "Yes," I say, "it will. It is because the nerve was cut."
>
> She nods, and is silent. But the young man smiles.
>
> "I like it," he says. "It is kind of cute."
>
> All at once I *know* who he is. I understand, and I lower my
> gaze. One is not bold in an encounter with a god. Unmindful, he
> bends to kiss her crooked mouth, and I so close I can see how he
> twists his own lips to accommodate to hers, to show her that their
> kiss still works. I remember that the gods appeared in ancient
> Greece as mortals, and I hold my breath and let the wonder in.[3]

"To accommodate to hers." To accommodate to his. The story tells us more than the words explicitly say. I dream it may symbolize for you the endless story of two-in-one, the sensitivity that makes for joy in the very heart of sorrow.

There is another dimension to the other. I mean the others who will surround you, invade you, torment you as long as you two shall live. Some can be difficult to love as much as you love yourself. For these are not always attractive, engaging, at times are not "our kind." I mean so many of our children: the 40,000 babies who die each year before their first birthday; the five and a half million who hunger for the scraps from our tables; the child who does not look like the Christ child because he has Down's syndrome or has been sexually abused. I mean our teen-agers: untold youngsters crushed by crack and coke; the highest adolescent pregnancy rate in the Western world; a teen-age suicide rate triple that of 30 years ago; more teen-age boys dead of gunshot wounds than from all natural causes combined.[4] I mean our dear elderly: those without access to healthcare; those who rummage for food in garbage cans; those threatened by euthanasia. I mean the jobless and the uneducated, the homeless and the hopeless—all those who experience far more of Christ's crucifixion than of his resurrection.

I dream that your privileged background—family, education, work experience, Catholic spirituality—will thrust you together to the service of God's unfortunates. In Scripture they command God's love in special fashion, for they stand most in need. I dream that the love you lavish on each other will expand to those whom love rarely touches. Paradoxically, as routine dulls somewhat the gloss of your love, the love you two lavish on others may well deepen your love for each other, may even prove your salvation.

III

Finally, a word to all of you. Today's sacred ceremony is not a spectator sport. Each of you has been invited to this lovely house of God because you have played some part—large, medium, or small—in the story that reaches a prominent peak today. But I must warn you, your task is not finished. This day's celebration, I have suggested, challenges Greg and Nancy to a three-phased love that can be daunting: to experience God's love and respond to it with all their mind, soul, and strength; to keep their love for each other alive, throbbing, despite the routine inevitable in long relationships; and to move their love for each other out to others, even walk a bit in the shoes of the unfortunate.

This would be a "mission impossible" were it not for a God who loves them—not from outer space but deep within them. God's help

they can count on. What they need as well to live that level of love is
. . . you. Not so much fondue forks or Waterford crystal; rather, your
support, your love, your strength. Perhaps especially the example of
husbands and wives who, for one year or 50, have lived their commitment through dark days and bright, have laughed and wept, have
slaved and enjoyed, have told us by their lives what it means to love
God, to love each other, to love the less fortunate.

So then, when Greg and Nancy join hands to become husband
and wife, I would ask the wedded among you to join your own hands
and murmur quietly, with even richer understanding, those words
that meant so much to you in the beginning: "I take you . . . to have
and to hold . . . for better for worse . . . for richer for poorer . . . in
sickness and in health . . . until death do us part." No more treasured
gift can you give your dear Nancy and Greg.

St. Andrew's Church
Pasadena, California
January 4, 1992

Anniversaries

21
TEACH AND ADMONISH IN ALL WISDOM
Homily for a Jesuit's Golden Jubilee

- Colossians 3:12–17
- John 15:9–12

I'm afraid this homily must zero in on Jesuits; our genial jubilarian leaves me no choice. But it's so hard to generalize about Jesuits; we have our paradoxes and our contradictions. Peter Canisius founds 18 colleges to ignite the Counter Reformation, ex-prince Aloysius Gonzaga dies at 23 while nursing the plague-infected. Matteo Ricci sells the gospel through Western science in Peking, Francis Xavier baptizes ten thousand in a single month in the Indies. Peter Claver is slave of the slaves in Latin America, Francis Regis has an apostolate among prostitutes. Miguel Pro dies at 36 before a firing squad in Catholic Mexico, Pedro Arrupe survives the first atom bomb in Hiroshima only to lie a living death for years in Rome. You find Jesuits gracing the Vatican in cardinals' robes, six Jesuits brutally murdered within the University of Central America. You find confessors to kings and martyrs to kings, Army chaplains and all-out pacifists, Jesuits on the golf course and Jesuits on the waterfront, Jesuits in clown suits and Jesuits in jail, Jesuits in costly classrooms and Jesuits in stinking slums—the whole gamut of human and inhuman living. And sprinkled among the pack, large as life, you find that endangered species . . . the Jesuit moralist.

Is there anything that links all these disparate characters, that gives rich meaning to their poverty and chastity and obedience, that even makes "golden" sense of a Richard McCormick? With almost six decades of Jesuit existence behind me, let me try my homiletic hand at a response. In typical fashion, three points. A Jesuit, every Jesuit, should be (1) a man open in mind and heart, (2) a man of the Church, (3) a man of faith that does justice. A word on each.

I

First, a Jesuit ought to be *open*. I mean, incredibly accessible, splendidly responsive—to God and to all God's images on earth. Our divine calling and our humanistic training should shape such a man. For from the very human tragedies of the Greeks to the *Divine Comedy* of Dante, from God's revelation in Christ to God's self-disclosure today, from medieval essentialism to contemporary existentialism, through our experience of a Martin Luther King and a Nelson Mandela, on our knees and at our computers, our human learning and our divine yearning have aimed at one product: a man of prayer and piety, of knowledge and love, of competence and compassion, to whom naught that is human is a stranger, who will move in a moment wherever the Church of Christ and the Society of Jesus want him, so caught up in Christ and kin to men and women that he will risk all, life and honor included, to make earthly existence more human, human existence more Christlike.

Richard McCormick is impressively open, accessible, responsive. On a very human level, to ballerinas and airline attendants, to gourmet chefs and powerful politicians. But just as open to those whose ideas change the world. In the forefront of a revolution in ethics and ethical thinking, he has opened his ears respectfully but not slavishly to ethicists Catholic and Protestant, dialogued with men and women of medicine, crossed swords with successors of Peter and the apostles, learned from constitutional lawyers, overleaped language barriers into Germany and France, Italy and Spain, the Netherlands.

He has, in consequence, changed the face of moral theology. Not only in its cold textbook content, but just as importantly by the power of his Christian personality, by his clarity, his courage, and his compassion. Listen to him as he describes his vision of the moral/ethical enterprise seen through the lens of abortion:

> Abortion . . . demands a most extraordinary discipline of moral thought, one that is penetrating without being impenetrable, humanly compassionate without being morally compromising, legally realistic without being legally positivistic, instructed by cognate disciplines without being determined by them, informed by tradition without being enslaved to it, etc. Abortion, therefore, is a severe testing ground for moral reflection. It is transparent of the rigor, fulness, and balance (or lack thereof) that one brings to moral problems and is therefore probably a paradigm of the way we will face other problems in the future. Many of us are bone-weary of the subject, but we cannot afford to indulge this fatigue, much as

the inherent risks of the subject might be added incentive for doing so. . . . [1]

Perhaps, like Rembrandt, a self-portrait?

II

Second, a Jesuit is a *man of the Church*. Till time is no more, our
friends will laughingly distinguish between Jesuit and Catholic, the
more conservative of our enemies will identify us with off-the-wall
liberals, and fearful sinners will seek a Jesuit confessor because he's
likely to be easy on them. Popes have told us to "shape up," and one
pope suppressed us. And still, the Society of Jesus exists, makes sense,
only within the Church, only because we are in service to the Church.
Even if we are no longer the pope's light cavalry, we are by profession
his faithful servants. A principle that was primary for Ignatius and his
first companions must remain directive of our own efforts today: "To
be sure of the Spirit one must listen to the Church."[2]

The problem lies in that momentous monosyllable . . . Church.
The passage of centuries has brought with it an increasingly vivid
realization: The Church is not simply its leaders; the Church is the
totality of God's people. The laity are not simply sheep propelled by a
shepherd's staff; the laity too can speak in the Spirit. The Church is
not simply divided into "the teaching Church" and "the learning
Church"; the whole Church, from pope to peasant, is ever and always
a Church that learns.

In such a Church, conflict is inevitable. More than two decades
ago, Karl Rahner put on the pen of St. Ignatius a letter to a modern
Jesuit giving some account of himself and the task that faces Jesuits
today. In a section on "Devotion to the Church" Ignatius is made to
speak of conflicts with officeholders in the Church. One poignant
paragraph runs like this:

> . . . do not think that in my devotion to the Church I was spared the
> experience of such conflicts or that I managed to bypass them with
> a false devotion. I was no Janizary [personal slave, principal de-
> fender] of the Church and the Pope. I was in conflict with Church
> officials in Alcalá, Salamanca, Paris, Venice and Rome. I was locked
> up for weeks by the officials in Alcalá and Salamanca; in Rome too
> all the uproar when I defended my devotion to the Church cost me
> a terrible amount of time and effort. When the Eternal Father
> promised me in La Storta that he would keep me in mind in Rome,

one of the possible forms which I imagined this 'favour' might take was a crucifixion in papal Rome. All the bones in my body shook when Paul IV was elected Pope. It was he who ordered the police to search my house even though I was already the General of an Order which had papal approval. I would have liked his blessing on my deathbed, in order to make an unassuming and courteous gesture towards him even at that hour, since I was dying without the sacraments; but when Polanco brought the blessing, I was already dead and the Pope's reaction on hearing the news was not exactly amiable.[3]

Like his beloved founder, Richard McCormick is a man of the Church. His specific service for most of his priestly life has focused on that extraordinarily difficult task: the life of the Catholic scholar, the effort to fuse revelation and reason, to fathom the meaning of Christian morality, to help men and women live as risen Christians. It has involved agony and ecstasy, the struggle to weld tradition to progress, because for him tradition is the best of the past wedded to fresh insights of the present with a view to a more Christian future.

At times his service has involved him in conflict with the official Church. In conflict not because he sets himself up on a hierarchical pedestal, not because he arrogates to himself an authority given by Christ to Peter alone. He jousts, tilts, clashes with authority because, as a theologian, he is in service to the whole Church, in service to God's Word within the Church, in service to the Spirit who is the Church's soul. He clashes only when he sees faith and the faithful poorly served. And in his opposition he is no less respectful than was Paul when he "opposed [Peter] to his face" on the need for circumcision (Gal 2:11); no less respectful than was Catherine of Siena when she told Pope Gregory XI that if he would not use his power to correct injustice, "it would be better for you to resign what you have assumed."[4]

A man of the Church indeed—a man who might well echo the outburst of the apostle Paul: ". . . on frequent journeys, in danger . . . from my own people, . . . danger in the city, danger in the wilderness, . . . danger from false brethren; in toil and hardship, through many a sleepless night. . . . And . . . there is the daily pressure upon me of my anxiety for all the churches" (2 Cor 11:26–29). For *all* the churches.

III

Third, a Jesuit is a man of *faith that does justice.* In 1974 the Jesuits' 32nd General Congregation proclaimed:

> The mission of the Society of Jesus today is the service of faith, of
> which the promotion of justice is an absolute requirement. . . . In
> one form or another, this has always been the mission of the Soci-
> ety; but it gains new meaning and urgency in the light of the needs
> and aspirations of the men and women of our time. . . . We are
> confronted today . . . by a whole series of new challenges.[5]

Although that mission did not appear in such language 450 years ago,
the idea behind the expression triggered the apostolates of Canisius
and Aloysius, Xavier and Claver, Ricci and Francis Regis. Granted, in
1943 the representative of the Jesuit General in the United States
castigated an American Jesuit for intruding into the Spiritual Exercises of St. Ignatius a series of "brilliant talks on social subjects. . . .
Such subjects [he thundered] have no place in the Spiritual Exercises."[6] Admittedly, the neighbor and the wider society do not domi-
nate the text of the Spiritual Exercises, but the crucial meditation on
the Two Standards makes Christian sense only if we grasp and articulate the social and political meaning of greed, honors, and pride.[7]

Not every Jesuit is ecstatic over this "mission of the Society of
Jesus today," this intimate linking of faith and justice. Father General
Pedro Arrupe admitted in Manila in 1983 that the inseparable unity
of the two—propagation of the faith and promotion of justice—was
"the concept which has been most difficult to put across."[8] However
that may be, Richard McCormick's adventures in moral theology illus-
trate admirably how scholarship fed on fervent faith can serve the
cause of social, political, and economic justice.

We all know that "ideas have consequences." Only God knows
fully the consequences of this man's ideas, how his moral analyses
have seeped into the human mainstream to affect human living, how
many myopic eyes have seen more clearly, how many deaf ears have
opened. Only God knows how many fetal lives have been spared and
how many of the terminally ill have died with dignity; how many good
people have ceased to rape God's good earth and how many of the
powerful have ceased to manipulate their brothers and sisters; how
many physicians have learned not simply to cure but to care and how
many lawyers have added to their love of law the law of love; how many
healthcare administrators can serve their communities with a more
sharply honed conscience and how many confessors now counsel
more compassionately. If the powerful of this world, from the labora-
tories for genetics to the halls of Congress, are willing to listen to
Christian reason, it is largely because Christian reason is incarnate in
moralists and ethicists like today's jubilarian. And with all this goes a

humility born of the conviction that within a pilgrim Church he is a pilgrim theologian. As in life, so in scholarship, he has not arrived; he is still, and always, on the way.

A man open in mind and heart, a man of the Church, a man of faith that does justice—little wonder that our Eucharist today is literally a thanksgiving. We thank God for giving us a man, a Jesuit, a priest, a scholar who lets "the word of God dwell" in him "richly," who "teaches and admonishes" us "in all wisdom" (Col 3:16), who lives each day what he murmurs each day, what he will murmur in a few short moments: "This is my body . . . given for you."

St. John's High School
Toledo, Ohio
August 31, 1990

22

LISTEN . . . AND DO
Fifty Years a Priest, Sixty Years a Jesuit

- Micah 5:1–4
- Romans 8:28–30
- Matthew 1:18–23

I suspect some of you are puzzled, and justifiably so. Why fix on a feast of our Lady to celebrate a Jesuit jubilee?[1] Oh, it's not utterly unreasonable. The mother of Jesus has been intimate to Jesuit existence ever since ex-soldier Ignatius Loyola yielded his sword to her and went to sleep wrapped in her rosary. But the link lies much deeper, and this is the heart of my homily. Our Lady is a powerful symbol—perhaps our most powerful sheerly human symbol—of what it means to be a Christian, a disciple of Jesus. Lest I disappoint you, three points, three persons: Mary, I, and you.

I

First, Mary. Why Mary today? Because in Luke's Gospel she is the perfect disciple. You see, to be a disciple is to follow. In our case, follow Jesus. Not in being virginally conceived; not in fleeing to Egypt to escape a tyrant; not in walking sandal-shod the paths of Palestine; not in being stretched out on twin beams of bloody wood. Then how? Our Lady shows us. She is the perfect disciple for an incredibly simple but profound reason: She listened to God's word, and what she heard she did. *There* is the whole Christian "thing"; there is "where it's at." Listen and do. It began when a teen-ager in Nazareth heard God's invitation: Will you mother my Son? Yes. It continued when she lost her 12-year-old in Jerusalem: Will you let my Son go? Yes. It came to a climax on Calvary: Will you give my Son back to me? Yes.

But far more important than Mary's sheer yes was its back-

141

ground. Her yes did not stem from a scenario, a Hollywood-type script detailing her life-with-Jesus and telling her how to act each scene. Mary said yes to God without knowing all that her yes would involve. I doubt that when the angel Gabriel said she would conceive "the Son of the Most High" (Lk 1:32), he gave her a crash course on the Trinity—three persons, one God. I know from Luke that when her preteen escaped from her for a seminar with Jewish teachers in the Jerusalem temple, she was terribly hurt and "did not understand" (2:50). I am sure no angel said to her beneath the cross, "Dry those tears, honey. This is just a passing phase. He's going to rise on Sunday." The angel simply told her, "Don't be afraid, Mary" (Lk 1:30). A Protestant preacher phrased it well: "She is not to be afraid of all that lies beyond her wallless room—a lonely birth on a winter's night, a child she was never to understand and who never had time to give her much understanding, the death she was to witness more lonely and more terrible than the birth."[2]

Mary's yes was a yes to a shadowed future, a yes to whatever God might ask—somewhat like Abraham leaving his country, kindred, and father's house, going to a far country, he knew not where—going because God said, "Go to the land that I will show you" (Gen 12:1). Don't be afraid—for one good reason: Always, wherever, God will be there. Don't be afraid; for, as St. Paul would declare decades later, "We know that in everything God works for good with those who love God" (Rom 8:28).[3]

II

Such, I have discovered, has been my Jesuit and priestly existence. At 16 and a half—not much older than Mary—I had no crystal ball, no angel, to reveal the 60 years to come. It sounded simply adventurous, not yet troublesome, that Jesuits go at a moment's notice wherever superiors send them. It was only years later that I heard of the Jesuit who protested an assignment, was told tersely by his provincial superior, "What I have written, I have written," and wrote in reply, "From the representative of Christ I expected the words of Christ, not of Pilate." I could not suspect that the seminary to which I gave my mind and heart for 28 exciting years would be closed—closed against my "better" understanding, against my "God-directed" will, against my deepest feelings. I had no premonition that the Church in which I had grown up would change so radically, a one holy Body of Christ torn by more factions than Paul found in Corinth; that priesthood would have so different an image, priests leave the priesthood by the thousands, priests prove guilty of pedophilia; that dear Jesuit friends would be torn within by changes in the Order, find that this was no longer the same Society in which they had vowed poverty, chastity, and obedience.

Which summons up a crucial element in discipleship. To follow Jesus is to encounter change, cope with change. Mary's life changed radically as the years moved on—from quiet adolescence to an angel's visit, from parturition in a stable to the home of a carpenter, from a cross on a hill to an empty tomb, from life without him on earth to life for ever with him in heaven.

There is no instant remedy, no push button, for coping with change: change in the Church, change in the Jesuits, change in wedlock, change in the work force, "good times and bad, sickness and health, poverty and wealth." Like Mary, we have to listen, at times agonizingly, to what God is saying. Not ordinarily on the wings of an angel; more often, what God tells us through God's own Book, through the events of our history, in the silence of our hearts.

It took me a long time to grasp what someone expressed so simply: "When a door closes in your life, God opens a window." Had the seminary called Woodstock not been closed, I would never have experienced the challenges of Georgetown and the delights of Holy Trinity. Only by passing control of the journal *Theological Studies* to another after 45 years was I forced to think creatively not of sedate retirement but of a fresh career: moving a mountain of social-justice issues, human affliction, more effectively into all the Catholic pulpits of the nation. Only by leaving highly-charged Georgetown for the contemplative Severn, abandoning D.C. for the only capital city of our country without an airport, without a train station, without a bus terminal, have I been able to think imaginatively of my project *Preaching the Just Word*, been forced to focus on conversion and spirituality in the preacher rather than sheer information and skills. Only through turmoil in the Church, from Communion in the hand to women at the altar, has theology become increasingly real, an anguished effort to understand what God is trying to tell me—about myself, about God's people, about God's self. Only through dear friends who have left my religious community have I been compelled to analyze my own vocation, struggle with the demands of celibacy, come to deeper insight into the agony and ecstasy of playing priest in the footsteps of Jesus and Ignatius. No angelic visitation; only with God's grace and Mary's inspiration that twin struggle to listen to the Lord and to do what I hear.

Failures? Of course. Shortcomings? Sinfulness? Stubbornness? Deafness? More than you who read only my headlines and homilies will ever know. I have experienced what it means to pick myself off the floor of my own humanity, to stand like the tax collector in the temple, beat my breast, and cry silently, "O God, be merciful to me *the* sinner" (Lk 18:13).[4]

And always there, never taking a holiday, is the ultimate change. I mean the death against which even the Son of God cried out. A half century ago I stood at the graves of my father and only brother, dead within three weeks of each other. Three weeks ago I stood at the grave of a dear friend in Portland, Oregon, father of two Georgetown graduates, dead at 54, his private plane crushing his flesh beyond human recognition. And I wonder how (to borrow from Welsh poet Dylan Thomas) I shall "go . . . into that good night"—"go gentle" or "rage against the dying of the light." These days I pray with Teilhard de Chardin:

> . . . When the signs of age begin to mark my body (and still more when they touch my mind); when the ill that is to diminish me or carry me off strikes from without or is born within me; when the painful moment comes in which I suddenly awaken to the fact that I am ill or growing old; and above all at that last moment when I feel I am losing hold of myself and am absolutely passive within the hands of the great unknown forces that have formed me; in all those dark moments, O God, grant that I may understand that it is you . . . who are painfully parting the fibres of my being in order to penetrate to the very marrow of my substance and bear me away within yourself. . . . It is not enough that I should die while communicating. Teach me *to communicate while dying*.[5]

Frankly, I am not anxious to die. Why not? One reason among several: I love this life, love you people, so agonizingly that I don't want to have to wait for you in a distant heaven. Annapolis is far enough. . . .

III

And what might all this say to you—this wedding of Mary's experience and mine, this experience of change? It would be so easy to stress the obvious: Listen to the Lord and then do what you hear. But in our time the obvious is of little help. Today confusion reigns not only among Democrats and in the Soviet republic, but in Catholicism as well. Hard as they listen, John Paul II and countless Catholics hear different voices, different angels, different Christs on so many issues that tear the Church we love: on married priests and the ordination of women, on homosexuality and abortion, on divorce and remarriage, on contraception and Communion in the hand, on the closing of elementary schools and what makes a college Catholic. It is with different ears that Catholics pick up the cries of the poor and the black, the Hispanic and the Haitian, the Jew and the Arab. It is with contrasting ears that American Catholics listen to their bishops on war and peace, on capitalism and the economy. And whose voice do our young actually hear when they see the official Church not so much as an authority but at best a resource, one among many, helpful at times but hardly infallible?

I have no instant solution. Listening is an arduous art. It's difficult enough to grasp accurately what another *human being* is trying to tell us (take three-point homilies); it's dreadfully more difficult when *God* is struggling to get through to us, when Church and conscience conflict, when our needs and desires, our loves and hates cloud our perspective, block the ears of our heart, of our faith. What suggestions might come from a half century uncommonly rich, by God's gracious giving, in study and contemplation, in peace and struggle, in laughter and tears, in faith and hope and love—love for the Lord and his mother, love for the thousands I have been privileged to touch in so many different ways, who have touched me lightly and profoundly?

First, within Catholicism, till time is no more, there will always be divisions. If St. Paul found division in Corinth a quarter century after the crucifixion—"I belong to Paul," "I belong to Apollos," "I belong to [Peter]," "I belong to Christ" (1 Cor 1:12)—be not surprised at dissension 20 centuries after.

Second, dissension, difference, dispute, while regrettable, will only be destructive if it destroys love. I'm afraid it sometimes does. I have seen Catholics claw one another like cats in a sack. My good friend the archbishop of Milwaukee has been blasted by his people for *listening* to the agonizing cries of prochoice Catholics. The hate mail I receive from "good" Catholics would make your flesh crawl. Passion, yes; hate, never. You can steal into heaven if you are sincerely prochoice; you cannot pass Peter if your heart is a harbor of hate. You can be one with God even if you kill Iraqi soldiers or defend capital punishment; you cannot be one with God if you do not echo the words of the Lord in Ezekiel: "As I live, I have no pleasure in the death of the wicked" (Ezek 33:11)—no pleasure in the death of Marcos or Saddam Hussein.

Third, let no one divide your religion and your justice. The Lord's words through the prophet Micah are still valid: "What does the Lord require of you? Act justly and love steadfastly" (Mic 6:8). There are still *two* great commandments: Love God above all else, love your brothers and sisters as you love yourself, as Jesus has loved you (cf. Mt 22:37–39; Jn 15:12). And the second commandment, Jesus trumpeted, "is like" the first (Mt 22:39). In a paradoxical country of wondrous wealth and unlimited promise, where a million and a half innocents are aborted each year, where one out of every five children grows up below the poverty line, where untold thousands of the young are incestuously abused, where the elderly rummage for food in garbage cans, where the helpless and hopeless are threatened with euthanasia, where crack and coke stunt minds and massacre bodies, where black and white live in smoldering mistrust, the Lord asks once again what he asked of Cain, "Where is your brother? Where is your sister?" And no Christian, no human dare respond cynically with Cain, "I don't know. Am I my brother's/my sister's keeper?" (cf. Gen 4:9).

Fourth, hope. With God, all is possible. One year ago, you would have been a candidate for a padded cell if you had predicted that Russia would go democratic, the Baltic states declare independence, East and West Germany unite—and religion arise from the ashes of Communism. If these are sheerly human achievements—which I doubt—then think what can happen when God intervenes. And God does—each day; for the Christ who died for you lives in you, lives in the man or woman next to you. This I know not from abstract theology but from my experience of you, from the impact each of you has had on me as a priest, as a Jesuit, as a man. Even in your darkest moments, when you feel terribly weak, remember the words of the Lord to St. Paul begging to be relieved of his special misery: "My grace is sufficient for you, for my power is made perfect in weakness." And Paul's response: "I am content with weaknesses . . . ; for when I am weak, then I am strong" (2 Cor 12:9–10). Even when change in the Church makes little sense to you, let it not destroy the peace of Christ in you. For all our reverence, our hope is not in a pope; our hope is in the Lord.

Fifth, and incomparably important, once more central to Catholicism must be the Eucharist. The obstacles are daunting: sermons difficult to characterize as "the word of God," celebrants who fail to celebrate, Communion on hand or tongue, songs only Pavarotti could sing, St. Louis Jesuits or J. S. Bach, all-male performers. All true, and still the charge of Jesus remains dominant: "Unless you eat the flesh of the Son of man and drink his blood, you have no life in you" (Jn 6:53). No life.

With that in mind we move on to the liturgy of the Eucharist. For there we shall re-enact, re-present, the most remarkable love in human history, the love that brings us together as nothing else can, the love that alone makes sense of my half century as a priest of Christ, my six decades as a son of Ignatius. Today, for me, this Eucharist is singularly what the word means: thanksgiving. Today I give thanks: thanks to God for giving me your love, thanks to our Lady for teaching me how to listen, thanks to each of you for showing me in your own lives the faces of Jesus.[6]

Holy Trinity Church
Washington, D.C.
September 8, 1991

23
MY GOD, WHAT A LIFE!
Homily for Jubilees of Priests

- Sirach 2:1–11
- Mark 9:30–37

When many of us gray heads or bald pates were ordained, a common-place on ordination cards was a paragraph from the famed Dominican preacher Lacordaire. At the close of an impassioned paragraph on the exalted state of a priest, the quotation closed with an equally passionate "My God, what a life!"

This priestly life that evokes so equivocal a reaction—what dare I preach about it at this advanced stage in our vocation?[1] Strangely perhaps, I shall not place priority on our past. We are indeed jubilarians, and that in itself calls for felicitation. We have survived so much: the cross fire between Rome's rescripts and parish expectations, the paranoia in a church changing, the ravages of aging. I shall focus on our future, on what we jubilarians, active or retired, can do and must do, can be and must be, if the Church's ministry is to be effective in an age singularly confusing for the faithful, less than promising for priesthood.

John Coleman, professor of religion and society in the Jesuit School of Theology at Berkeley, suggests that what priests need today is not a new or renewed *theology* of priesthood; there are enough of those to line a respectable sacerdotal shelf. What we need is "a new way of imagining or imaging the priest—a new metaphor for our contemporary understanding of priests."[2] As a sort of spin-off on this observation, let me suggest three images I would like to see prominent in priests, specifically priests ordained in 1931, 1941, 1951, and 1966. Hardly new images; still, images that need revitalizing, because they are frightfully important for the spirituality of our people, the success of priestly ministry, a resurgence of vocations, and our own deep

148

happiness. Nothing in what follows falls under infallible definition; its value is simply one man's half century of experience.

I

The first image? *A man of joy.* I would want people who see me, hear me, touch me feel that I joy in my priesthood, that I would not exchange it for, literally, the world. Yes, there is so much more I would like to have: a counterpart like Eve to make me more fully human; children to carry on my name and "ooh-ah" at videos about me; more intimate sharing in what Vatican II called "the joys and hopes, the griefs and anxieties of the men and women of this age."[3] But, somewhat like that remarkable Catholic short-story writer Flannery O'Connor, dead of lupus at 39, I have to be aware of human limitations; each vocation involves a surrender of so much that is good, and each human is restricted by self and circumstances.

Here what is of high importance is that people *sense* my joy. It is not enough that my whole heart is in my Mass in point of fact, if my countenance suggests I have inadvertently ingested a sour pickle. Of old we faced the congregation but rarely; now we are "on center stage" for both acts—word and Eucharist. Every gesture, every word, every look says something to a single soul or a thousand. Let it say, "I'm delighted to be here—delighted to be with you." But not only at the altar. In a wheel chair or on a hospital bed, on the phone or at a party, wherever, let people sense that I too have said to Someone, "I take you for better for worse, for richer for poorer, in sickness and in health, as long as life shall last." And I joy in the taking.

My brothers, I am convinced that vocations will grow when youngsters can look at us the aging and say, "That's what I want to be like when I grow old." Smile, O priest of God, even when it hurts—especially when it hurts. The future of the American Church depends on it.

II

The second image? *A man for others.* Oh yes, we *are* for others in principle and in point of fact; you and I know that. As with Jesus, that has been the motivating force of our entire existence. As with Jesus, "for others" has brought us to a cross, to many a cross: absence of appreciation, frequent frustration, pain of flesh and spirit. You may have read Paul Wilkes's book on the daily pastoring of Father Joseph Greer of Natick, Massachusetts—originally a *New Yorker* profile. He tells the young priest interns in his parish:

> You have to be nuts to go into the priesthood. It's an awful job. The pay is terrible, the hours are worse. People not only do not look up to you. They look down. You have to love God, and if you don't, it will grind you up. Remember, no trumpets will sound. And you are going to spend more time being a carpenter than a priest.[4]

But at this point in our lives many of us cannot be "for others" as we once were. You may remember the famed German Lutheran Dietrich Bonhoeffer, hanged in 1945 in a concentration camp for conspiring to overthrow Hitler. One of his prison poems is titled "Stations on the Road to Freedom." The third of his stations is hauntingly pertinent to the aging:

> A change has come indeed. Your hands, so strong and active,
> are bound; in helplessness now you see your action
> is ended; you sigh in relief, your cause committing
> to stronger hands; so now you may rest contented.
> Only for one blissful moment could you draw near to touch
>   freedom;
> then, that it might be perfected in glory, you gave it to God.[5]

Most of us here—not all, but most—are at an age when perhaps the most significant sentence in God's inspired Word is the declaration of St. Paul, "I rejoice in my sufferings for your sake, and in my flesh I complete what is lacking in Christ's afflictions for the sake of his body, that is, the Church" (Col 1:24).

The freedom in which youth exults, the freedom the Jewish philosopher Philo called a "portion" of God's own freedom, paradoxically expands as we the aging allow God to strip from us so much that bound us to earth, so much that actually enslaved us to creatures: health and possessions, strength and vigor, brilliance of mind and beauty of body, yes so many we loved. In my own case, frankly, a "place in the sun," the world's recognition, audience applause. Only by letting go—of the past, of where I've been—can I grow into Christ and help the Church to grow. Not forgetting the past—yesterday is part and parcel of my today; simply refusing to live in it. Even for the aging, life is now, life is here. It is the plea of the Psalmist, "O that today you would hearken to God's voice!" (Ps 95:7b). Only if we are not prisoners of our past, only by moving *today* a step closer to the fulness of humanness that is Christ—Christ crucified and risen—can we the aging continue to serve the Church.

Once again, however, we are not dealing with abstractions, with a renunciation that simply in fact expands my freedom. People have to *sense* that "I rejoice in my sufferings for [their] sake," that I rejoice in my aging—the young especially. The cry of Paul should echo in me, "When I am weak, then I am strong" (2 Cor 12:10); for "I can do all things in him who strengthens me" (Phil 4:13).

III

The third image? *A man of prayer.* Sounds trite, doesn't it? Of course we are men of prayer. How else could we continue obedient bachelors? But I do not mean simply a mediator between God and God's images, indispensable as this is—one who, in the age-old adage, "brings God down to men, men up to God." I do not even mean the symbolism for us in the words of consecration: Jesus took us, blessed us, broke us, and gave us. I am much more concerned for a personal relationship, a relationship of love, a relationship that is a living experience, a relationship that cannot be imprisoned but must move out to touch others.

I assume that after 25, 40, 50, or 60 years of priesting, that relationship exists; it is there. But once again I submit that what is imperative is that people—the faithful and the unfaithful—*see* us as men of prayer. I am reminded that over 150 years ago—in 1838, to be precise—Ralph Waldo Emerson delivered an address to the graduating class of the Harvard Divinity School in which he said in part:

> I once heard a preacher who sorely tempted me to say, I would go to church no more. . . . He had lived in vain. He had no word intimating that he had laughed or wept, was married or in love, had been commended, or cheated, or chagrined. If he had ever lived and acted, we were none the wiser for it. The capital secret of his profession, namely, to convert life into truth, he had not learned. Not one fact in all his experience, had he yet imported into his doctrine. . . . Not a line did he draw out of real history. The true preacher can always be known by this, that he deals out to the people his life,—life passed through the fire of thought. . . .[6]

If the preacher must come through as a man who lives, the priest must come through as a man who prays. Not a string of Hail Marys, for all their importance; rather, a ceaseless living in God's presence. But once again, not simply an objective fact known to God and the angels; rather, so rich an experience of the living God that it cannot be imprisoned, must burst the bonds of my individual self, tells others mutely or eloquently that I love God with all my soul and strength, love the crucified images of Christ as he himself loves them. Even in our aging, perhaps especially in our aging, we speak without words about the God *we* love. What is it our aging says?

Men of joy, men for others, men of prayer—such is our privilege and our burden. Perhaps more profoundly than on the day of our ordination. For we come together with the wounds of our passion seared into our hands and hearts. And, it seems, with the joy that, Christ promised, no human being, nothing on earth, would take from us (cf. Jn 16:22). And now—now we enter the holiest of holies, that action which more than any other has been the purpose of our priesthood—that moment when we murmur once again what we have murmured ten thousand or twenty thousand times to God and God's people: "This is my body, given for you."

Yes, my brothers, with such memories, with such actualities, with such a challenging future, our Eucharist is indeed a thanksgiving. We can cry out with fresh accents, "Yes, my God, yes indeed, what a life!"

St. Mary's Seminary
Baltimore, Maryland
May 21, 1991

24

HUMOR, YOUNG ONES, EUCHARIST
Homily for a Golden Wedding Anniversary

- Numbers 6:22–26
- Philippians 1:3–11
- John 15:9–17

If there is one thing Mary Ann and Pierce do not want today, it is a eulogy. Eulogies can be embarrassing; what is worse, golden-anniversary eulogies sound like advance obituaries. And yet, this is still their day—a day for remembrance, for celebration, for thanksgiving. And so I simply must speak of them, but in a context broader than their individual and united selves. Let me tell you, simply and artlessly, how one friend sees them after almost a quarter century—a limited vision indeed, but very real and loving. I shall do so in three stages— each stage suggested by a picture.

I

My first picture hangs inside the entrance of their lovely home near Gibson Island. It goes back to June 10, 1974. It was taken in a castle near Cork, and it shows a fearless Pierce Flanigan held by the knees as he hangs head down to kiss the Blarney stone. Mary Ann is nowhere to be seen; I suspect she was close by, torn between prayer for a headstrong husband and back-seat instructions to the Irishman holding in his hands Pierce's limbs and his life.

I set this picture before you not because the Blarney stone evokes the smooth talk of the Irish; rather because it evokes a quality of Flanigan life which has much to do with their half century of marriage. I mean their sense of humor. By humor I do not mean a belly laugh. Good humor was perhaps best defined by the English novelist William Makepeace Thackeray: He called it "a mixture of love and wit." One without the other is perilous, especially in wedded existence. For love without wit can be terribly grim and unattractive; wit without love can be sheer sarcasm, a savage thing, can hurt, draw blood. But the two together give us what is so delightful in TV's M*A*S*H: Hawkeye has a keen eye for what does not fit, what doesn't quite make sense, what is absurd—in himself and his colleagues, in military brass and war itself. He mocks it boisterously or gently, but always, I think, with compassion—another word for love.

What I have discovered without fail in our golden jubilarians is a wedding of wit and love. They can appreciate what is comical or incongruous, absurd or ridiculous, in an idea, a situation, an event—even in a person. They can see what is humorous, what doesn't fit, in themselves, in a child or grandchild, in the world around them, talk wittily about it, laugh lovingly over it. For 23 years I have experienced Pierce's "needle"—a form of acupuncture that is amazingly on target and, even more amazingly, never really hurts.

The point is, the same laughter that restored health to the body of famed *Saturday Review* editor Norman Cousins[1] can bring invigorating life to the wear and tear of a marriage. It doesn't mean that Mary Ann and Pierce can laugh everything off. There are moments in all our lives when wit must simply yield to love. The Jesus who must have smiled when little children cuddled up in his arms did not smile when he came upon a mother mourning her only son. The Jesus who must have smiled when the sommelier at Cana wondered where the good wine had come from did not smile when a soldier offered him vinegar on the cross. The Jesus who must have laughed when Peter put his foot in his mouth or when he saw Zacchaeus up a tree did not laugh when Judas left the Last Supper to sell him for silver. Only Pierce and Mary Ann know at first hand the tears that bedew 50 years of life together, Swinburne's "seasons that laugh or that weep."[2] But the miracle of seasons shared as they have shared is the serene smile that invariably bathes us all in its love—even or especially when the love is salted with tears.

II

My second picture adorns another wall at Windswept. It is a striking family photo: Pierce and Mary Ann are surrounded by five children who could have stepped out of *Vogue*. It was taken in September 1966. Pierce III is 24, Anne 22, Kathie 20, Eileen 17, John all of 12 and looking amazingly like TV's Doogie Howser, M.D. Each time I contemplate that portrait, I realize how uncommonly Pierce and Mary Ann have been blessed, the uncommon blessing they have been. In our time any family that has five children grown, intelligent, married to loving and lovable spouses, all with good jobs, all with children, all happy, all friends to one another, that family is fortunate. And when the grandchildren get along like reasonably human beings, a fresh miracle has sprouted.

Fortunate indeed, but it did not happen by sheer luck. It happened because 50 years ago a young woman and a young man took seriously those remarkable words of God that open human history: "Be fruitful and multiply . . ." (Gen 1:28). Shape images of yourselves, images of God. Not sheer multiplication, but all that parenting involves—from the first diaper through teen-age rebellion to the flight from the nest.

As you know, Mary Ann and Pierce have lived and still live a well-rounded life: faithful friends such as crowd Lady Chapel this evening; interest in education and the arts; minds filled with what is true, spirits with what is beautiful, hearts with what is good. They have walked the roads of Portugal and France, England and Ireland, Italy and Greece; they have sailed the Aegean Sea and the Caribbean, the Chesapeake Bay and the Atlantic Ocean, the English Channel and (less happily) the Trégière River. But when the chips are down, the richest joy in which they rest is a Thanksgiving or a Christmas, at Windswept or in Bethesda, in Ruxton or Lincoln; for here is the center of their existence—family.

Over the centuries, civilized people took for granted that the basic building block of civilization is the family. Not only because without fathering and mothering humanity obviously has no future. More importantly because the way families live determines the extent to which a nation is civilized, is human. The family photo on Windswept's wall tells not all but awfully much. This family is a gift, not only to us who know and love them, but to a nation that wonders whether anyone can any longer say "for ever."

III

My third picture does not hang on a wall; it is enshrined in my memory. I mean each Christmas morning at Windswept. Each December 25 for many years, I have been privileged to celebrate the Eucharist with Mary Ann and Pierce at a small table in their living room overlooking the water. That Eucharist symbolizes for me their profound spirituality—I mean their relationship to a God who is very real to them, very near to them, intimate to their life together. Without that relationship, without the ceaseless presence of the risen Jesus, their lives would be not perhaps empty but surely less meaningful. In that Christmas Eucharist they bring together on a simple table all the many-splendored gifts God has given them—their love for each other, their children and grandchildren, their relatives and friends, those who have gone before them with the sign of Christ's peace, those whom God is about to call—and offer all to the Lord who gave them all this and so much more. Here, in a special way, is their experience of God. Not a vision, not an apparition; simply an unusual awareness of God all about them, in them, as real to them as the air they breathe.

That is why, for Pierce and Mary Ann, this evening's Eucharist is the center of their celebration. Not the whole celebration, simply its center from which all else radiates. For their wedded existence, like the Eucharist, takes its shape from the crucial sentence Jesus spoke to his disciples the night before he died for us: "This is my body given for you" (Lk 22:19). In this Eucharist which means "thanksgiving," we thank God not only for a God-man who gave his life for us, but for a man and a woman whose whole life has been . . . gift. A gift to their children and their children's children; a gift to all of you whose presence here is a living witness to that gift; a gift to so many others whose lives have intersected with theirs; a gift to me.

Their Eucharist, you see, is not a private party. It takes them from liturgy to life, from church to world, to become "eucharists" (small e) for the life of others. For, like the Eucharistic Christ, their life too has been a real presence. They have been present, really present, to untold hundreds who have needed them. Totally present—not only their money but their minds and hearts. Present to people's needs—for food or affection, for understanding or love, yes for God. This may be news to them (they know no other way to live), but it is hardly news to us. Even the friends who do not share all their faith sense a hidden Presence in their lives that bases their presence to a whole little world.

Pierce does not wave religious banners: "Look at us—we believe." Mary Ann does not parade a protest sign I once saw: "Eve was framed." Aware that their Church has its share of the warts that disfigure all human institutions, they still love it, joy in it, because here they find, as nowhere else, the risen Christ ceaselessly murmuring, "This is my body given for you." This, in large measure, has made it possible for them to say together to a whole little world through half a century, "This is my body, here we are, given for you."

Mary Ann and Pierce: I suspect I have just proven how inadequate to this occasion are words woven of human rhetoric. This being so, I suggest that all of us who surround you here borrow a leaf from the Lord and pray together the blessing God ordered Moses to murmur over a chosen people:

> May the Lord bless you and keep you.
> May the Lord make His face to shine upon you,
>   and be gracious to you.
> May the Lord uncover His face to you,
>   and bring you peace.
>
> (Num 6:24–26)

Lady Chapel
Cathedral of Mary Our Queen
Baltimore, Maryland
February 23, 1991

25

CHRIST BEHAVES AS ONE WHO LABORS
Opening of the Ignatian Year, Cincinnati

- Ezekiel 18:25–28
- Philippians 2:1–11
- Matthew 21:28–32

Good friends in Christ: Your persuasive pastor has placed on my slumping shoulders an unbearable burden. How does a mere mortal speak intelligently, in a quarter hour, on the founder of the Jesuits, on the Company he founded, and on his sons in Cincinnati? How move from 1491 to 1540 to 1840 to 1990–91?[1]

Fortunately, a homily is not a history; I shall not bore you with a barrage of dates and facts. A homily, at its best, focuses on one or other of God's wonderful works in the story of salvation, issues a challenge to a Christian congregation, demands a response. In harmony with that, I shall zero in on God's most unexpected break-in, irruption, incursion into our earth, extract from it a profound meaning stressed by St. Ignatius, and lay it before you for your own lives. I shall (1) look back deeply into the distant past, (2) look swiftly into our present, (3) look forward to the years that lie ahead. In other words, I shall talk successively about Ignatius, about Jesuits, about you. And the climate, the context, the atmosphere within which I shall speak is today's second reading. I mean Christ Jesus. Though he was God's Son, he "emptied himself," took to himself our flesh, "lowered himself still further, becoming obedient unto death, even death on a cross. Therefore God has highly exalted him and bestowed on him the name which is above every name, that at the name of Jesus every knee should bow . . . and every tongue confess that Jesus Christ is Lord . . ." (Phil 2:6–11).

I

I begin by looking back. Back to Ignatius. What was so central to his thinking and living that it distinguishes him? There is much that attracts men and women to Ignatius. Some are mesmerized by a mystic who was eminently practical. Others are seduced by a soldier turned saint. Still others are taken by the "organization man" who revolutionized much of Europe with his "counterreformation." But what makes him perennially relevant, always contemporary to every Christian—lay and cleric, woman and man, young and old, rich and poor, theologian and teacher, CEO and sanitation worker? I suggest you will find it in the final meditation of his Spiritual Exercises, the Contemplation for Learning to Love Like God. Here Ignatius asks of you something quite surprising: "Consider how [Christ[2]] works and labors for me in all creatures upon the face of the earth, that is, he behaves as one who labors."

What you discover in Ignatius is the ceaseless presence of Christ to our earth, the Incarnation not only in Nazareth back two millennia but in our midst this very moment. In startlingly concrete language Ignatius compels us to revamp a narrow theology which implies that, when the risen Jesus rose to his Father, this earth somehow lost him, save for a vague something called sanctifying grace and a mysterious presence under the appearances of bread and wine. Ignatius forces us to surrender a spirituality that looks up to heaven for God's grace. No, "consider how Christ labors for me in all creatures."

Not that the Son of God takes flesh of Mary each day. He did that once for all in Bethlehem, carried that flesh of ours with him when he returned to his Father, will never lay it down. What Ignatius saw with uncommon vividness and expressed with striking concreteness is that Christ is not only risen, not only enjoys in his very body the bliss of the Holy Trinity. He behaves like a worker, like a laborer, in every single creature in creation.

How is it that billions of stars can fly the heavens more speedily than light? Because an all-powerful Christ gives them *being*. Not once for all, but continuously, day after day. How is it that over four thousand varieties of roses can grow and perfume our earth? Because an imaginative Christ gives them *life*. How is it that your long-haired Labrador can look hungrily at you, hear your faintest whistle, smell you out, lay paws on your shoulders? Because a sensitive Christ gives it *senses*. How is it that you can shape an idea at Xavier University, construct the Tyler Davidson bronze fountain,[3] transplant a human heart, live as one flesh with another man or woman? Because a still human

Christ gives you *intelligence and love*. And how can you believe that the Son of God died a bloody death for you, how can you confidently expect to live forever, how can you give yourself unreservedly to God and your brothers and sisters? Because a living Christ infuses faith in you, fills your flesh with hope, inflames your very bones with a unique love not of this world.

And all this, Ignatius saw, Christ does not from some majestic throne in heaven he shares with two other divine persons. He reminds Ignatius of a skilled, enthusiastic worker—very much alive, always in touch with his creation, ceaselessly concerned, today more imaginative than yesterday, terribly in love with all he shapes. In a special way, alive within each of you. For, as he told his disciples, "If you love me, my Father will love you, and we will come to you and make our home with you" (cf. Jn 14:23).

Very simply, to Ignatius Jesus Christ was real, was alive. Alive not in outer space but in every single work of his loving hands. Alive not only yesterday but at each moment of each creature's existence. The world is charged with the presence of Christ, with the labor of Christ.

II

This moves me into the present, the Company Ignatius created. Specifically, the Society of Jesus in the Cincinnati area. It has a fascinating history that encompasses 150 years. It includes a flourishing university begun in 1840 on a shoestring and trust in God; a high school that touches a benign dictatorship to over a thousand of "the young and the restless"; a university chapel that serves a still broader constituency; a retreat house that brings the Ignatian vision to the workaday world; a renewal center that trains spiritual guides and retreat directors for an increasingly complex world; and this impressive house of God that traces its Jesuit lineage back 145 years.

Unlike Mark Antony in Shakespeare's *Julius Caesar*, I come not to bury these activities but to praise them. It is a type of praise that may not be obvious even to those who are active in them. I want to pay tribute to them for the Ignatian vision that inspires them. Not just in general, with a flabby wave of the hand in Ignatius' direction. I mean specifically the Ignatius I have just described to you. For in their different ways these six institutions exist to impregnate their people with Ignatius' Contemplation for Learning to Love like God.

Sound strange to you? Then please think along with me. Xavier University and St. Xavier High School do a superb job educating men and women in significant areas of human thinking and living, from the humanities, through the sciences and business, to philosophy and theology. But to be authentically Jesuit they must do more. Someone has asserted acutely, "Education is what is left over after all you have learned in school has been forgotten." That is not cynicism; it is realism. What *is* "left over" after school is forgotten? It is learning *how* to learn that is "left over," that enables us to continue to address the continuous questions that arise. How do you go about discovering for yourself? How do you discover the age of our earth or the rate of unemployment, how discover the microbes in human flesh or the ethics of surrogate motherhood, how discover what lifts and lowers the Dow Jones and what cards Napoleon played in exile on St. Helena, how discover what it means to be alive, how discover where truth lies, where beauty, where goodness?

In a special way, Xavier grads should leave us with a vivid awareness of how to find *Christ*, how find him everywhere, in all things. How discover Christ at work, like a laborer, in the things they touch—the telescope and the microscope, the chemical elements and the computer, the Milky Way and the Grand Canyon. Christ at work in the slender blade of grass and the giant redwood, in the frogs they dissect and every endangered species, in the proud eagle and the ever-busy bee. Christ at work in the ideas their minds generate and the love their hearts liberate. Christ at work in every man, woman, and child on this earth's face, from Adam to Saddam, from Eve to Mother Teresa, and beyond.

Unreal? Quite the contrary. In the Jesuit vision of education there is nothing so real as Christ, nothing so important as awareness of Christ. Not only in chapel, on your knees. Rather, a worldview in which no creature, for all its freedom, is so independent of Christ that it can simply be or stay alive or love for long without him.

Our parishes and pulpits, our retreat and renewal centers—these exist indeed for constant conversion to Christ, a day-by-day opening of hearts and minds to Christ crucified and risen. But not in a narrow sense, a me-and-Jesus spirituality that is neither *of* this world nor *in* it. Ignatian spirituality at its best sends retreatant and parishioner from church to world, from contemplation to action. Out to the only world they have, *their* world, a bewildering world that is actually never without Christ but simply does not recognize him.

III

Finally, let me look forward to the years that lie ahead. Here allow me to address all of you: Jesuit, Jesuit-educated, Jesuit-pock-marked, Jesuit-immune. It matters not. For all of you, the insight of Ignatius is indispensable.

You see, you and I live in a world, in a culture, that has been steadily secularized. Now secularization is a big word but not a bad word. Secularization is not secularism. Secularism is a view of life, a way of thinking and living, based on a rigid premise: The religious dimension of human living should be ignored or excluded—certainly it has no place in the public arena, in politics or education. Secularization is a process. The fact is, religion, the churches, have increasingly ceased to be the primary "mover and shaker" in society. Other institutions, other disciplines, with their own legitimate autonomy—law, medicine, university—have taken over responsibilities that the Church used to have, functions that the Church used to control. Now "religion has no direct influence over the large corporate structures which have emerged in the last four hundred years—big government, big business, big labor, big military, big education."[4]

All the more reason, then, why the individual Christian, why each of you, must struggle to discover the Christ who is actually there, without whom there would be no government, no business, no labor, no military, no education. It is simply harder to find him there, far harder than in the medieval marriage to Christ, when the culture was more clearly impregnated with Christ.

The point is, once you discover Christ where you live and work and have your being, once you realize that Christ is acting like a worker in your acre of God's world, a heavy responsibility rests on you. For his activity to bear its fruit, you have to work with him. For his crucifixion to change human hearts, to change our culture, he needs you. Christ has so arranged his work of redemption that he needs coworkers with him. Like Ignatius, you have to learn to love like God, to love like Christ.

You see, God's scenario for the story of salvation is not a one-man show. Christ indeed plays the starring role, but featured is every man and woman ever baptized into him. You labor with him not only within the Eucharist, when I murmur "The body of Christ" and you respond "Amen, So be it." You labor with him each time you feed the hungry Christ and slake the thirsty Christ, when you house the homeless Christ and clothe the naked Christ, when you visit Christ imprisoned on a bed of pain or behind bars. You labor with Christ when a broker resists the temptation to insider trading or the easy buck from Savings & Loan, when a husband is ceaselessly faithful to wife whatever the powerful attraction from without, when a lawyer serves the impoverished without pay, when the child in the womb and the aging near the tomb are as dear to a doctor as the injured Cincinnati Bengal,[5] when the rock star sings his way into the hearts of his adorers rather than their loins, when a teacher strikes intellectual fire in the mind of his students, when a psychologist plumbs the depths of a tortured soul, when a lover of God's creation fights to preserve earth's natural beauty, when black Sister Thea Bowman races her brain cancer in a wheelchair across the nation murmuring "I'm too busy to die."[6]

The point is, each moment in the drama of salvation features two irreplaceable characters: Christ and another human being, Christ and you, the two laboring together. The splendidly human actions I have described, these *you cannot* sustain for long without Christ, and *Christ will not* work his best in them without you.

If, dear friends, you would celebrate this Ignatian Year with more than a token Mass, let Ignatius involve you, mind and will, heart and hand, in this exciting scenario of salvation—the world's salvation and your own. Exciting because everything you touch is already touched with Christ, everything is electric with his presence—except for sin and, possibly, subpar golf. Your privilege and your burden is twofold: first, to be *conscious* of the Christ who labors for you in all creatures; second, to *collaborate*, labor with Christ in simply everything you do.

With such consciousness and such collaboration your life will take on fresh meaning; at least three effects will surround you. First, nothing you do need be dull; nothing you achieve must you accomplish by your solitary wit and wisdom; nothing you suffer will you suffer alone. Second, you will transform the turf on which you dance so lightly and agonize so heavily. You will live what Vatican II called the laity's "special obligation,"[7] your distinctive apostolate, "to penetrate and perfect the temporal sphere with the spirit of the gospel."[8] Because of you, your acre of God's world will be different. Third, St. Ignatius will love you, for you will have captured his vision. If being dubbed Jesuit or jesuitical fails to turn you on, then glory simply in being Ignatian. It only means you are intelligently and passionately Christian.

St. Xavier Church
Cincinnati, Ohio
September 30, 1990

26

WHATEVER YOU NEED, DEAR BODY OF CHRIST
Maryland Jesuits' Celebration of the Ignatian Year

- Acts 4:8–12
- 1 John 3:1–2
- John 10:11–18

As I was struggling to connect the Society of Jesus with today's Gospel, agonizing to relate today's Jesuits to Jesus' contrast between the model shepherd and the hired hand, an unexpected article came to my assistance. It was written, very recently, by a freshman in one of our Jesuit colleges, and the first paragraph ran in part as follows:

> When one reviews the recent history of the Jesuits, he is reminded of these lines from Paradise Lost: "As one great furnace flam'd, yet from those flames/No light, but rather darkness visible." For approximately the last twenty-five years the Jesuits have striven, quite successfully, to divorce themselves from the previous four hundred years of their existence in order to establish a new mission which has replaced their traditional role as the most articulate defenders of Catholic doctrine and the Papacy itself with the more politically correct and intellectually chic role of being missionaries (mercenaries?) for "political and social justice." . . . The order, which once brought stability to a troubled Church and truth to a doubting world, has now rejected much of that truth, and has siphoned that poisonous doubt which plagues our world into the very bloodstream of the Holy Church.[1]

Now a homily is not a debate. I quote our young friend not to refute him, but because his rabid rhetoric compels me to reflect prayerfully on 1540 and 1991, what it means to be a Jesuit whether in the 16th century or the 20th, how we may distinguish the model shepherd from the hired hand, still link Jesuit to Jesus. Lest I let you down, three stages to my reflection. (1) What was a Jesuit in the mind of

164

Ignatius? (2) Have we changed all that radically in our time? (3) How do I personally look at Jesuit existence?

I

First, what was a Jesuit in the mind of Ignatius? There was much in Jesuit existence that was traditional among religious orders: A Jesuit was vowed to poverty, to chastity, to obedience. Much was original, innovative: no high office in the Church, no choral recitation of the Divine Office, no obligatory penances, no distinctive habit, no third order, no female branch. And all types of apostolic endeavor in all parts of the world.

But that tells you terribly little; you must probe more deeply within. Even the Society's rules reveal relatively little; for it was only because Rome demanded it that Ignatius "wrote any rules except on a domestic level for the good order and harmony of the house."[2] A Jesuit after the heart of Ignatius was a man of the Spiritual Exercises, captured and held by a spirituality centered in Christ—"the only guidance" his followers needed.[3] In the Exercises his very first companions, men of the stamp of Francis Xavier, had heard the call of the Eternal King: "It is my will to conquer the whole world, and thus to enter into the glory of my Father. Therefore, whoever wishes to join me in this enterprise must be willing to labor with me, that by following me in suffering he may follow me in glory."[4] They had asked Christ through our Lady to receive them under his standard, had asked for "the most perfect kind of humility . . . in order to imitate and be in reality more like Christ our Lord: . . . poverty with Christ poor, rather than riches; insults with Christ loaded with them, rather than honors; . . . accounted as worthless and a fool for Christ, rather than . . . esteemed as wise and prudent in this world."[5] They had asked, meditation after meditation, to see Christ more clearly, love him more dearly, follow him more nearly. In the Contemplation on Learning to Love Like God, they had pondered "with great affection" how much Christ had done for them, how much he had given them of what he has and is; and reflecting on what "according to all reason and justice" they ought to offer in return, they had bent low before him and prayed:

> Take, O Lord, and receive all my liberty, my memory, my understanding, and my entire will, all that I have and possess. You have given all to me; to you, O Lord, I return it. All is yours; dispose of it

wholly according to your will. Give me your love and your grace; for this is enough for me.[6]

And after long deliberation and prayer each elected to live this manner of life in the company of like-minded men . . . in the Company of Jesus.

II

Second, have we changed all that radically in our time? Would Ignatius recognize us as legitimate sons? Are Jesuits still good shepherds ready to lay down life in order to give life, or have they turned into hirelings who care nothing for the flock, are reluctant to risk? Only a history, not a homily, can answer that question adequately. Let me simply speak prayerfully to you as one who has lived through Jesuit change, has suffered personally from it, has even found some change difficult to accept intellectually.

You cannot grasp the issue of change if you focus only on *what* Jesuits are doing, on specific apostolates. Ignatius' Company was genuinely Jesuit before Peter Canisius helped construct 18 colleges across the face of Europe, and his American sons can claim Ignatius for father even if we are compelled to surrender all of our 28 colleges and universities. Even were it true—and it is not—that "the faith that does justice" had its birth in 1975, the charge is irrelevant. As the teen-age virgin of Nazareth, asked by an angel to mother God's Son, had for scenario not a script chiseled in stone, but only "Whatever you want, dear Christ," similarly for Ignatius. What his sons would do before his death and beyond, what they would have for mission in 1991, would be determined not in abstraction but by the demands of the Church at a given moment in history: "Whatever you need, dear Body of Christ." And our fidelity to Ignatius would rest not on reproducing what he or Xavier or Canisius did, but on our total self-giving in the spirit of the Spiritual Exercises: "Take and receive, O Lord. . . . "

So then, our primary task, in 1991 as in 1540, is not exhausted in any specific area, in any single ministry. Our mission is to be of service to God's children however and wherever the Church calls. Put another way, our calling is to be sacraments of Christ. I mean visible signs that God is here, persuasive proofs in our own person that God loves every man and woman from Adam to Antichrist.

But visible signs in a typically Jesuit way. Our calling and our training should shape a man who is incredibly open: open to God and to all God's images on earth. From the agonizingly human tragedies of the ancient Greek dramatists to the philosophies and theologies that have shaped us, from Dante's *Divine Comedy* to Kevin Costner's *Dances with Wolves*, from God's revelation in Christ to God's latest self-disclosure in the signs of our times, on our knees and at our desks, our human learning and our divine yearning have aimed at one product: a man of prayer and play, of competence and compassion, to whom naught that is human is a stranger, who will move in a moment wherever the Church wants him, so caught up in Christ and kin to men and women that he will risk all, life included, to make earthly life more human, human life more Christlike.

And so we have our paradoxes and our contradictions: Army chaplains and all-out pacifists, Jesuits on the golf course and Jesuits on the water front, Jesuits in night clubs and Jesuits in jail, Jesuits in costly classrooms and Jesuits in stinking slums, Jesuits on the left and Jesuits on the right, Jesuits co-opted by governments and Jesuits massacred by governments—the whole gamut of human living. Why? Because everywhere there is a human person crying out for Christ.

And so we change. We get up later than Ignatius and at times our hair is longer than his; we walk in picket lines and every so often someone even says no to Rome. Not because the Society is dead, but because Jesuits are alive—alive especially to the anguished plea from wasted bodies and parched minds.

And so we make mistakes, possibly more mistakes than we've ever made before. Not because obedience is now for the birds, but because the human situation is so much more complex and the name of the game is risk . . . because the name of Jesus is risk.

III

This leads to my third question: How do I personally look at Jesuit existence?[7] This year I celebrate two anniversaries: 60 years a Jesuit, 50 years a priest. What keeps me here? There are surely those who will say I'm in a rut, or I'm not about to surrender my nonsocial security, or I'm too blind to see that the Jesuits are outmoded, a thing of the past. In point of fact, my Jesuitness goes much deeper than any of that.

I am not unaware of the human face of the Society. In fact, my experience leads me to apply to the Society of Jesus what that fine French Jesuit Henri de Lubac once said about the Church of Christ:

I am told that she is holy, yet I see her full of sinners. I am told that her mission is to tear man away from his earthy cares, to remind him of his eternal vocation, yet I see her constantly preoccupied with the things of the earth and of time, as if she wished us to live here forever. I am assured that she is universal, as open as divine intelligence and charity, and yet I notice very often that her members, through some sort of necessity, huddle together timidly in small groups—as human beings do everywhere. She is hailed as immutable, alone stable and above the whirlpools of history, and then, suddenly, under our very eyes, she upsets many of the faithful by the suddenness of her renewals.[8]

Yes, we are a society of sinners, even with the grace of God. Our vision is myopic, and so we do not always discern the divine, we misread the signs of the times; at times we close up the wrong school! Our wills are weak, and so we do not always live the logic of our commitment. Despite all our grandiose professions, we can be as small as the next man. No doubt we American Jesuits would be better than we are, our efforts more fruitful, if our freedom had been nailed to the crosses that for half a century pinned our brothers in Russia and Poland, in Czechoslovakia and Hungary, in Lithuania and Albania and Romania, if martyrs like Walter Ciszek rather than theologians like Walter Burghardt had been the seed of Christians.

And still, here is where I want to be. Not only because here I find myself fulfilled. That is indeed true. But in a society committed to the greater glory of *God* sheer self-fulfilment can be perilously selfish. I delight in this Company of Jesus because through six decades I have experienced the "great things" a "mighty" God can do through those who, like Mary, murmur an unreserved yes to divine invitation. I have come to know literally thousands of Jesuits of whom—despite the young critic of my introduction—Ignatius must be terribly proud. Why? First, because they are men of the Exercises; I mean men whose center is Christ, who "seek only to will and not will as God our Lord inspires them, and as seems better for the service and praise of the Divine Majesty."[9] Second, because they are men for others; I mean men who can honestly repeat what St. Paul proclaimed to the Christians of Corinth: "I will most gladly spend and be spent for your souls" (2 Cor 12:15). Third, because they are men of the Church; for even in the agonizing events of the 80s, Jesuits to a man bowed their heads with dear Pedro Arrupe to a papal decision that cut many a loyal heart to the quick.[10]

I love this Company of Jesus, these companions of Jesus. In large measure because they are how they are, different from me yet one with me in Christ and for others, I remain a Jesuit—and, if God graciously grants it, expect to die a Jesuit.

St. Ignatius Church
Baltimore, Md.
April 21, 1991

27

MOTHER OF JESUS, MOTHER OF JESUITS?
Feast of the Blessed Virgin Mary,
Mother of the Society of Jesus

- Galatians 4:4–7
- Matthew 1:20b–23

Today's feast confronts us with a problem. If you can credit the liturgical books of the Society of Jesus, the mother of Jesus is the mother of Jesuits.[1] Is this anything more than piosity, devotion run hog-wild? To make Christian sense of this in the Ignatian Year, I want to talk about (1) our Lady and Ignatius Loyola, (2) a significant shift in devotion to our Lady, and (3) our devotion in the decades that lie ahead.

I

First, our Lady in the life of Ignatius.[2] No, he never said our Lady was "mother of the Society of Jesus." He did not race around Rome waving Marian banners to arouse devotion to her. And yet, the mother of Jesus was central to his spirituality—quietly, very naturally, without ostentation.

It began at Loyola, when he was convalescing from the cannon ball that shattered his right leg and damaged the left. Our Lady appeared to him with the Child Jesus—an appearance that proved a profound conversion experience, gave him a loathing for the life he had so far misspent. At Loyola, too, he copied in blue Mary's words in the Gospels.[3]

Especially significant were Mary's shrines. The place names fashion a mosaic of Ignatian devotion. *Aránzazu*, where the pilgrim kept a prayer vigil, placed his plans and problematic future in Mary's hands. *Navarrete*, where he spent money to repair and decorate a neglected image of Mary. *Montserrat*, where he kept his vigil of arms at the feet of the Black Virgin, spent the whole night in prayer. *Manresa*, while reciting the Hour of our Lady, when he had the illumination of the Trinity that so profoundly affected his whole life—and saw our Lady too. *Barcelona*, where he prayed before the image of Our Lady of the Way. *Jerusalem*, where he visited the Church of the Dormition (falling asleep) of Our Lady. *Rome*, where he prayed at the long-sacred shrine of Loreto. *Montmartre*, in the little chapel dedicated to Mary, where on the feast of the Assumption 1534 Ignatius and six companions pronounced the vow that would orient their life to come. *La Storta*, where the Father answered his prayer to our Lady, "Place me with your Son."

There is so much more. Do you remember how in his bravado days Ignatius was tempted to slip a few dagger digs to a Moor who questioned Mary's virginity after Bethlehem? Do you remember how he would have loved a Jewish ancestry, so as to be related in flesh to Jesus and his mother? Do you remember that on this very day 450 years ago, in Rome's Basilica of St. Paul-outside-the-Walls, Ignatius and five companions pronounced their profession in the Society of Jesus "in the presence of [God's] virgin mother and the whole heavenly court"? Do you remember how, while composing the Constitutions, he saw "now the Father, now all three persons of the Trinity, now our Lady who was interceding for him or sometimes confirming what he had written"?[4] Do you remember the votive Masses he said in honor of our Lady? How he slept with the rosary on him?

And if you have ever experienced the Spiritual Exercises, you could not escape our Lady: on sin, on the kingdom, on Jesus embryo and infant and adolescent, on his passion. So insightfully when Ignatius asks all who meditate on the Two Standards to converse with our Lady, ask her "to obtain from her Son and Lord the grace to be received under his standard. . . ."[5] For in his mind Mary was "the very embodiment of the victory over Satan and the world."[6] So touchingly, the appearance of the risen Jesus to his mother—not indeed recorded in Scripture, but "Scripture supposes that we have understanding,"[7] that a risen Jesus bypassing his mother, Jesus without his mother, makes no sense.

Is it fanciful to suggest that, in the mind of Ignatius, the *sheerly human person* most responsible for his decision to found a Company of Jesus was the mother of Jesus?

II

This triggers my second point: Four centuries later, in our rough-and-tumble 60s, what happened to our Lady? Put bluntly, we lost her. Not only American Catholics at large, but unnumbered Jesuits as well. Point the finger where you will—at the Second Vatican Council, at Protestant pressure to put Mary "in her place," at Catholic emphasis on essentials—word and worship, sacraments and sacrifice. The reasons are complex; the result was patent: Mary faded into the background of Catholic devotion. Rosaries disappeared not only from pious fingers but from religious habits. Evening novenas played second fiddle to prime-time TV. Statues of Mary were retired to the sacristy. "Lovely lady dressed in blue" became a fun line for sophisticates.

Some losses we need not regret. We did bury some long-lived superstitions: Jesus administers justice, Mary ministers mercy; if you really want to get a friend out of hell, ask Mary. We are less facile in calling our Lady "our life, our sweetness, and our hope." We may well have succeeded in subordinating rosary to liturgy, Mary to Mass, mother to Son.

But in the process all too many rushed all too hastily to an un-Catholic extreme. They forgot, if they ever knew, that Catholicism, for all its stress on intelligence, is not a cult of cold reason; that knowledge, even grace-full, is not identical with holiness; that a saving spirituality, oneness with God, must link heart to mind, emotion to understanding, passion to purpose. In the process of purification, too many unwittingly betrayed God's Word, the Church's theology, and a Catholic art.

God's Word. Like it or not, I learn from the New Testament that Mary is not only mother of *Jesus*. Contemplate Jesus, Mary, and John on Calvary: "When Jesus saw his mother there with the disciple whom he loved, he said to his mother, 'Woman, here is your son.' In turn he said to the disciple, 'Here is your mother' " (Jn 19:26–27). It is not wishful thinking but solid scholarship that declares: The "beloved disciple" is not simply the apostle John; the "beloved disciple" is the Christian, all Christians. Those who believe in Jesus are reborn in his image. As sisters and brothers of Jesus, you and I, as well as John, have Mary for mother.[8]

The Church's theology. Unless I have stopped growing, I learn from Vatican II that God's Mother "is a model of the Church in the area of faith, of love, and of perfect union with Christ."[9] It goes back to a precious tradition theologians have recovered from the early and medieval Church: Mary is a type and figure of the Church. What Mary was and is, that the Church and each individual Christian is expected to be. Put another way: Mary, as Luke's Gospel intimates, is the first disciple, the most remarkable model of what Christian disciples should be, what you and I should be. For she lived, more perfectly than any other human, the essence of discipleship, a ceaseless "Let it happen to me as you say" (Lk 1:38). She laid at God's feet the yes that altered history—carried it into eternity with her.

A Catholic art. To thrust the Mother of God into a religious attic is to lose sight of the painting and poetry, sculpture and architecture, music, dancing, and dramatic art that have nourished the Catholic imagination for centuries, more powerfully than our philosophy and theology. It is to forget Michelangelo and Botticelli, Chaucer and Chartres, Bach and Brahms. In brief, it is to forget what power there is in the way poet Gerard Manley Hopkins compared our Lady to the air we breathe:

> . . . men are meant to share
> Her life as life does air.
>   If I have understood,
> She holds high motherhood
> Towards all our ghostly good
> And plays in grace her part
> About man's beating heart,
> Laying, like air's fine flood,
> The deathdance in his blood;
> Yet no part but what will
> Be Christ our Saviour still.[10]

III

This leads into my third point: Mary in our future. Jesuits of course, but actually the wider spectrum of Catholics, indeed of Christians. Here a homilist tiptoes around land mines. A distinction is all-important: There are devotions, and there is devotion. No homilist dare tell you, Jesuit or not, what devotions you must practice, what specific acts of piety you must perform to be Catholic: Way of the Cross, Nine First Fridays, Novena to the Sorrowful Mother or the Holy Face of Jesus, Our Lady of Guadalupe. So much of that depends on different cultures, changing times, personal likes and dislikes. I dare not dogmatize, dare not declare that if you are meditating on the glorious mysteries of Jesus and Mary, you do it best while your fingers are caressing a rosary.

But devotion is something else again. One spiritual writer called it "the total religious élan [thrust] directly towards God."[11] I may legitimately stay away from Medjugorje and Lourdes, from Fatima and Czestochowa; but I risk a rift in my spiritual life if Mary is not intimate to me. Why? Because Mary, this Jewish woman who gave birth to the world's Savior, this woman who at this moment is gloriously alive in soul and body, this woman is one of the most powerful symbols the Christian possesses, and symbols are what give life to our belief. Let me explain.

What is a symbol? A sign. Not just any sign, like "Baltimore 40 miles." A symbol is a sign that "works mysteriously on [our] consciousness so as to suggest more than it can clearly describe or define." It is "pregnant with a depth of meaning which is evoked rather than explicitly stated."[12] And God has revealed God's self especially through symbols: Abraham as father of God's people, the burning bush seen by Moses, the brazen serpent in the desert, the "kingdom of God" in the preaching of Jesus, the cross on Calvary, Jesus' resurrection, the descent of the Holy Spirit.

And Mary? Mary is a remarkable symbol. Not "just a symbol," that devastating expression. She is remarkably real as a person, and that is why she is so significant a symbol. But what does Mary reveal about God that is so terribly important—reveal not so much in words as more eloquently in who she is?

I said above that Mary reveals what it means to be a disciple. Her life discloses what is sometimes called a feminine principle, but a principle that is crucial for man as well as woman. Mary's life is an open-ended yes to life as it unfolds. Our God is a God of surprises. If you haven't experienced that as yet, I promise you that you surely will. Your spirituality, your life with God, is not a matter of ever onwards, ever upwards. It is an adventure wherein you can promise yourself only two certainties: (1) The Holy Spirit will ceaselessly surprise you, and (2) God will always be there. Symbol supreme of such open-endedness is the mother of Jesus—from an angel's surprise in Nazareth, through a ceaselessly surprising youngster in Nazareth, to a dead Christ cradled in her lap and a risen Christ leaping from the rock. But you will not discover this unless our Lady is more than a swift Hail Mary, unless you warm up to her as to your own mother.

Here let me stress something even more profound: Mary our

mother reveals God's own mothering. Lest you think this a sample of Jesuitry, listen to Pope John Paul I: God is not only Father but "even more so Mother, who . . . wants only to be good to us," wants only to love us, especially if we are bad.[13] Mary takes us beyond herself as Mother of Mercy, Mother of Divine Consolation, Refuge of Sinners, Comforter of the Afflicted. She *is* all these, but she ceaselessly points to God as the one to whom these qualities most properly refer.

> All that is creative and generative of life, all that nourishes and nurtures, all that is benign, cherishes, and sustains, all that is full of solicitude and sympathy originates in [God]. Maternal fruitfulness, care and warmth, and indispensable mother love has its source in [God]. She exercises a maternity that does not leave us orphans.[14]

It is no longer a judgmental Father who is led to smile at us by a mother's prayers; *God* is the most loving of all mothers, far more maternal than even Mary could possibly have dreamed of being. God's justice need not be tempered by Mary's merciful intercession. To forgive is indeed divine. It is the compassion of *God* that is disclosed in this merciful, compassionate woman. But I shall not discover this by memorizing the words of Mary in Luke—only if the mother of Jesus is genuinely my mother, only if I am as close to her as was John beneath the cross.

Good friends: Have I gotten away from Mary Mother of the Company of Jesus? In a sense, yes. Our Lady was indeed an active lady in the Society's prehistory, in what happened between a cannon ball in 1521 and the birth of Jesuits in 1540. And we Jesuits are still privileged to pray to her, "Place me with your Son." But the Mother of the Society of Jesus may work her best in us if this feast has a twin effect. I mean, if it not only revives in *Jesuit* hearts a Mary too long put "in her place," but does not set us on a Marian pedestal "far from the madding crowd's ignoble strife." The mother of Jesus reminds us that the "mighty" God who "has done great things for [her]" (Lk 1:49) is mother not only of Jesuits but of all who claim to be Christ's, that her ceaseless role in redemption is to hold her Son out to all of us, that her value as a divine sign and symbol is that she more than anyone was endlessly open to a God of surprises, that her gifts as mother reflect a God who is not only Father but "even more so Mother."

As we Jesuits promote justice to the unfortunates of earth, would we not be well advised to restore to her just place in our lives the woman who was closest of all to Jesus, the woman who typifies all we as Christians should be, the woman who will never cease to be our mother, even into eternity?

St. Aloysius Gonzaga Church
Washington, D.C.
April 22, 1991

Medley

28
HANDS NAILED DOWN
Memorial Mass for Pedro Arrupe, S.J.

- Philippians 2:5–8
- John 12:20–26

In the closing years of his life, the German theologian Karl Rahner focused ever more intensely on "the cross . . . erected over history."[1] What St. Paul phrased so baldly and economically in his letter to the Christians of Philippi in Macedonia—"Christ Jesus became obedient unto death" (Phil 2:8)—Rahner expanded in packed and poignant paragraphs. Jesus surrendered himself

> in his death unconditionally to the absolute mystery that he called his Father, into whose hands he committed his existence, when in the night of his death and God-forsakenness he was deprived of everything that is otherwise regarded as the content of a human existence: life, honour, acceptance in earthly and religious fellow-ship, and so on. In the concreteness of his death it becomes only too clear that everything fell away from him, even the perceptible security of the closeness of God's love, and in this trackless dark there prevailed silently only the mystery that in itself and in its freedom has no name and to which he nevertheless calmly surren-dered himself as to eternal love and not to the hell of futility. . . .[2]

Rahner argued that if you seek where concretely, for any and every Christian, independently of time and circumstance, Christ is to be followed, we must answer in one only proposition: "the Christian, every Christian at all times, follows Jesus by *dying* with him; following Jesus has its ultimate truth and reality and universality in the following of the Crucified."[3]

But following the Crucified, Rahner noted, is not limited to the

179

close of our earthbound existence. Whatever it is that pricks my pride, assails my lustiness, intimates my mortality, takes the joy from my very bones—"In all these brief moments of dying in installments we are faced with the question of how we are to cope with them." Do "we merely protest, merely despair . . . become cynical and cling all the more desperately and absolutely to what has not yet been taken from us"? Or do "we abandon with resignation what is taken from us, accept twilight as promise of an eternal Christmas full of light, regard slight breakdowns as events of grace"?[4]

Good friends: Today we pay tribute tearful and cheerful to a man who followed the Crucified. From a life packed with "dying in installments," I pluck three moments: 1945, 1965, and 1981. I mean: a bomb, a ballot, and a blood clot. A word on each.

I

First, a bomb. On August 6, 1945, wrote Pedro Arrupe, the clock on the wall of the Hiroshima novitiate stopped at 8:10 in the morning: "it seemed to have its hands nailed down."[5] Hands nailed down. In a few moments, six kilometers away, a malignant mushroom in Hiroshima's serene sky would wound our world for ever. Before Don Pedro's eyes, his city and his people were ablaze. 75,000 dead or dying; 200,000 in need of medical care; 150,000 fleeing the holocaust in terror.[6]

Through that Calvary Pedro and his brothers walked, tiptoeing on ruins under which the embers still felt warm. Here a little boy, glass imbedded in his eye; there a mother on fire as her son tugs in vain at the wooden beams that imprison her; 200 children dead in a school. With a razor blade Pedro removes 50 fragments of glass from a Jesuit's back. His ears ache with the cries of the drowning as the river rises in the night. Former student of medicine, he has no anesthetics —only aspirin and iodine, only bicarb of soda and boric acid. Time and again, Pedro and his brothers pile up pyramids of once-human flesh, 50 or 60 at a time, pour fuel on them, set them afire.[7]

Five years later, in Bogotá, Pedro watched Hiroshima's holocaust on film.

> In an hour and a half I saw . . . the horror and tragedy I had lived during several months. My vision became clouded with tears and I could stand it no longer; I left my seat and walked out. . . . What I withstood in all its terrible reality, overcame me completely in the

unreality of a celluloid film. My nerves, which I had thought were made of iron, were shattered before that emotional onslaught.[8]

Hands nailed down. Hiroshima was for Don Pedro an installment in dying. The morning after the bomb, in the house chapel littered with irradiated bodies, he turned to murmur "Dominus vobiscum" ("The Lord be with you") to tortured unbelievers who stared at him without understanding. "I do not think I have ever said Mass with such devotion."[9] And still, in his own words, "Even from destruction God knows how to draw life."[10] A young man reborn by baptism after Pedro had attended to his festering wounds—inspired later to priesthood.[11] An 18-year-old girl found by Pedro after 15 days, her body one gangrenous mass, reduced to "a wound and an ulcer," with only one question from her dying lips: "Father, have you brought me Communion?"[12] He had.

The stories are beyond counting, the lesson strikingly the same: In Hiroshima as outside Jerusalem, hands nailed down could still reach out to touch flesh and spirit in agony, to give life.

II

Second, a ballot. On May 22, 1965, on the third ballot, Pedro Arrupe, provincial of Japan, was elected 28th superior general of the Society of Jesus. From the rubble of World War II a new world had been born, a world of paradox and contradiction, of promise and peril, of freedom and chains. 1965? The year India and Pakistan were at war, Rhodesia declared independence of Britain, and bloody coups erupted in Indonesia, Algeria, and the Congo. When American boys began bleeding in Vietnam. When Martin Luther King Jr. led slaves from Selma, fire and blood devastated Watts, and Malcolm X was shot to death. When two Soviet cosmonauts were the first to walk in space, the Beatles wowed us with "Nowhere Man," and Medicare was born. When the young were terribly restless—in the world, in the Church, in the Jesuits. When a world-wide council of bishops was fashioning a fresh face for Catholicism, and much of the Church was not ready for it, some of the Church already unhappy and hostile.

This kind of world foreshadowed Pedro Arrupe's 18 years as superior general. For all the Jesuits who loved him dearly and found him inspiring, many, he knew, complained that Arrupe's Society was not the Society they had entered, not the Society of their vowed obedience. Never one to condemn, he still wept over hundreds of his brothers who found Jesuit existence unfulfilling, unbearable, and like an earlier set of Christ's disciples "walked no more in his company" (Jn 6:66). He himself walked a thin, courageous line when he asked us for intellectual submission to the encyclical on birth control, but only if we could submit without violence to our intellect. A small group of Spanish Jesuits asked Paul VI for a new juridical status, directly dependent on the pope; the papal no did not make for peace. This man, molded to the mind of Ignatius as few before him, had to read in the secular press the prediction of a Jesuit that just as the Society was founded by a Basque, by a Basque it would be destroyed.

But I suspect that the cross which more than any other wedded for Don Pedro gladness and sadness, high hope and deep discouragement, was the Society's new emphasis in response to the signs of the times. I mean the commitment declared in 1974 by our 32nd General Congregation: "The mission of the Society of Jesus today is the service of faith, of which the promotion of justice is an absolute requirement."[13] The inseparable unity of the two, Arrupe admitted in Manila, is "the concept which has been most difficult to put across."[14] Arrupe knew that on this issue some of our most loyal friends and benefactors thought us traitors to the Ignatian ideal. He knew that more than a few Jesuits thought "the faith that does justice" nonsensical, naive. He knew that many of his sons echoed the remark I overheard in a Jesuit recreation room about the desperate plight of Latin America's poor: "not unjust, simply unfortunate." He knew there were idealistic Jesuits who carried the struggle to extremes, to a violence hardly in conformity with the cross of Christ. Yet he never wavered in his core conviction, the memorable message John Paul II proclaimed in Puebla: "The Church has learned that its evangelizing mission has as indispensable part (como parte indispensable) action for justice. . . . "[15]

Installments in dying. Only those who, like Vincent O'Keefe, shared his days can describe in detail the nails that held Don Pedro's hands. But the nails, they all agree, are only half the story. More wondrous still was Arrupe's inner serenity. Only if you knew the madness that flooded his office each day could you appreciate his deep-seated tranquility. Only he, O'Keefe tells me, was not "chewing nails." It reached a high point—this combination of profound peace, high spirituality, and moral leadership—in 1974–75, during the 32nd General Congregation. With all the incredible miscommunications between the Society and Paul VI, he kept the Congregation facing up to its problems, determined to live his Company's genuine charism.

III

Third, a blood clot. It was August 7, 1981, six in the morning, when Don Pedro's plane from Bangkok landed in Rome. Greeted by Father Louis Laurendeau and Brother Luis García, he reached down to pick up his small suitcase; but he could not close his right hand around the handle. He managed a puzzled smile; but he could not keep his balance, started to sweat profusely. At Salvator Mundi Hospital the diagnosis was distressing: a cerebral thrombosis; his right side was partially paralyzed.

From that day to his death—almost ten years—Don Pedro was nailed to a fresh and final cross. But here too there were installments in dying. Apostle to the world, this dynamic man who had circled the globe six times had to be helped from bed to chair and back to bed again. As Jesus had said to another Peter, "Truly, truly I say to you, when you were young, you girded yourself and walked where you would; but when you are old, you will stretch out your hands, and another will gird you and carry you where you do not wish to go" (Jn 21:18). "This," the evangelist observed, "This [Jesus] said to show by what death [Peter] was to glorify God" (v. 19). Hands nailed down.

Apostle of the word, fluent in Japanese and German, in Latin and Italian, in English and French and Spanish, a man whose charism was oral communication, Don Pedro could now form words in Spanish alone—and that with dreadful difficulty. You may remember that when he was elected superior general in 1965, his first words to his electors and to the Society were borrowed from the first chapter of Jeremiah. Elected by the Lord "a prophet to the nations" (Jer 1:5), Jeremiah protested: "Ah, Lord God! Look, I don't know how to speak" (v. 6). When Arrupe's resignation was accepted on September 3, 1983, his farewell address to the Society had to be delivered by a stand-in. It began with a deliberate, heart-rending allusion to 1965 and Jeremiah: "As you see, I cannot even address you directly."[16] I don't know how to speak. Hands nailed down.

While still superior general, this man of the Church, this son of Ignatius to whom the "Rules for Thinking with the Church" were second nature, this powerful leader had to listen in his paralysis while Agostino Cardinal Casaroli read aloud a letter from Pope John Paul II committing the Society's care to someone else, to a personal delegate of the pope. Not because the general of the Jesuits was so painfully ill, but because John Paul did not care for the way Jesuit life was moving. It hurt him beyond telling; I know this for a fact. And still he managed a faith-filled yes—"Not my will but thine be done" (Lk 22:42)—for himself and for 25,000 men inspired by him to echo his response. Hands nailed down.

Installments in dying, indeed. Only Don Pedro knows how many, how devastating. But as in the rubble of Hiroshima, so in the rubble of his final, drawn-out, crucifying holocaust, he sensed that "even from destruction God knows how to draw life." Through these ten years, only God knows how many of us Jesuits are genuinely alive—alive to God, alive to God's crucified images on earth—because Pedro Arrupe's hands were nailed down. Only God knows how many; I know . . . one.

Good friends of Pedro Arrupe: We have been uncommonly privileged. We have known a man, a Christian, a Jesuit, a priest who lived with serenity, often with joy, a spirituality of the cross. From an atom bomb in a Japanese city, through a world-wide leadership of thousands of multicolored Jesuits, to years of near-speechless helplessness on a Roman bed of pain, he showed us how to live and how to die—the dying/rising of his Lord. He lived the frightening phrase of Jesus on the cost of discipleship, "If you want to come after me, you have to take up your cross *every day*" (Lk 9:23). And he revealed in his flesh why this is so: "If a grain of wheat does not fall into the earth and die, it remains alone [a solitary grain of wheat]; but if it dies, it bears much fruit" (Jn 12:24).

My sisters and brothers: For a spirituality of the cross, "the cross erected over history," the cross erected over your flesh and mine, listen to Don Pedro's final message, his final words, to the whole Society of Jesus, to all of us, spoken mutely, spoken from another's lips, spoken with hands nailed down, back in 1983:

> For myself, all I want is to repeat from the depths of my heart: "Take, O Lord, and receive all my liberty, my memory, my understanding, my whole will, all I have and all I possess. You gave them to me; to you, Lord, I return it [all]. It is all yours; dispose of it entirely as you will. Give me your love and your grace; this is enough for me."[17]

God's love and God's grace: Is this enough *for me*?

St. Ignatius Loyola Church
New York, N.Y.
February 19, 1991

29

NEW CHRISTIAN, NEW COMMUNITY
Homily for the Baptism of an Infant

- Galatians 3:27–28

Infants play a special role in Christ's Church—a role adults do not play quite as effectively. Infants compel a homilist to say what he has to say . . . briefly. So then, if only from fear of rousing the wrath of Frans-Joseph James Patrick Maria, I shall speak swiftly of him and what is happening to him today.

St. Paul has put it pungently: "As many of you as were baptized into Christ have put on Christ. There is neither Jew nor Greek, there is neither slave nor free, there is no male-and-female" (Gal 3:27–28). That sentence says something explicitly about Frans-Joseph, and what it says about him suggests a word about the rest of us.

I

First, Paul is saying something about Frans-Joseph. In my early days as a priest, the big bugaboo about baptism was original sin. Pious parents rushed their babies to the baptismal bath, lest sudden death overtake their child and send the infant to a limbo less fearful than hell but quite a distance from God.[1] Today the stress, the emphasis, is wonderfully different. Not that we have jettisoned original sin, thrown it off the bark of Peter; there is a dark side to humanity that goes back to our beginnings, all the evil that has come down to us since then, all the heaped-up sins and sinfulness into which each infant is born.[2] And so there is a need for healing, for new strength poured into children who will have to confront the devastating evil that surrounds them.

Still, what we emphasize now is not so much our sinfulness in an old Adam as our healing through the risen Christ. Frans-Joseph will be "baptized into Christ." What does this mean? It does *not* mean that before a certain gray-headed Jesuit splashes water on him he is numbered among God's enemies. No, Frans-Joseph was beloved of God on January 18 and for more than nine months before. But through that year something significant was lacking: He was not-yet-in-Christ. Today he will begin that wonderful adventure we call "belonging to Christ." He puts on Christ, like the white garment he will don to symbolize it.

The adventure will never end this side of eternity, for Frans-Joseph should never stop growing into Christ, can always be more Christlike than he is at any given moment. But today it begins. The God who shared Frans-Joseph's first birth with Frans and Cathleen will take him into His arms, much as his dear mother does, for a fresh birth, a rebirth, as adopted son of God, in the image of the one Son who died for him, rose to life for him, will live in him days without end. When blessed water bathes his brow, we shall be able to say for him with St. Paul, "It is no longer I who live; Christ lives in me" (Gal 2:20).

But that is not all. Belonging to Christ, Frans-Joseph becomes part of the Body of Christ, is incorporated into the community of believers. He is one with all others who believe. This leads into my second point: you and me.

II

You see, you and I are about to do something to Frans-Joseph without a "by your leave." At this early stage of his existence, there is already much we must do to and for him without asking his permission—feed him, burp him, evacuate him; otherwise he will not live. This afternoon there is something quite different we feel we must do for him, do to him; otherwise he will not live the way the God who gave him life wants him to live. Let me explain.

I believe it was Thomas Merton who said, "No man gets to heaven all by himself." (No woman either.) From Abraham to the last human alive, the way God has arranged salvation is in the context of community. We Catholics do not reach God as 900,000,000 individuals each with a me-and-Jesus spirituality. We reach God within a community of faith, hope, and love—through a people of God's own choosing with a creed, a cult, and a code. A creed: I mean a people whose minds are enlightened by one same core of truth revealed by God in Christ. A cult: I mean a people whose spirits are nourished by the flesh and blood of a God-man. A code: I mean a people whose lives are lived in harmony with a morality that has for ideal Jesus' Sermon on the Mount.

It is this community that Frans-Joseph enters today without anything more than an infant wail of protest. This forced entrance into a community we have chosen for him lays a heavy burden on us who know and love him. As he grows into childhood and adolescence, he will have to grow into faith, into hope, into love—in a word, grow into Christ. How he grows into Christ will depend not simply on a Christ he cannot see; it will be powerfully affected by the dear ones he *can* see—by father and mother, by godfather and godmother, by relatives and friends, by each of us and so many more who rejoice in the name Christian.

The question? What will Frans-Joseph actually see in us? A community so committed to Christ that we believe on his word what passes proof, or a set of individuals who choose for ourselves what we will accept, what reject? Will he see a community that sets its hope on God and God's grace, or a group of Sunday Christians who rely on the marvels of technology for our salvation? Will he see a community that compels from unbelievers the ancient pagan cry, "See how these Christians love one another," or churchgoers who claw one another like cats on a hot tin roof?

Good friends: This is a solemn moment—solemn but thrilling as well. For this helpless infant, like the Christ child in Mary's arms, might well do as much for us as we do for him today: He can make us want to be better than we are. For our own Christlife and for his. So then, as we share the joy of Frans and Cathleen, as we celebrate this latest living link between the Netherlands and the United States, I suggest that we thank God for the gift *all of us* have received this day. For, as centuries ago in Bethlehem, so here today: A child has been born *for us*. . . . For us.

Holy Trinity Church
Washington, D.C.
April 7, 1991

30
JESUS TOOK A CHILD IN HIS ARMS
Homily for the Baptism of Two Infants

• Mark 9:33–37

This day we do, under God, two remarkable things. One is totally thrilling, the other is somewhat scary. A word on each.

I

The thrilling thing we do today? I like to think of it the way the Gospels describe a touching scene in Jesus' life: Jesus "sat down and called the Twelve. . . . And he took a child and put him in the midst of them; and taking him in his arms, he said to them: 'Whoever receives one such child in my name receives me; and whoever receives me receives [the Father] who sent me' " (Mk 9:35–37).[1] Today Jesus takes William Winters and Matthew Kyle into his arms. Not indeed physically, but actually more profoundly still. For today we see with eyes of faith what St. Paul proclaimed: "As many of you as were baptized into Christ have put on Christ" (Gal 3:27). In a few short moments these two infants will "put on Christ." Towards the close of this ceremony I shall say to them: "You have become a new creation and have clothed yourself in Christ. See in this white garment the outward sign of your Christian dignity."

The white garments are symbols: They are being clothed with Christ.[2] What does this mean? Paul put it in "heavy metal" theological language that merits our meditation: "Through baptism we have been buried with [Christ] in death, so that just as Christ was raised from the dead through the Father's glory, so we too might live a new life. For if we have grown into a union with him by undergoing a death like his,

188

we shall certainly be united with him in a resurrection like his" (Rom 6:4–5). Baptism—being plunged into blessed waters—is like being buried with Christ so as to rise with him into a new life.

Today these two children begin "a new life." Melissa and Scott, Mary Ann and Pete, you have already experienced personally an endless miracle that never grows stale: what it means for a child to be alive. You mothers experience it uniquely: the movements within, the life growing inside, the feeding on you, the oneness with your life. You fathers feel it each time you hold your child, look into his eyes, see him smile, hear him cry. For your child to be alive means that he grows, matures, sees with new eyes, hears with new ears, touches and tastes and smells. Each day he experiences new life.

Today that life is enriched beyond measure. Today that life becomes life in Christ. If you are in Christ, St. Paul says, you are "a new creature" (2 Cor 5:17). These children of yours now belong for ever to Christ; Christ lives in them. They will not feel it, but when the waters of baptism flow over their foreheads, they will begin a new relationship with Christ; his life will flow through their veins. Now it begins. And as the months and years go on, they will be able to live ever more fully the life that is given them today.

They are alive, to you and to God, even though it will take time for their gifts to develop. On a natural level, here are the muscles that one day will sink a basket or light up a hockey net, the mind that one day will begin to think, the heart that one day will know what it means to love. Similarly, their new life in Christ. This is the mind that one day will say, "I believe in one God, in Jesus Christ, in the Holy Spirit." This is the spirit that one day will actually hope: hope for God's grace through the bittersweet of human living, hope for life without end. This is the heart that one day will try to love God above all else, love its sisters and brothers at least as much as it loves itself.

The gift of God, life in Christ, is there from this day on; it will only need time to activate it. And that brings me to my second point. For the challenge to these children, "See in this white garment the outward sign of your Christian dignity," goes on: "With your family and friends to help you by word and example, bring that dignity unstained into the everlasting life of heaven."

II

Today we do something quite frightening. We bring these two infants into our believing community, into the Catholic Church. We

don't ask their permission; we don't wait till the age of reason for them
to make up their own minds on whether it's a good idea or not. We
believe it is, and so we do it.

The problem is . . . the community. As these two infants grow,
what will they discover? Somewhat as you have to be concerned about
what kind of parents they will discover, you must be anxious about the
religious community they will find. As faith grows in their minds, will
they discover a vibrant, enthusiastic community of faith, a community
that accepts wholeheartedly what God took flesh to tell us, gives itself
without reservation to God "in good times and bad, in poverty and
wealth, in sickness and health"? Or will they find us people who believe only what we see, are afraid to say an unreserved yes to whatever
God asks? As hope comes to life in them, will they find themselves
among fellow worshipers who pray in the words of the Psalmist, "For
God alone my soul waits in silence, for my hope is from Him. He only
is my rock and my salvation, my fortress; I shall not be shaken" (Ps
62:5–6)? Or will they find our community placing its hope in man and
woman, in political power, in the triumphs of technology? As their
love moves from sheer feeling to awareness of the other, will they
discover a community that lives the commandment of Christ, "Love
one another as I have loved you" (Jn 15:12)? Or will they see in our
midst Christian cats clawing at one another, jealous of one another,
convinced that in today's rat race the race is to the swift, the shrewd,
the savage?

I am only suggesting the burden that baptism lays—on parents,
on sponsors, on the community. Especially in their younger years,
William Winters and Matthew Kyle will be uncommonly influenced by
what they see and hear in the community that claims to be Christian. If
that is true, I suspect that we—all of you and I too—might well make a
resolution today. Not only will we feed these children with Captain
Crunch, Sugar Pops, Gummy Bears, Happy Meals. We will build up
their childlike faith, their young hopes, their natural love with our
own deep faith in the God who shaped us in a divine image, our trust
in a Christ who died for us, our love for the heartsore and the homeless, the destitute and the disadvantaged.

So then, today's joy has to be tempered with sober reflection. We
who with justice are dismayed when each year 50 million living beings
are prevented from coming fully alive, we must be equally concerned
that they who come to birth through our bodies and our spirits grow
not only with all the earthly blessings our gifted lives can provide, but
also in imaging the Christ who takes them into his arms today. It is a
tough task all of us assume today: to collaborate with our dear Lord in

shaping children who will love as he loved. To do that, we ourselves have to love as Jesus loved. So, why don't we pray quietly in our hearts for that kind of love? After all, Matthew Kyle and William Winters deserve no less.

Holy Trinity Church
Washington, D.C.
August 4, 1991

31
ACT JUSTLY....
Homily for a Red Mass

- Micah 6:6–8
- Matthew 20:25–28

As we gather for worship, the legal profession is under attack. From Washington, from Hollywood, from the streets. Two months ago the Vice President of the United States raised some Bar Association hackles in Atlanta. Dan Quayle asked: "Does America really need 70 percent of the world's lawyers? Is it healthy for our economy to have 18 million new lawsuits coursing through the system annually? Is it right that people with disputes come up against staggering expense and delay? The answer is no."[1] A highly popular film, *Regarding Henry*, suggests that "lawyers, should they care to join the human race, need a shot in the head."[2] Perhaps more devastating still, lawyer "jokes" are crisscrossing the country like wildfire, savage you, file you somewhere beneath terrorists and laboratory rats, on a level with sharks.

Although homilists too, like the Hebrew prophets, may be justified in castigating systems on occasion, such is not my intent this evening. Unlike Mark Antony over the corpse of Caesar, I come not to bury your profession but to praise it[3]—and to challenge you. I intend to take the splendidly human gifts that adorn your legal vocation and link them to the divine gifts that grace your Christian calling. Let me develop swiftly three related themes, three questions: (1) What role do the laity play in the Church? (2) How does the lawyer, the judge, fit into that role? (3) What does your legal life suggest for your broader, wider Christian existence?

192

I

First, the general question: Who are you laity? Almost 125 years ago, in 1867, Msgr. George Talbot, adviser to Pope Pius X on English affairs, wrote a letter to the archbishop of Westminster, Henry Manning. That letter asked a profound question and supplied a provocative reply. "What," he asked, "is the province of the laity?" His response? "To hunt, to shoot, to entertain. These matters they understand, but to meddle with ecclesiastical affairs they have no right at all."[4]

Almost a century later, in 1965, the bishops of the Catholic Church in solemn council proclaimed:

> . . . The mission of the Church is not only to bring to men and women the message and grace of Christ, but also to penetrate and perfect the temporal sphere with the spirit of the gospel. . . . The laity must take on the renewal of the temporal order as their own special obligation.[5]

This "temporal order" is not some vague, gossamer, abstract idea. The temporal order is CBS and CIA and C&P, Pentagon and public school, board room and courtroom, media and medicine, Merrill Lynch and the Bank of Credit & Commerce International, Calvin Klein and Thompson Advertising, the country club and the local slum. The temporal order is this absurd little earth, where a billion humans fall asleep hungry while millions grow fat, where the war on the womb takes more lives in a year than two world wars, where men and women die for one another and kill one another, where more blacks languish in jail than are in college, where "equal justice for all" is an ideal rather than a reality.

It is this concrete order that has indeed its own proper purposes, yet demands to be sanctified. I mean, it must be directed to justice, to peace, to love. Only devoted, enthusiastic laymen and laywomen can do this effectively. Not only because this is your world, the only world you have, the world in which you live and move and have your being. Even more importantly, here lies your God-given task: to move your acre of God's world a bit closer to God's kingdom. Here is where you fulfil your distinctive function as Christians, where you play out your spirituality, where you express and deepen your oneness with God, your love relationship with Christ. And here—take careful notice— here you are not substitute players for a decimated priesthood, to be returned to the sidelines if vocations to the Roman collar return to normal. This is your specific vocation, even if our seminaries were to burst their seams. In that world you, above all, are the Church's presence—Christ's presence.

II

This leads into my second question: Who are you within this general lay vocation? On the face of it, you are men and women whose lives center around a single significant word: justice. Justice under law. An unforgettable focus, for without justice the anarchist reigns, or the despot. You are incredibly powerful people. Because of you, human lives change. Because of you, this man languishes behind bars for life, that woman goes scot free. Because of you, a Colonel North is convicted, and a Colonel North's conviction is overturned. Because of you, the insider trader, ideally, has no more clout in court than the homeless and hopeless. Because of a Thurgood Marshall, a whole race finally has its day in court. In your ears the words of the prophet Micah should ring loud and clear:

> With what shall I come before the Lord,
>   and bow myself before God on high?
> Shall I come before Him with burnt offerings,
>   with calves a year old?
> Will the Lord be pleased with thousands of rams,
>   with ten thousands of rivers of oil?
> Shall I give my first-born for my transgression,
>   the fruit of my body for the sin of my soul?
> [The Lord] has showed you, O man [and woman], what is good.
>   And what does the Lord require of you?
> Act justly, love steadfastly,
>   and walk humbly with your God.
>
> (Mic 6:6–8)

"Act justly." Within Catholic ethics, to act justly is to give each man or woman what is his or her due. Within American law, what is "due" is a risk-laden presumption that honors your profession. Before the law, the presumption is for innocence. No one is guilty until proven guilty. We rightly despise the Mafia, but unless an Edward Bennett Williams had been free to defend "godfathers," none of our liberties would be safe. The press may already have written "rapist" indelibly on Dr. William Smith's bio, but it is a courtroom that will definitively write "Guilty" or "Not guilty" beside his name.

A powerful profession indeed, a perilous profession, where you hold lives and reputations, prison bars and freedom, within your knowledge, your skills, your judgment. What you must never forget, however, is that this role you play is not simply a secular task, an ethical demand; it is a Christian responsibility. This is your singular way of penetrating and perfecting the temporal sphere with the spirit of the gospel. And the basic obligations the gospel lays on the law, Christ on lawyers, are, I suggest, three.

1) Competence. Lawyers and judges who are content with the expertise of their law-school days are as dangerous as priests who close their last theology book the day of their ordination. Here, in a singular way, not to go forward is to go backward. And with disastrous consequences for human living. How bring the spirit of the gospel into the law? To transfer a favorite Army slogan, "Be the best that you can be." To transfer a tough precept of Jesus, "Be perfect" (Mt 5:48) —as perfect as human nature will allow you, as perfect as the grace of Christ will endow you.

2) Compassion. The Bakkers and the Boeskys[6] may well deserve what the law exacts. That response of the legal head does not exempt you from a response of the Christian heart. If the Lord God can say, "As I live, I have no pleasure in the death of the wicked, but that the wicked turn back from his way and live" (Ezek 33:11), then surely sadness should supersede triumph whenever an image of God, however disfigured, must be severed from civilized society.

3) Service. Here today's Gospel is frighteningly pointed: "You know that the rulers of the Gentiles lord it over them, and their great men exercise authority over them. It shall not be so among you; but whoever would be great among you must be your servant, and whoever would be first among you must be your slave; even as the Son of man came not to be served but to serve, and to give his life as a ransom for many" (Mt 20:25–28). No less than president or policeman or priest, the good lawyer is perilously tempted: to see others, especially the less fortunate, the powerless, as subjects or enemies or clients—somehow under you, in your grip or power. Even if you and I, lawyer and priest, resist that temptation, how profoundly do we see ourselves as servants, as men and women committing our very lives to those we serve?

III

My third question: What does your legal life suggest for your broader, wider Christian existence? How can your love of law lead to the law of love? Let me focus on the imperative proclaimed to you today from God's own prophet Micah: Act justly.

You see, the justice the prophets preached was not simply an ethical construct, did not mean merely giving to others what they deserved, what they could justifiably demand because it was clear from philosophy or was written into law. The Jews were expected to father the fatherless and watch over the widow, to protect the powerless and succor the stranger, not because the needy deserved it, but because this was the way *God* had acted toward *them*. In freeing the oppressed, the Jews were mirroring the God who had freed *them* from oppression. In loving the loveless and unloved, they were imaging the God who time and again wooed Israel back despite her infidelities. Israel's justice was to reflect not the justice of man or woman, but the justice of God.

What should this say to you? Although your professional life is the law, you dare not limit your life to living by the law. For two forceful reasons. (1) Because human law, for all its value, cannot save you, cannot make you one with your God. Only love can do that. Not loving law; only loving God above all that is not God, loving your every brother and sister at least as much as you love yourself. (2) Because the equality you dispense at the bar of justice is not enough to unite woman and man, black and white, Jew and Arab, the haves and the have-nots, the restless young and the rest-home aged, the crack pushers and the police who imprison them. Only the Sermon on the Mount can do that, not Blackstone's *Commentaries*.

The challenge? To link in your lives dear Lady Justice and the Judeo-Christian just. I mean, give to each what each deserves and give to all more than they deserve; give to each what you have covenanted with the law to give, and give to all what you have covenanted with the Lord to give.

Good friends in Christ: I am not suggesting that civil/criminal law and the gospel should be one and the same thing. I am not arguing that forgiveness, the quality of Christian mercy, cancellation of all debts, "forgive and forget," is acceptable legal method. I do claim that the human law you serve so admirably can be (1) enriched and (2) surpassed. Enriched because, without emasculating human justice, you surround it with the compassion that human weakness should evoke, embrace it not as lord of all you survey but as servant in the image of Christ the Suffering Servant. Surpassed because in the totality of your living you transcend what sheer human law demands.

Live the law that way, and Thomas More will delight in his successors. Live that way, and our Lord Christ himself will delight in receiving you into the kingdom of justice you are preparing.

Cathedral of St. Peter
Wilmington, Delaware
October 17, 1991

32

MIND, MASS, MISSION
Homily for a Conference on Catholic Social Thought

- Jeremiah 18:18–20
- Matthew 20:17–28

Have you read the latest figures on "the global village"? If our world were a village of 1000 people, that village would have the following residents:

> Asians 564,
> Europeans 210,
> Africans 86,
> South Americans 80,
> North Americans 60.

Of those people,

> 60 would control half the income,
> 500 would be hungry,
> 600 would live in shantytowns,
> 700 would be illiterate.[1]

Good friends: On May 15 the Catholic world will celebrate a centenary. One hundred years ago Pope Leo XIII gave us the first of the great social encyclicals, *Rerum novarum*. There's a peril here. May 15 can prove to be just another anniversary, take its place with January 15, February 22, June 6, July 4, October 12, November 11, December 7. Sound and fury indeed, but nothing changes. If the Catholic social theory that moves from Leo to John Paul is to revolutionize the global village, is to touch what Karl Rahner called "the cross erected over history,"[2] if Catholics are in significant numbers to be men and women come "not to be served but to serve" (Mt 20:28), this year must begin to turn us inside out. For us, May 15 must be "May day, May day," a desperate cry to us from the living-dying for help, for survival.

But how? Spurred in large measure by that most imaginative of practical priests Bryan Hehir,[3] I submit that, as Catholic servants of justice, our service will be most effective if it weds three facets of the human spirit: the intellectual, the spiritual, and the social; thought, worship, and action; mind, Mass, and mission. A word on each.

I

First, the intellectual dimension. I mean thought, knowledge, reflection, understanding. Here we focus on what Bryan Hehir calls the American Catholic "center," the "postimmigrant" Catholic community, "a church pervasively present in white, upper-income suburbs," as distinguished from the "newly immigrant church . . . persistently present in inner-city communities, largely black and Hispanic."[4] What is demanded of these—the college-educated, technically-trained, well-fed, well-heeled, well-clothed? Intelligence informed by faith; a faith that yearns for understanding; Christian imagination.

A sad, perhaps fatal facet of contemporary American Catholicism is massive ignorance. Most of our educated Catholics, including clerics, lack a sense of Catholic tradition. Lawrence Cunningham, professor of religion at Florida State University, found himself frustrated in the classroom because

> students lack any sense of the historical perspective of Western culture in general and the part Catholicism played in the formation of that culture in particular. They . . . have no sense of the kind of church which existed before the Second Vatican Council. Students have this strong conviction that what is important happens now and the "now" has little or no link with the past. They tend to see the life of the church rather as they see the surface of a video game screen: active, immediate, and graspable as a whole. . . .[5]

Cunningham's experience can be transferred to American Catholicism in general. The results are tangible: a generation of educated Catholics who know Augustine only as a born-again Catholic who foisted on us a hellish doctrine of original sin and a pessimistic view of marriage; who cannot spell Chalcedon, even though a quarter century ago Harvey Cox argued that apart from Chalcedon technopolis is unintelligible;[6] who can anathematize Aquinas and scuttle scholasticism without ever having read a word thereof; who sneer at the mere mention of "medieval," as if the Middle Ages were darker than our own; who couldn't care less about a papal pronouncement, much less peruse it. During a half century of theology I have watched our incredibly rich tradition pass slowly but surely into museums, or at best into the hands of appreciative Protestant sisters and brothers.[7]

This lamentation is not irrelevant to our present purposes, to your agenda these four days.[8] Our "postimmigrant church" is incredibly ignorant of 20 centuries of rich social doctrine: from Christ's proclamation of "good news to the poor" (Lk 4:18) to John Paul's warning against an unbridled capitalism; from the insistence of early Fathers of the Church that God's good earth was given to *all* men and women, not to a favored few, to the U.S. bishops' pastoral plea for "economic justice for all." Without some such appreciation the global village is not likely to change for the better. In fact, each time the pastoral on the economy is even breathed from the pulpit, the educated faithful will continue to rise up in wrath or sink back in indifference.

II

But understanding is not enough; an intelligent faith must be fed by worship. For, as Vatican II insisted, "the liturgy . . . is the fountain from which all [the Church's] power flows. . . . The renewal in the Eucharist of the covenant between the Lord and men and women sets [the faithful] afire."[9]

How does the Eucharist mold the faith experience of the Catholic people? Not primarily by introducing political, social, or economic themes. Liturgy used for specific political ends is at odds with the essential nature of liturgical action. The Eucharistic signs and symbols do not of themselves change oppressive structures, do not speak directly to complex issues of poverty and justice, of statecraft and technology. The liturgy does not of itself make Christian Democrats in Italy or make for constitutional amendments in the States; it is not a substitute for sociology, economics, or political science.

How, then, does liturgy effect change? Above all, by its own inner dynamic. For the temporal order can be changed only by conversion, only if men and women turn from sin and selfishness. And for Catholics the primary source of conversion is the Mass. The Mass should be the liberating adventure, the freedom experience, of the whole Church, the sacrament that unshackles us from our inherited damnable concentration on ourselves, fashions us into sisters and brothers agonizing not only for a church of charity but for a world of justice as well.

Good liturgy frees the faithful to sort out the issues we have to decide. How? Because it makes us aware of our addictions and illusions, casts a pitiless light on myopic self-interest, detaches from a narrow selfishness, facilitates Christian discernment. In that sense liturgy evokes rather than teaches; we let God transpire, come to light; God shakes us, shivers us, turns us inside out.

III

This leads naturally into my third point: The wisdom of faith and the experience of Eucharist—word and sacrament—are not given us solely for our personal use, for our individual movement to God. "We are fed by word and sacrament *so that* we can be light, leaven, and salt."[10] Christ's challenge—be salt, be light, be leaven—is not an invitation; it is a command. It makes a bit more concrete Jesus' second great commandment, "You shall love your neighbor [at least as much] as you love yourself" (Mt 22:39). It is a command to recognize that the homeless who crowd the country's shelters are our brothers, that the women who are inhumanly abused are our sisters, that the children who grow up stunted below the poverty line are our children as well as God's.

But recognition is only a beginning. What the vast majority of the Catholic faithful have still to learn is a realization that is written into the flesh of this conference, the programmatic sentence proclaimed in Puebla by Pope John Paul as he opened the Third Assembly of the Latin American Bishops 12 years ago: "The Church has learned that its evangelizing mission has as indispensable part (*como parte indispensable*) action for justice and those efforts which the development of the human person demands. . . ."[11]

Action for justice. Not mine to spell out in a homily what any individual Christian should do, where act, how. That depends on God's call, on personal charisms, on specific situations. But this much I dare say: I find it hard to think of any Christian—short of a permanent vegetative state—who is not called to be salt or light or leaven. What is needed on a massive scale is a Catholic conversion. Not from unbelief to belief; not from languid, lackadaisical Catholicism to Sun-

day religion. Rather, from a me-and-Jesus spirituality that still plagues
our parishes to a burning yearning to transform a small acre of God's
sin-scarred earth into God's garden of peace, of justice, of love.

I take it that you who have crowded the Mayflower this week do
not need so radical a conversion. Your task, I suggest, is to be apostles
of those two Latin words, *rerum novarum*. They wed two meanings
intimately linked: something new and something revolutionary. I
mean Christ's "good news to the poor" in a rhetoric that burns and
blesses, wounds and heals, in actions that run counter to our culture.
Your task and mine is to break through the apathy, the indifference,
the hostility of uncounted Catholics where "the poor" are concerned,
the consumer mentality that rivals the contraceptive mentality for its
challenge to a church genuinely "for others."

The task is incumbent on cleric and lay. Brian Hehir neither
wastes nor minces words when he declares of the parish priest:

> Failure to meet [the expectations of a church "at the center"] is not
> only a pastoral catastrophe, it is a social loss; it is to miss the possibil-
> ity of engaging those at the center of American society with the
> content of social teaching. To have "the center" before us each
> week and fail to grasp the opportunity is dereliction of pastoral and
> social duty.[12]

But when the chips are down, priests will be whistling down the wind
unless the faithful in the pews catch fire. Here is where the example of
lay apostles is extraordinarily effective. I mean men and women like
yourselves who not only treasure our tradition but live it and spread
it—in soup kitchens and offices of peace and justice, in shelters for
the homeless and speeches to the heartless, through your own cries of
pain for today's Christ child, today's Christ crucified.

In closing, I can do no better than to ask you to pray with me the
prayer that opens the Mass for the Development of Peoples, the
prayer with which John Paul II closed his encyclical *On Social Concern*:

> Father, you have given all peoples one common origin, and your
> will is to gather them as one family in yourself. Fill the hearts of all
> with the fire of your love, and the desire to ensure justice for all
> their brothers and sisters. By sharing the good things you give us,
> may we secure justice and equality for every human person, an end
> to all division, and a human society built on love and peace.[13]

Mayflower Hotel
Washington, D.C.
February 27, 1991

33
OBLATES: BE WHAT YOU ARE CALLED
Homily for an OMI Seminar on Justice

- Micah 6:6–8
- Luke 4:16–21

Back in 1979, a challenging book was authored by an Oblate surely known to many of you. Its title: *The Eucharist and Human Liberation.*[1] Tissa Balasuriya insisted that, since Eucharistic worship is at the center of Christian life, the Eucharist must affirm and promote the biblical imperative of human liberation. But, he found, almost without exception the Eucharist has been a place where the oppressor joins the oppressed with impunity; the Eucharist has been used in co-operation with and support of colonizing powers; even today liberating movements do not find affirmation in Eucharistic worship. Whatever the defects of the book, it compels a crucial question: How is it possible to celebrate Eucharist if it is not expressing the real oppressions of our people, if it is not molding a faith that liberates from all enslavements?

A homily is not a history, not a lecture, not a debate. But the challenge above does force on each Christian at least three probing pieces of self-examination: (1) What is the Eucharist supposed to do to and for the worshiping Christian? (2) What has it done to and for me? (3) What demands does it place on the Christian for the years that lie ahead?

I

First, what is the Eucharist supposed to do to and for the worshiping Christian? In its perhaps most succinct expression, Eucharist, as the central act of Catholic worship, should play a significant role in gracing us to live the two great commandments of the law and the gospel: Love God above all else, and love the human images of God at least as much as you love yourself (Mt 22:37–40; Deut 6:5; Lev 19:18). That second commandment, Jesus claimed, "is like" the first (Mt 22:39). Loving others is like loving God.

But loving is not simply a feeling. The First Letter of John is terribly strong:

> This is the message which you have heard from the beginning, that we should love one another, and not be like Cain who . . . murdered his brother. . . . Whoever does not love remains in death. . . . By this we know love, that [Jesus] laid down his life for us; and we ought to lay down our lives for our brothers and sisters. But if anyone has the good things of the world and sees his brother [or sister] in need, yet closes his heart against him [or her], how does God's love abide in him? Little children, let us not love in word or speech [alone] but in deed and truth.
>
> (1 Jn 3:11–18)

But how does liturgy increase Christian love for others, help us to love in deed and truth? Not because it provides principles of solution for complex social issues. Not because it tells me how to get rid of a world's hunger, how to stop the traffic from Colombia in coke and crack, how to house San Antonio's homeless and clothe its naked, how to keep death from the 150 million children who will perish needlessly during this decade alone. Liturgy does not deduct trillions from our nation's deficits, create jobs for General Motors, overturn Roe *v.* Wade.

How, then, does liturgy become a social force? Through its own inner dynamism, by its incomparable power to turn the human heart inside out, free me from my damnable inherited focus on myself, fling me out unfettered to the service of sisters and brothers enslaved. A celebrant who effectively celebrates the transcendent puts God's people in touch with that which transcends all their burning concerns, their particular perplexities. Good liturgy frees them to sort out the issues they have to decide, because it makes them aware of their addictions and their illusions, casts a pitiless light on myopic self-interest, detaches from a narrow selfishness, facilitates Christian discernment.

No, the Eucharistic signs and symbols do not of themselves change social, political, and economic structures, do not speak directly to complicated issues of poverty and justice, of statecraft and technology. But they should change millions of Catholic hearts and minds, grace us to admit the oppressions for which we are responsible, inspire us to struggle with others for the coming of a kingdom characterized by peace and justice and love. Good liturgy makes for conversion, graces us to want to respond passionately to the challenge of the prophet Micah: "What does the Lord require of you? Act justly, love steadfastly, and walk humbly with your God" (Mic 6:8).

II

All of which brings me more directly to myself. I wonder if I have not, for all too many earlier years, reveled in a liturgy utterly inoffensive, a peaceful service where oppressor and oppressed can escape from the furies and passions of the week, simply confess inwardly a handful of private peccadillos, praise God for God's wonderful works in the story of salvation, forgive others their failure to recognize how wonderful I am. I know that for almost four decades my celebration of Eucharist did indeed challenge people to love God and neighbor, but rarely with the awareness of Eucharist as a conversion—not for the people and, naturally, not for me. Rarely with the agonizing awareness of the world outside theology.

It was only about 1980 that I was pierced by the programmatic text from Isaiah with which the Lucan Jesus begins his public ministry in Nazareth's synagogue: "The Spirit of the Lord is upon me, . . . has anointed me, has sent me to preach good news to the poor, to proclaim release for prisoners and sight for the blind, to set at liberty those who are oppressed" (Lk 4:18; Isa 61:1).[2] Only then was I penetrated with the realization that such is *my* vocation, *my* ministry. It did not come in a flash, lightning-like. It grew in large measure from graced insight into what I was doing at the altar. I mean the penitential rite: "I confess to Almighty God and to you, my sisters and brothers, that I have sinned . . . *in what I have failed to do*." I mean the words of consecration, not merely a memory but a self-giving: "This is *my* body given for *you*." My body . . . for you. I mean fresh awareness that "Deliver us, Lord, from *every* evil" includes not only my personal failures "but also distorted social structures which deprive people of their human and religious dignity, rights and development."[3] I mean the endless repetition of the Eucharistic dismissal: "The Mass is ended. Go in peace, to serve the Lord, especially in your sisters and brothers." The Mass is ended—but really it has only begun.

Each Mass, I realized, ends with a dismissal. Not simply a sending *away:* Now you may legitimately leave the church building. A sending *to:* a movement from church to world. The recessional is not a triumphant roundabout return to the sacristy; for me, it symbolizes with startling vividness the Christian pilgrimage: from the Calvary of the Mass to the calvaries that dot this world's landscapes. Congratulations on my homily are still appreciated on the church steps, but now most gratefully when a man or woman says in some fashion, "You really made me look inside myself, outside to others."

Still, experience of Eucharist had to be touched to experience of people, of the men and women and children for whom the body I feed on was given. Theological theses had to be enfleshed. There was the sightless black lady on a hospital bed, leg amputated, smiling dazzlingly at me for all God's gifts to her. The teen-age girl I had baptized as a child, now gang-raped. The Iraqi soldier incinerated on top of a tank. The *Time* photo of the Croatian boy sobbing at the funeral of his father, a policeman killed by Serbian guerillas—"A simple child," wrote Wordsworth, "That lightly draws its breath. . . . What should it know of death?"[4] The 54,000 poor whom Mother Teresa picked up from the streets of Calcutta, 23,000 of them dying in a single room. The elderly woman rummaging in a garbage can for the food we throw away. The bodies broken, minds maimed, spirits smothered by drugs and alcohol. The homeless beggar whom, like the priest in Jesus' parable, I "passed by on the other side" (Lk 10:31). My schizophrenic cousin.

III

All of which suggests my third question: What of the future? What demands does Eucharist-cum-experience place on the Christian for the years that lie ahead? I dare not declare what precisely our Lord Jesus expects of any individual Christian, cleric or lay. That depends on who you are, where you are. It calls for self-examination and consultation, for imagination and creativity. It demands ceaselessly the simple yet agonizing prayer of Saul hurled to earth by God: "What shall I do, Lord?" (Acts 22:10). I can only relate my own most recent experience, my ultimate dream.

Theology has been the air I breathe for more than half a century. That is why I taught theology for 32 years, edited the journal *Theological Studies* for 45, helped inaugurate the Woodstock Theological Center—created to touch theology to social, political, and economic issues. Since 1974 the Center has touched large numbers through research and conferences, seminars and workshops, articles and books. But two years ago, when I asked in the twilight of my existence, "What shall I do, Lord?", I was answered in my understanding. If the

Church's best-kept secret, her social gospel, is to reach the Catholic people as a whole, research and publication are not enough. The theology has to be *preached*—preached Sunday after Sunday, preached persuasively, preached courageously, preached with "fire in the belly." Hence my project *Preaching the Just Word*, a systematic effort to blanket the 22,000 parishes of our country with the second great commandment, to touch love of the less fortunate "in deed and truth" to all the faithful who actually share in the liturgical mystery.

If a homily is not a history, neither is it a commercial. Not my task here to "sell" you on my project. I strongly suggest, however, that the Oblates of Mary Immaculate are peculiarly positioned to preach the just word. Not only from a pulpit. Your first objective, indeed, was to preach missions to the poor of rural areas.[5] But more broadly, you direct retreat houses where men and women should be liberated from a me-and-Jesus spirituality, persuaded with Vatican II that their singular vocation is to transform their turf into an acre of justice and love.[6] You run schools where you can channel the energy and passion of the young away from the rugged individualism that stalks our nation, challenge them as crucified Christians to bring the crucified Christ to the crucified who surround them. You have parishes from coast to coast where thousands of the faithful must hear from your lips that the "option for the poor" is not a fad of off-the-wall liberationists, that the whole gospel is social.

I urge you, from the depths of my heart, to be what you are called: Oblates, *oblati*, Christians "offered up." Offered to God, offered in sacrifice to the least of your sisters and brothers. Yes, it is with special significance that you murmur each day to heaven and earth, "This is my body [and it is] given for you."

Oblate School of Theology
San Antonio, Texas
January 8, 1992

34
LET COMPASSION TAKE WING
Baccalaureate Homily for an Air Force Academy

- Deuteronomy 4:32–34, 39–40
- Romans 8:14–17
- Matthew 28:16–20

Graduates of 1991: You take wing from Colorado Springs during momentous months in American history. Momentous, yet perplexing. On the one hand, American air power has brought a dictator to heel with unexpected speed; on the other, a situation of homelessness and hopelessness, of fear and futility, of disease and starvation in the defeated country must mute our cries of victory and force tears from the steeliest of eyes.

A homily is not a debate; it is not my function to argue the merits of American intervention—Grenada or Panama or the Persian Gulf. A homily is an effort to touch your actual life to the demands of Christ. It is not to argue, to prove, to refute; it is to evoke a Christian response by a Christian challenge. Since your response rests on my challenge, let me tell you how I propose to challenge you.

I begin with an assumption. I take for granted that you are people of peace; I mean men and women who yearn for peace rather than war. Nothing less can justify war, military might, an arsenal, an air force, "smart" bombs. But what is it that makes men and women of peace? How can you judge whether you are peacemakers, whether you fall under the beatitude proclaimed by Jesus, "Blessed are the peacemakers, for they shall be called sons and daughters of God" (Mt 5:9)? Suppose we explore the problem in three stages, with three questions. (1) What basic quality underlies a peacemaker? (2) How do you latch onto such a quality? (3) What might all this say specifically to airmen and airwomen as you fly from peaceful classroom to unfriendly skies[1]?

208

I

First, what basic quality underlies a peacemaker? A profound respect for life. So deep a respect that no man's death, no woman's death, is an unqualified blessing, a good thing in every way. Even the death of a Hitler or a Stalin. God, Jesus declared, is a "God not of the dead but of the living" (Mk 12:27).[2] Remember God's own declaration in the book of Ezekiel, "As I live, says the Lord God, I have no pleasure in the death of the wicked, but that the wicked turn from his way and live" (Ezek 33:11). If our God does not rejoice in the death of the sinner, neither should we. The death of Saddam Hussein may well be a blessing for the Western world; to Hussein it might be martyrdom or devastation; in the eyes of God who permits it, it is the antithesis of all God has in mind when God fashions a man or woman in His own likeness, breathes life human and divine into an unrepeatable organism, sent His own divine Son to die for so strange a creature.

That is why the model of the Air Force is not a Rambo I or II or III; *he* enjoys killing. Not so the Christian. It's a difficult way of life, and I would be surprised if you did not agonize over it: to take life justifiably, yet regretfully; to do what you have to do and still not take pleasure in it; to recognize that in the Christian perspective there are innocents among the enemy; to condone "collateral killing" and still weep over it.

Is it possible without affecting your effectiveness? I do not know; my specialized field of combat is theology. But this I do know. Massive killing has a way of blunting our sensitivities; a body count becomes sheer statistics; body bags, especially of the enemy, do not command the same respect as a dear one in a funeral parlor. A hundred thousand cycloned in Bangladesh evoke pity, but not the horror when we saw on TV a single Vietnamese girl racing down a street aflame with napalm, when a starving Kurdish child stares out at us from eyes that no longer see.

In God's eyes each life is precious—like a child to its mother, however deformed by Down's syndrome, however devastated by AIDS, however destroyed by crack or coke. Jesus himself wept—not only over his dear friend Lazarus, but over the city of his crucifixion. If peace is to blossom from war, it can only happen because, for all your unparalleled ability to destroy, for all your ethical capability to justify violence for freedom's sake, your profound respect for life, for all life, for enemy life molds you into men and women of compassion. Com-passion: You "suffer with" all who suffer.

II

This compels my second question: How do you latch onto such a quality, so profound a respect for all life that you become men and women of compassion? How can you possibly combine violence with compassion, war with peace, death with life, killing with sensitivity? Not by your own naked efforts. Only if the weakness that plagues every human intellect and will is fortified somehow by a more potent presence. Against all the odds, today's feast helps tremendously. For today's feast celebrates a Trinity.[3] I mean a God who is at once the Mystery of mysteries and a God for us. True, this feast proclaims perhaps the most difficult mystery Catholics are privileged to believe: a God who is genuinely three persons, and yet there is but one God. The Father is not the Son, and neither Father nor Son is the Holy Spirit. Each is a distinct person; each is God; and still there is only one God.

But the thrilling thing about the Trinity is that God is a God for us. If you doubt it, recall the exciting sentence from the Gospel of John, "God so loved the world that He gave His only Son, that whoever believes in him should not perish but have eternal life" (Jn 3:16). What is this eternal life? Not simply life after the grave. Eternal life, life with and in God, has its beginning now. It is summed up in the thrilling promise of Jesus the night before he died: "If [you] love me, . . . my Father will love [you], and we will come to [you] and make our home with [you]" (Jn 14:23). More than that. Because the apostles would be desolate after he left them, Jesus promised them and us: "I will pray the Father, and [the Father] will give you . . . the Spirit of truth, whom the world cannot receive, because it neither sees Him nor knows Him; you know Him, for He dwells with you and will be in you" (Jn 14:16–17). This is the Spirit St. Paul proclaimed to you in today's second reading. You who are led by the Holy Spirit are children of God. You are no longer in a state of slavery, enslaved to fear, to the flesh, to deeds of death. Within you is God's very self. Within you is the Holy Spirit, the Spirit who makes possible what is impossible to sheer human nature.

There, precisely there, is your eternal, endless life: the living God—Father, Son, and Holy Spirit—living within you. This is not pretty poetry. This is Christianity; here is the "new thing" that Christ brought, that God's own Son died a bloody death to bequeath to you. Right now each of you should take delight in St. Paul's question: "Do you not know that you are God's temple and that God's Spirit dwells in you?" (1 Cor 3:16). And his striking follow-up: "God's temple is holy, and that temple you are" (v. 17).

III

This leads into my third question: What might all this say to you as you fly from classroom to battleground? What pertinence does God's presence in you have for the problem I raised earlier: How reconcile the Pentagon and compassion, death-dealing missiles and respect for life? The point is, the Trinity resident in you is not just a passive presence within you—like a statue in a church. Indeed God's presence transforms you into a temple; but God is there to transform not only who you are but what you think and do. It is because God is extraordinarily active within you that you can believe what passes belief: one God in three persons, a crucified Son of God, bread that is not bread but the body of Christ. It is because God is active in you that you can hope against hope: for life after death, for the resurrection of your flesh. It is because God is active within you that you can love God above all things, love your neighbor as you love yourself, love others as Jesus loves them, love even unto crucifixion.

Here, my friends, is the Christian clue to your dilemma. It is because God is active within you that you can dare to live as Jesus lived. It is because the Holy Spirit—the Spirit of light, of life, and of love—is active within you that you can think like a Christian, live like a Christian, love like a Christian.

In the concrete, because Jesus lives within you, you can actually live what he commanded: "You have heard that it was said, 'You shall love your neighbor and hate your enemy.' But I say to you, Love your enemies and pray for those who persecute you, so that you may be sons [and daughters] of your Father who is in heaven. . . . For if you love [only] those who love you, what reward have you?" (Mt 5:43–46). Because the God of compassion is active within you, the God who *is* Compassion, the God who, says the Psalmist, "does not deal with us according to our sins, nor requite us according to our iniquities" (Ps 103:10), you can become men and women of compassion even in the paradoxical life that stretches before you.

The problem is, it does not happen automatically: God in you, therefore compassion. Like all virtues, all good habits, you have to work at it. For compassion is not a weakness; it is a feeling, a "suffering with," that is born in the depths of your being. And you have to want it, want it fiercely, with all the fire in your belly. It will not be easy. For our Western culture harbors a chilling conviction: A compassionate society is a sick society. The compassionate person is abnormal. See the world through the eyes of the unfortunate, those who are not free, and you threaten "the highest value of civilization: individual freedom."[4]

No, good friends. For the years that lie ahead—years hidden from your eyes—the natural gifts your calling demands must be complemented by compassion, the compassion God in you stands ready to give you. For your country's sake, lest we lapse into barbarism. For your Church's sake, lest we divide at dreadful extremes between the pacifists and the killers. For your own Christian personality, to conform yourself ever more closely to the Christ who could cry for those who crucified him, "Father, forgive them, for they do not know what they are doing" (Lk 23:34).

Why, on this graduation day, so much emphasis on a charism such as compassion? Simply because compassion is another word for love —but love among the ruins, love in the grime and grit of human dying. And, as St. Paul put it pungently, you can talk like an angel, fathom mysteries, have enough faith to move mountains, give away all you have, even your life—but all this, without love, without compassion, is worthless (see 1 Cor 13:1–3).

So then, good friends in Christ, go forth from Colorado Springs with high confidence. You have good reason so to fly off. For you go forth with three Cs: (1) a professional *competence* communicated by a remarkable academy; (2) a profound *courage* that is part of your God-given nature; and (3) a growing *compassion* that links you intimately to Christ, that stems from the dynamic presence within you of a Trinity whose blessing it is my privilege to wing to each and all of you. May Father, Son, and Holy Spirit keep you always in the shelter of *Their* wings.

Catholic Chapel
United States Air Force Academy
Colorado Springs, Colorado
May 26, 1991

35
TO KNOW, TO SERVE, TO RISK
Baccalaureate Homily for a University

- Jeremiah 9:23–24
- Galatians 5:1, 13–14
- Matthew 25:14–30

There is no way a baccalaureate homily can sum up the four years that have fled or unfold the far future that beckons. Nevertheless, under peril of putting your hops on hold for a quarter hour, I shall take the three liturgical readings I have chosen and tie them to intelligent Christian living. My thesis? USF will have opened your eyes to "the good life" if you leave Ignatian Heights (1) knowing what knowledge is, (2) free to love and serve, (3) ready to risk.

I

First, the challenge from Jeremiah. To an ancient society that prized three possessions above all else—wisdom, power, wealth—the prophet thundered: "Thus says the Lord: 'Let not the wise glory in their wisdom, let not the mighty glory in their might, let not the rich glory in their riches; but let those who glory glory in this, that they understand and know me, that I am the Lord who practice steadfast love, justice, and righteousness in the earth; for in these things I delight, says the Lord' " (Jer 9:23–24).

"Let those who glory glory in this, that they understand and know me." This is not a jesuitical ploy to return theology to the top of the academic mountain—"queen of the sciences" rather than their servant. It is not a declaration that all you have learned at USF is dross and dung. These four years, for all the sleep they have murdered, have been a remarkable adventure of the mind. For with this mind of yours you looked into a microscope and were filled with the wonder of life the naked eye cannot see. With this mind you sped over oceans more swiftly than the jet and touched men and women from Siberia to Zaire, from Ethiopia to East Germany. With this mind you fled back into the past and rediscovered a universe multibillion years old, redis-covered an America five centuries young. With this mind you plucked meaning from the strings of a harp and the whisper of the wind, from a sonnet and a sonata, from Michelangelo's *Pietà* and the Mona Lisa, from Beethoven's *Pastoral Symphony* and Tchaikovsky's *Swan Lake* bal-let and Verdi's *Aïda*—yes, from Madonna and The Grateful Dead. With this mind you looked into the minds of philosophers from an-cient Greece to modern Britain, from Plato's world of ideas to White-head's experience and process, to share their tortured search for what is real, for what is true. With this mind you grappled to grasp the economics that makes the world go round, from Adam Smith through Karl Marx to Alan Greenspan. With this mind you looked into the mind of God revealed in creation, on a cross, and in the lines of God's own book.

The search does not cease with a sheepskin; ideally, it should never end. More importantly, your struggle to grasp God's creation should bring you gradually to grasp the God of creation. But not simply as an idea, a concept, a definition. Not a theology of God, but the much more mysterious and mighty God of theology. For, as meta-physician Jacques Maritain saw so clearly, the culmination of human knowing is not conceptual; it is experiential: "Man/woman *feels* God."

You see, knowing God is not the same as knowing *about* God. In half a century I have learned a great deal about God—from philos-ophy and poetry, from a divine Word and human reflection. With Aquinas, I have learned that God is Immovable Mover, Uncaused Cause, Necessary Being, Absolute Perfection, Supreme End. With St. Paul, I have risen from "the things that have been made" to God's "invisible nature" (Rom 1:20). With the evangelist John, I believe "God so loved the world" as to give an only Son (Jn 3:16), gave him to a crucifying death that I might have life. I thrill when I read in Jesuit poet Gerard Manley Hopkins that I can find God in man and woman, that "Christ plays in ten thousand places,/ Lovely in limbs, and lovely in eyes not his/ [plays] to the Father through the features of men's faces."

But good as this is, it is not good enough. The Christian quest is not primarily for ideas about God; the Christian quest is for God, for oneness with a personal Trinity, for a relationship of love more inti-mate than ever was man's love for woman. And so, for the years that lie ahead, I urge on you a burning, humbling question: For all you know *about* God, have you truly encountered the living and true God? Have you "felt" God? If you never do, I do not predict that you will be unhappy or unsuccessful. I do claim that you will miss much of the thrill in human living, run a greater peril of finding existence unexciting, may never come to understand how a God who does not need you was anxious to die for you.

II

So much for knowledge. But St. Paul takes our knowledge a giant step forward. "You were called to freedom, my brothers and sisters; only do not use your freedom as an opportunity for the flesh, but through love be servants of one another" (Gal 5:13).

I suspect that the word "servant" does not turn you on. We associate servant with low income and menial labor, with Topsy in *Uncle Tom's Cabin* or the old-time maid in apron and minicap, at best with the aristocratic British butler. The Christian servant is a far nobler calling: To serve is to image Christ. It goes back to what Jesus said to his apostles: "[I] came not to be served but to serve"—in fact, "to give [my] life as a ransom" (Mt 20:28).

Why else, do you think, did the Son of God choose to be born of a teen-age Jewish girl in a stable? Why did God-in-flesh walk the roads of Palestine for three rough years healing the sick and raising the dead? Why did he make friends with prostitutes and the poor, with sinners and outcasts? Why did he let his enemies beat his back with whips, crown his head with thorns, nail him between two robbers, curse him till he gasped his life away? Because he loved every woman and man he had shaped in his image; because he wanted to experience what they were going through; because he cared—cared enough to live for others and to die for them. Because without his caring the whole world would have gone to hell.

Note especially that Jesus was a *suffering* servant—along the lines of the suffering servant portrayed by Isaiah: "He was despised and rejected by men, a man of sorrows, and acquainted with grief; and as one from whom men hide their faces he was despised, and we esteemed him not" (Isa 53:3).

As you exit USF, I trust you will exit uncommonly free. Not free simply from Jesuit bondage, from the terrorism of blue books and the great grade rush. Free rather, through Christ, from one suffocating enslavement St. Paul had in mind: the slavery that is self, a smothering imprisonment where human living revolves around me—my successes

and my failures, my wealth and my poverty, my power and my impo-
tence, my heartache and my hiatus hernia. Free *from* this, but *for* what?
Paul told you: for loving service—living for your brothers and sisters.
Like Jesus, a man or woman for others.

No need to spell out the crises that cry out to you. First-rate
sociologists insist that we are witnessing a resurgence of late-19th-
century rugged individualism, where my ultimate responsibility is to
myself, where the ideal is to get to the well first before it dries up,
where the race is to the swift, the shrewd, and the savage, and the devil
take the hindmost. It shows up on Wall Street, in Savings & Loan, in
the halls of government, in the consumerism and waste that shame our
"sweet land of liberty." It shows up as one out of every five children in
our fair land grows up beneath the poverty level, mind stunted and
body bloated; in the feminization of poverty; in second-class citizenship for African Americans; in the violence that explodes on TV and
on our streets. It shows itself in the tears wherewith uncounted refugees water the world's roads, in half the human family hungry for
bread or justice, for peace or freedom, for understanding and compassion, for a God who does not seem to be there.

One example says it all. About two years ago *Time* magazine ran
an ethics article on the NIMBY syndrome.[1] NIMBY is an acronym for
Not in My Back Yard. It's a form of antisocial activism. Today you
have more and more people who cannot care for themselves: "more
homeless, more AIDS victims, more drug addicts, more prisoners,
more garbage, more toxic waste." Everyone admits, we have to take
care of these. "But," as New York City's then-Mayor Edward Koch
complained, "when you need a facility, they say, 'Not in my backyard.'" Or, as some suggested about a proposed drug-treatment
center, "Put it in Nancy Reagan's back yard!"[2]

Not so for you. If USF's "faith that does justice" flows through
your bloodstream, a whole little world will be your back yard. I mean
the world that would preoccupy Jesus were he to walk today's dust. On
the one hand, the have-nots: the homeless and the hopeless, the drug-
addicted and the AIDS-infected, mothers on relief and pregnant
teen-agers too young to mother, youngsters with no road to travel
save hate and crime. On the other hand, the haves, those who crassly
exploit money or power or fame: the Boeskys and the Milkens with
their multibillion-dollar white-collar wickedness; the Marcoses and
the Noriegas who keep whole nations enslaved; the rock and rap stars
who thrill young America with a fresh foul-mouthed culture.

I do not fly from East to West with a hatful of answers, a program for social justice. I come to you with the plea of Paul: "through love be servants."

III

The "faith that does justice" projects me into my final point. So far, knowledge and freedom. But to know what knowledge is, to feel free to love and serve—this is not enough. You are still poised on the rim of action. You can take the route of servant number 3 in today's Gospel. Unlike two fellow servants, shrewd operators who bulled the market and doubled their master's money, the case of the cautious servant shows us a man afraid—afraid because his master was "a hard man" (Mt 25:24) who did not look kindly on failure. So instead of investing the money, he buried it. That way, no loss. No gain, but no loss. Or so he thought—till his master returned: "You knew what I am like, how I react when money is involved. As a servant, you're worthless. Into 'the darkness outside' you go!" (cf. vv. 26–30).

You can play life safe or you can risk. To risk, the dictionaries tell us, is to expose yourself to loss or injury, to disadvantage or destruction. The fact is, the whole human bag is a risk. In the measure that you are actually alive, you are risking; for you take all sorts of chances without knowing how they will come out. To marry is to risk: You surrender your safe private self to a small community of selves, lose your individual life in the hope of finding it more fully with another; and today the odds are at best 50–50. To be a top-flight doctor or lawyer, to enter politics or business, is to risk: You may end up terribly narrow or one-sided, closed to everything save a damaged heart or a court case, public applause or the Dow Jones. To be a priest is to risk: Too many of us are crotchety, peevish, self-centered bachelors incapable of loving or being loved. Simply to be free is to risk: You can say no to God, betray your dearest friend with a kiss. In a word, to live humanly is to launch out into a large unknown.[3]

At this fascinating, frightening, bewildering, engaging hour in human history, how ready are you to risk all to share in the crucifying vision of Christ? You already risk much in your commitment to Christ. You see a criminal on a cross, and you cry "My Lord and my God!" You hear words from a book, and they turn for you into the word of God. You taste bread, and you eat the body of Christ.

But if you risk in committing yourself to a Christ you cannot see, you risk more in committing yourself to a church you can see. For this is a pilgrim church, a community on the way, not yet there; a body of sinful, sinning men and women, at times in startling contradiction to the Lord who heads it, to the Spirit who gives it life. And still it is Christ's community; here is where he expects you to experience him. And not only to endure it but to love it, to take it for better or worse, for richer or poorer, in sickness and in health, until death. Otherwise you are no different from the cautious servant. You play it safe, hedge your bets, stay out of trouble, live a comfortable Christianity, don't get involved. When things get rough, you can lay the blame on someone else: a harsh pastor, a Roman document on birth control, paranoid nuns in parochial schools, uninspired liturgies, marriage laws, Catholics who go piously to church but don't live it—the thousand and one reasons that keep us from looking inside ourselves.

You are men and women with talents—some of you with extraordinary gifts, entrusted to you by a Master at once demanding and loving. How much are you ready to risk—not for riches or power or fame, but to bind a bleeding church, to heal a wounded world? If not you, then who?

St. Ignatius Church
Ignatian Heights
San Francisco, Calif.
May 17, 1990

36
A KIND OF LOVING, FOR ME
Baccalaureate Homily for a Public High School

- Isaiah 40:29–31
- Psalm 138

The next 15 minutes could be painful for you. I don't know you, except that you seem to "soap" your way out of "The Young and the Restless";[1] and you don't know me, except that I obviously stem from a wrinkled stage of humanity. Your pop and rock are not my mix of music; and my *Swan Lake* ballet is not likely to turn you on. We speak a different language, dream different dreams, march to different drumbeats. And still I shall speak what just might speak to your hearts; for this afternoon I echo Rod McKuen when he sings:

> I make words for people I've not met,
> those who will not turn to follow after me.
> It is for me a kind of loving.
> A kind of loving, for me.[2]

At this crucial stage in your growing, as you move from adolescence to young manhood, young womanhood, what is the "kind of loving" I want to put into words? My springboard is the musical *Godspell*, a prayer that goes back to the 13th century, a prayer with three powerful points: "Dear Lord, these three I pray: to see more clearly, to love more dearly, to follow more nearly." See . . . love . . . follow.

I

First, see more clearly. Today, as in every age, there is a great deal of blindness around. We oldsters—all too many of us—close our eyes to what we do not want to see, what might shake us, shiver us, upset

219

our comfortable life-style, cause us to "toss our cookies." We read that one out of every five children in this "land of the free" is growing up below the poverty line; we read . . . and turn to the comics. We read that in Soviet Central Asia "thousands of infants die within 12 months of birth," that "countless others suffer more slowly, weakened by the heat and infected water, the pesticides from the cotton fields, a diet built on bread and tea and soup";[3] we read . . . and turn to the Style section. We read that teen-agers are turned on to drugs by the millions, and we shut our eyes, we suggest that our children "say no," and we get "bombed" on our more civilized cocktails. We read that each year in the U.S. 1.6 million unborn humans are destroyed in the womb, and we close our eyes to everything save my right to choose. We see on prime time a feast of violence and sex, Rambo and porno, and we shrug our shoulders; you can't *prove* it affects our children. We see single parents forced on welfare because it pays more than our shameful minimum wage, and we argue: If they weren't lazy, they could find a good job. We see how insider trading and junk bonds can butcher our national and personal budgets, and all too many shake their heads in admiration: "Wish I had thought of that!" And so on into the night.

Graduates of 1990: Don't grow up with blinders! Grow up with eyes wide open, with the peripheral vision you reserve for sports and the opposite sex. Get rid of those cataracts that lay a haze over your understanding. Don't see just what you want to see, what will justify your idea of a "good life," your rosy existence. Open your eyes beyond your back yard, your front lawn, your class, your college, your city, your country—beyond the Redskins and the Caps, beyond Eddie Murphy and The Grateful Dead. Open your eyes wide to *all* your sisters and brothers, black and white, yellow and brown—especially the pimped and the prostituted, the coked and the angel-dusted, those who hunger for bread or justice, for a tomorrow that might be less inhuman than today.

II

But seeing more clearly is not enough. Once you see more clearly, then love more dearly. Not easy. For one thing, "love" is a word much abused. We use it for the sacred covenant between husband and wife, and for the unbuttoned promiscuity of "Miami Vice" and the Movie Channel. We use it for the touching first meeting of adolescents' eyes, and for the one-night stands on "Love Boat." We use it for St. Francis of Assisi in love with birds and beasts, with sun and moon, and for every form of sexual abuse. We use it the way Amy Grant sings "Love of Another Kind," and we use it in the new filth that rages through rap and rock.

Genuine love is tough to squeeze into a definition. But if you want to test genuine love against its counterfeits, ask yourself time and again: Where is my focus? On myself or on the other? On my satisfaction or the other's advantage? Am I only a consumer, a taker, a sponger, a leech? Or is my mindset "How can I help? How much can I give?"

Real love is not puppy love; real love is a tough love. It's the tough love that enabled the mother of Detroit Pistons' Isiah Thomas to bring up nine children in an asphalt jungle. It's the tough love that lit up the Potomac in 1981, when Air Florida crashed against the 14th Street bridge, bodies were flung into the river, a helicopter kept dropping its rescue doughnut, and one drowning passenger kept lifting onto the doughnut one after another people he never knew, till the doughnut came down one last time, but he had disappeared beneath the icy waters. It's the tough love that impelled a young nurse-friend of mine to tend an AIDS-afflicted stranger when many a doctor would not go near him. It's the tough love of the Franciscan brothers in Springfield, Illinois, who give their lives for grown men with IQs from zero to thirty-five. It's the tough love of black Sister Thea Bowman, who never let brain cancer slow her wheelchair as she covered the country to bring hope and love to others, as she kept repeating, "I'm too busy to die." But she did—two short months ago.

Such is the mindset your less fortunate sisters and brothers expect of you. You are gifted beyond the ordinary. The vast majority among you will grace college campuses, some of the country's most prestigious—some even more glamorous than Georgetown! And there you can move either of two ways. You can opt for success 1990 style. I mean, you can roar into the great grade rush with the three goals declared by Harvard freshmen four years ago: (1) money, (2) power, (3) fame. You can decide that in life's game the race is to the swift and the savage, that the meek will never "inherit the earth" (Mt 5:5), that the gentle only ask to be stepped on, that love is for losers. Or you can echo St. Paul: "If I speak in the tongues of men and of angels, but have not love, I am a noisy gong or a clanging cymbal. And if I have prophetic powers, and understand all mysteries and all knowledge, and if I have all faith, so as to remove mountains, but have not love, I am nothing. If I give away all I have, and if I deliver my body to be burned, but have not love, I gain nothing" (1 Cor 13:1–3).

III

See more clearly, love more dearly. One need remains: Follow more nearly. Put more concretely, you need role models. I'm sure you have them, whatever you might call them. TV ads live off them, off your hero worship. For flying through the air with the greatest of ease, Michael Jordan. For stealing 90 feet of turf, Rickey Henderson. For a real man in your life, Kevin Costner. For a vibrant woman, Madonna. For a group to turn you on, Red Hot Chili Peppers.

I am not about to laugh at such role models; I refuse to knock them. They can be important for certain stages of your life, for aspects of who you are. I simply submit that at this turn in your life the people you need to follow after should be such as touch your deepest desires, your dearest dreams, people who inspire you to give yourself totally to a cause, to life at its richest, to others.

I mean Martin Luther King Jr. Whatever your color, here is a man you can follow with your whole mind and heart. Not reproduce every individual thing he did, every single march. More importantly, his dream that one day "all of God's children, black and white, Jews and Gentiles, Protestants and Catholics, will be able to join hands and sing, 'Free at last! Free at last! Thank God Almighty, we are free at last!' " And to work for that freedom not like another rampaging Rambo but without violence, with only the kind of love that is stronger than death. The kind of love that destroyed Dr. King's flesh and from his death raised up free men and women. The kind of love that made a white society weep for its racial sins.

I mean Mother Teresa. Whatever your religion, here is a woman you can follow with all your soul and strength. Not follow her to India; not pick up from Calcutta's streets 54,000 homeless and watch 23,000 of them die in your room; not ask for the unborn and newborn nobody wants; not even physically cradle the AIDS-infected. Rather, the conviction that each person whose path you cross—however outrageously he or she looks or talks or smells—is a child of God, shaped in God's image; that the standard of genuinely human living is not the millions you amass, the power you control, the fame that flings adoring teen-agers at your feet, but the way you treat the least of your sisters and brothers, how well you can walk in the shoes of the less fortunate.

For those of you who claim to be Christian, I mean, above all else, a man who was crucified between two thieves two thousand years ago. I mean the Jesus who wrote and sang, lived and died the best-selling, longest-lasting pop of them all: "Greater love than this no one has, to lay down life itself for friends" (Jn 15:13).

For those of you who follow the faith of Abraham, you who lost six million brothers and sisters in the Nazi Holocaust we Gentiles prefer to forget, you whose forebears have been tempted to conclude that "God died in Auschwitz," I give you the remarkable rabbi Abraham Joshua Heschel:

> To meet a human being is a major challenge to mind and heart. I must recall what I normally forget. A person is not just a specimen of the species called *homo sapiens*. He is all of humanity in one, and whenever one man is hurt we are all injured. . . . To meet a human being is an opportunity to sense the image of God, *the presence* of God. According to a rabbinical interpretation, the Lord said to Moses: "Wherever you see the trace of man there I stand before you. . . . "[4]

For those of you whose eyes are fixed on Islam, by all means follow "the Prophet." But follow him "more nearly." In harmony with your sacred Koran, submit yourself completely to the one only God; worship Him alone and live according to His law; don't be distracted by the idols of this world: riches, social position, pride, greed.

Am I giving the back of my hand to excellence? Not at all. I simply want you to grasp what human excellence really is. Am I denouncing money, power, fame? Quite the contrary. I simply want you to ask yourself a three-letter word: Why? Why money, why power, why fame? Money to line your own pockets, build a million-dollar condo, buy sex and crack, or to lift your sisters and brothers from the grime and grit of the slums? Power to lord it over others, muscle your way into the corridors of the mighty, or to give power to the powerless, hope to the hopeless? Fame to swell your ego, or fame to let the less privileged get to know you, to learn from you, to profit from your love?

A final word. St. Matthew's Gospel has a fascinating parable (Mt 25:14–30). A rich CEO goes off on a business trip. Before leaving for Dulles, he gives each of three employees a fair amount of money to invest. On his return he asks an accounting. The first two have done fabulously at the stock exchange: Their investment has doubled. "Well done, gentlemen!" Up comes employee number 3. "Sir, all of us know you're a hard man to please. I was afraid; so I hid your money; here it is, exactly what you gave me." The CEO blows a final fuse: "You worthless piece of garbage! Out you go into the darkness!"

What is the Gospel telling you? That to live the way God wants you to live, you have to risk. I mean, expose yourself to loss or injury, to disadvantage or destruction, perhaps even to death. You have to take chances. The critical question you must decide is: What's worth living for, risking for, dying for? How much are you willing to risk for your dream? Will you play it safe, always punt on fourth down and one? Or will you "go for broke," invest everything you have for a dream that grabs you, a dream shaped of love, a dream that just might make your little world more human?

A recent award winner at the Cannes Film Festival has a loser-friendly lover, Lula, claiming that the "whole world's wild at heart and weird on top."[5] That may well be. But from all I hear about you, I have high hopes that you may tame some of the wildness at the world's heart, humanize some of the weirdness at the top. In any event, now you know why

> I make words for people I've not met,
> those who will not turn to follow after me.
> For me it's a kind of loving.
> A kind of loving, for me.

South Lakes High School
Reston, Virginia
June 10, 1990

NOTES

Prologue

1. Walter Brueggemann, "The Preacher, the Text, and the People," *Theology Today* 47, no. 3 (October 1990) 237–47, at 237.
2. Pius XII, *Allocutio ad cultores historiae et artis*, May 9, 1956 (*AAS* 48 [1956] 212).
3. Decree on the Apostolate of the Laity, no. 5.
4. 1971 Synod of Bishops, *De iustitia in mundo* (Vatican Press, 1971) Introduction, p. 5. One may argue whether "constitutive" in the document means "integral" or "essential." What is beyond argument is that the Synod saw the search for justice as inseparable from the preaching of the gospel.
5. 1974 Synod of Bishops, "Human Rights and Reconciliation," *Origins* 4 (1974) 318.
6. International Theological Commission, "Human Development & Christian Salvation" IV (tr. Walter J. Burghardt, S.J., *Origins* 7, no. 20 [Nov. 3, 1977] 310–11).
7. Lawrence S. Cunningham, *The Catholic Heritage* (New York: Crossroad, 1986) 1.
8. J. Bryan Hehir, "The Church in the World: Where Social and Pastoral Ministry Meet," *Church* 6, no. 4 (winter 1990) 21.
9. Yves Congar, O.P., "Sacramental Worship and Preaching," in *The Renewal of Preaching* (Concilium 33; New York: Paulist, 1968) 60.
10. Karl Rahner, *The Shape of the World To Come* (London: SPCK, 1974) 77.
11. Text in *Origins* 21, no. 25 (Nov. 28, 1991) 393–404.
12. George Higgins, "The Problems in Preaching: Politics/What Place in Church?" *Origins* 2, no. 13 (Sept 21, 1972) 213.
13. Constitution on the Church in the Modern World, no. 43.

14. This Prologue updates material I have presented in my volume *Preaching: The Art and the Craft* (New York/Mahwah: Paulist, 1987) chap. 9: "Let Justice Roll Down Like Waters: Preaching the Just Word" (pp. 119–38), and in my article "Preaching the Just Word: Problem, Preacher, Project," *Modern Liturgy* 18, no. 2 (March 1991) 8–10.

Homily 1

1. An appearance to Jesus' mother is not mentioned in the Gospels, but, as St. Ignatius Loyola remarked, no one with "understanding" would doubt such an appearance.
2. Gerard Manley Hopkins, "S. Thomae Aquinatis Rhythmus ad SS. Sacramentum," in *The Poems of Gerard Manley Hopkins*, ed. W. H. Gardner and N. H. MacKenzie (4th ed.; London: Oxford University, 1970) 211.
3. Constitution on the Sacred Liturgy, no. 7.
4. Philip Elmer-DeWitt, "Is the Country in a Depression?" *Time* 136, no. 24 (Dec. 3, 1990) 112.
5. Ibid. [113].

Homily 2

1. For all its homiletic form, this was actually a conference given at an evening of recollection opening the Advent season for faculty and staff of Georgetown University.
2. William Shakespeare, *Hamlet, Prince of Denmark*, Act 3, Scene 1.
3. Marcos McGrath, CSC, "Social Teaching since the Council: A Response from Latin America," in Alberic Stacpoole, ed., *Vatican II Revisited by Those Who Were There* (Minneapolis: Winston, 1986) 324–36, at 325.
4. Pastoral Constitution on the Church in the Modern World, no. 43.
5. In a message (September 1990) to the World Summit for Children, quoted in an editorial by Anthony J. Schulte, O.F.M., "Make Room in the Inn for the World's Children," *St. Anthony Messenger* 98, no. 7 (December 1990) 26.
6. See Robert F. Drinan, "Too Greedy for the Needy, America No Place for Children," *National Catholic Reporter* 27, no. 38 (Aug. 30, 1991) 19. His figures come from Sylvia Ann Hewlett, *When the Bough Breaks: The Cost of Neglecting Our Children* (Basic Books, 1991); her sources for the figures in my text come from the Children's Defense Fund.
7. John Paul II, *On Social Concern* (encyclical letter *Sollicitudo rei socialis*, Dec. 30, 1987) no. 28.
8. Schalom Ben-Chorin, as quoted by Hans Küng, *The Church* (New York: Sheed and Ward, 1968) 149.

Homily 3

1. The occasion was the annual Mass on the feast of the Epiphany sponsored by the John Carroll Society, Georgetown University alumni/ae, and the Serra Club.
2. See my expository article "Isaiah 60:1–7: From Gloom to Glory," *Interpretation* 44, no. 4 (October 1990) 396–400, at 396–97.
3. In a message (September 1990) to the World Summit for Children, quoted in an editorial by Anthony J. Schulte, O.F.M., "Make Room in the Inn for the World's Children," *St. Anthony Messenger* 98, no. 7 (December 1990) 26.
4. Quoted ibid.
5. See *America*, March 24, 1990, 283.
6. The Church in the Modern World, no. 31.
7. Schulte, "Make Room" (n. 3 above) 26.

Homily 5

1. Note that "you" is plural here. The rebuke is addressed to all whose faith is founded on signs and wonders alone.
2. A noontime Mass for college students on a class day.
3. Here I am primarily indebted to Raymond E. Brown, S.S., *The Gospel according to John (i–xii)* (Garden City, N.Y.: Doubleday, 1966) 525–32, esp. 530–31.
4. Brown's translation, ibid. 126; see the problem of John's meaning here, ibid. 127.
5. Brown's translation, ibid. 422.
6. Gregory Dix, *The Shape of the Liturgy* (Westminster, Eng.: Dacre, 1945) 744.
7. Gerard Manley Hopkins, "S. Thomae Aquinatis Rhythmus ad SS. Sacramentum," in *The Poems of Gerard Manley Hopkins*, ed. W. H. Gardner and N. H. MacKenzie (4th ed.; London: Oxford University, 1970) 211.

Homily 6

1. For the difficult question of the relationship between "the Twelve" and "the apostles" in the NT, see Joseph A. Fitzmyer, S.J., *The Gospel according to Luke (I–IX)* (Garden City, N.Y.: Doubleday, 1981) 253–57, 614–18.
2. I say "disciples" because "The circle of witnesses-to-be [Acts 1:6: "those who had come together"] appears to broaden beyond the chosen Eleven (v 2) to the larger gallery (Luke 24:33) from which the twelfth apostle will be chosen (vv 21–22)" (Richard J. Dillon, "Acts of the Apos-

tles," *The New Jerome Biblical Commentary*, ed. Raymond E. Brown, S.S., Joseph A. Fitzmyer, S.J., and Roland E. Murphy, O.Carm. [Englewood Cliffs, N.J.: Prentice Hall, 1990] 44:16, p. 728).

3. See Raymond E. Brown, S.S., *The Gospel according to John (xiii–xxi)* (Garden City, N.Y.: Doubleday, 1970) 763–64. Note his quotation from Barrett: ". . . the only hope for the *kosmos* is that it should cease to be the *kosmos.*"

4. See ibid. 615; cf. 1 Cor 9:1 and Gal 1:15–16.

5. See Raymond E. Brown, S.S., "Roles of Women in the Fourth Gospel," *Theological Studies* 36 (1975) 688–99,.esp. 692–93.

6. St. Augustine, *Confessions* 9, 9.

7. Quoted in William D. Miller, *Dorothy Day: A Biography* (San Francisco: Harper & Row, 1982) 341; emphasis mine.

8. Ibid. 343–44.

9. Léon-Joseph Suenens, *Coresponsibility in the Church* (New York: Herder and Herder, 1968) 31.

10. Decree on the Apostolate of the Laity, nos. 5 and 7.

11. Pastoral Constitution on the Church in the Modern World, no. 43.

12. Dreadfully harassed by the government of Saddam Hussein.

13. Devastated by a typhoon, with perhaps 130,000 dead at the present writing.

14. See Karl Rahner, S.J., *Ignatius of Loyola*, with an Historical Introduction by Paul Imhof, S.J. (London/New York: Collins, 1979) 12–13.

Homily 7

1. Frederick Buechner, *The Hungering Dark* (New York: Seabury, 1969) 45.

2. See also Mk 8:14–21. On the Eucharistic features in Jn 6:1–15, see Raymond E. Brown, S.S., *The Gospel according to John (i–xii)* (Garden City, N.Y.: Doubleday, 1966) 246–49.

3. Leo XIII, *Mirae caritatis*, Aug. 28, 1902 (DS 3364).

4. As this homily was being prepared, black judge Clarence Thomas' appointment by President George Bush to the Supreme Court was close to consideration by the U.S. Senate.

5. See *Time*, Dec. 17, 1990, 45.

6. See *Ethics and Public Policy Center Newsletters* no. 35 (summer 1991) 2, quoting from an address by Jean Bethke Elshtain.

7. SOME (So Others Might Eat) and Zacchaeus are Christian ministries in the District of Columbia.

Homily 8

1. I shall understand "the Lord" here as referring to Jesus rather than to Yahweh. For justification of this choice, see Joseph A. Fitzmyer, S.J.,

The Gospel according to Luke (I–IX) (Garden City, N.Y.: Doubleday, 1981) 385–86: "The hindsight with which the infancy narrative has been composed by Luke makes it likely that *kyrios* here would be understood by him as Jesus. That identification makes the canticle itself hang together better as a unit: Jesus is not only the horn of salvation in the house of David (1:69), the Dawn from on High (1:78), but also the *Kyrios* before whom John prepares the way (1:76)."

2. This homily was preached to 43 priests during the inaugural retreat of the project *Preaching the Just Word*, a national effort to move the preaching of social-justice issues more effectively into the Catholic pulpits of the United States.

3. Here I am indebted to Joseph A. Fitzmyer, S.J., *Luke the Theologian: Aspects of His Teaching* (New York: Paulist, 1989), specifically his chapter "The Lucan Picture of John the Baptist as Precursor of the Lord" (86–116). This chapter is the most useful single source I know for anyone preaching on the Baptist—not an easy task if one wants to make sense of the scriptural material.

4. Ibid. 107.

5. Fitzmyer, *Gospel according to Luke* 388.

6. See Fitzmyer, *Luke the Theologian* 91–95, for "four items [that] contribute to the plausibility of a temporary relationship" between John and the Essenes of Qumran.

7. Raymond E. Brown, S.S., *The Gospel according to John (i–xii)* (Garden City, N.Y.: Doubleday, 1966) 153.

8. So the Jewish historian Flavius Josephus, *Antiquities of the Jews* 18.5.2. Josephus and Mark do not agree on the reason for John's execution, but Josephus does support Mark's statement that John was imprisoned and executed by Herod.

9. Here I follow Abraham J. Heschel's *The Prophets* (New York: Harper & Row, 1962), especially the opening chapter, "What Manner of Man Is the Prophet?" (3–26). Actually, Heschel has seven characteristics; I omit two as not pertinent to my third point: the prophets' mighty exaggerations and their role as God's counselors.

10. Ibid. 4.

11. Ibid. 5.

12. Ibid. 19.

13. On divine pathos, for Heschel a unique category, see ibid. passim, but esp. 24, 221–31, 489–92. For a strong critique of this category, see Eliezer Berkovits, "Dr. A. J. Heschel's Theology of Pathos," *Tradition: A Journal of Orthodox Thought* 6 (spring-summer 1964) 67–104. He argues that Heschel's affirmation of divine pathos is based on a fallacious line of deductive reasoning and on a literalist interpretation of biblical texts.

14. Ibid. 231.

Homily 9

1. The occasion was a liturgy within the Jesuit community of Georgetown University to mark my departure from Georgetown after 12 years as theologian in residence, to direct a Woodstock Theological Center project entitled "Preaching the Just Word," briefly described in my third point.
2. Here I am indebted to Robert J. Karris, O.F.M., "The Gospel according to Luke," in *The New Jerome Biblical Commentary*, ed. Raymond E. Brown, S.S., Joseph A. Fitzmyer, S.J., and Roland E. Murphy, O.Carm. (Englewood Cliffs, N.J.: Prentice Hall, 1990) 43:68–72, pp. 691–92.
3. Ibid. 43:68, pp. 691–92.
4. References to the relocation of 100-year-old Woodstock College Seminary from Woodstock, Maryland, to New York City in 1969–70, and to the closing of Woodstock-in-New-York in 1974.
5. *Documents of the 31st and 32nd General Congregations of the Society of Jesus* (St. Louis: Institute of Jesuit Sources, 1977) 411, no. 48.

Homily 10

1. I am aware that there are three possible translations of this verse: (1) the one I have actually used, "In everything God works for good with those who love Him"; (2) "God makes all things conspire for the good of those who love Him"; (3) "All things work together for good for those who love God." See Joseph A. Fitzmyer, S.J., "The Letter to the Romans," in *The New Jerome Biblical Commentary*, ed. Raymond E. Brown, S.S., Joseph A. Fitzmyer, S.J., and Roland E. Murphy, O.Carm. (Englewood Cliffs, N.J.: Prentice Hall, 1990) 51:90, p. 855. But the point I am making is not affected by the choice of one version over another.
2. St. John Chrysostom, *Homily 50 on Matthew* 3–4 (PG 58, 508–9).

Homily 11

1. The special occasion was the celebration, within the 12:30 Sunday liturgical community in Georgetown University's Dahlgren Chapel and the 5:30 Sunday liturgical community at Holy Trinity Church, of my 50 years in the priesthood of Christ and 60 years in the Society of Jesus.
2. *Peter in the New Testament*, ed. Raymond E. Brown, Karl P. Donfried, and John Reumann (New York/Minneapolis: Paulist/Augsburg, 1973) 65. See the whole small section on "Peter's Confession of Jesus as Messiah (Mark 8:27–33)" (64–69).
3. Walter Shapiro, "Tough Choice," *Time* 138, no. 11 (Sept. 16, 1991) 54–60, at 54.

4. See Thomas McCarroll, "Down and Out: 'Discouraged' Workers," *Time* 138, no. 10 (Sept. 9, 1991) 56.
5. Francis Thompson, "Daisy," in *Francis Thompson: Poems and Essays*, ed. Wilfred Meynell (Westminster, Md.: Newman, 1949) 5.
6. Richard Schickel, "More Than a Heart Warmer: Frank Capra: 1897–1991," *Time* 138, no. 11 (Sept. 16, 1991) 77.

Homily 12

1. John Milton, *Paradise Lost* 9.958–59.
2. "One Hand, One Heart," from *West Side Story*, lyrics by Stephen Sondheim, music by Leonard Bernstein.
3. Catherine of Genoa; see *Vita mirabile e dottrina santa della Beata Caterina da Genova* (Genoa, 1551, 1847) 50b, quoted in Friedrich von Hügel, *The Mystical Element of Religion as Studied in Saint Catherine of Genoa and Her Friends* 1 (New York: E. P. Dutton, 1908) 265.
4. Kahlil Gibran, *The Prophet* (New York: Knopf, 1961) 15.
5. See Evelyn Whitehead and James Whitehead, "Christian Marriage," *U.S. Catholic* 47, no. 6 (June 1982) 9.

Homily 13

1. I use "St. Paul to the Ephesians" for simplicity's sake. I am well aware that many scholars deny or question Pauline authorship here, and that the letter may have been an encyclical or circular letter destined for several churches in the Roman province of Asia; see Paul J. Kobelski, "The Letter to the Ephesians," in *The New Jerome Biblical Commentary*, ed. Raymond E. Brown, S.S., Joseph A. Fitzmyer, S.J., and Roland E. Murphy, O.Carm. (Englewood Cliffs, N.J.: Prentice Hall, 1990) 55:2–3, pp. 883–84.
2. John's *eis telos* combines two meanings of that phrase: "to the very end" and "completely, fully, absolutely."
3. See Joseph A. Fitzmyer, S.J., "The Letter to the Romans," in *The New Jerome Biblical Commentary* (n. 1 above) 51:51, p. 844.

Homily 14

1. St. Augustine, *Confessions* 4, 6, 11.
2. O. Henry [William Stanley Porter], "The Gift of the Magi," in *The Complete Works of O. Henry* 1 (Garden City, N.Y.: Doubleday, 1953) 7–11.

Homily 15

1. A. S. Rosso, "Buddhism," *New Catholic Encyclopedia* 2 (1967) 847–57, at 847.
2. See ibid. 848. I am aware that these rules were formulated by the Buddha for monks and nuns, and that laypeople "were obliged only to abstain from killing, stealing, lying, intoxicants, and fornication. But they were exhorted to practice kindness, clean speech, almsgiving, religious instruction, and the duties of mutual family and social relations" (ibid. 849). A helpful introduction, brief and highly synthetic, is the article by Frank E. Reynolds, "Buddhism," *World Book Encyclopedia* 2 (1975) 555–57.
3. Catholic preachers should be aware of the short paragraph on Buddhism in Vatican II's Declaration on the Relationship of the Church to Non-Christian Religions: "Buddhism in its multiple forms acknowledges the radical insufficiency of this shifting world. It teaches a path by which men and women, in a devout and confident spirit, can either reach a state of absolute freedom or attain supreme enlightenment by their own efforts or by higher assistance" (no. 2; tr. *The Documents of Vatican II*, ed. Walter M. Abbott, S.J. [New York: Herder and Herder/Association, 1966] 662).
4. I am not implying that this is the meaning of divine likeness intended by the author(s) of Genesis 1. I have profited from some of the rich tradition in this area.

Homily 16

1. It is not clear whether this is a reference to Christ or to God.
2. See the commentary by Joseph A. Fitzmyer, S.J., "The Letter to the Romans," *The New Jerome Biblical Commentary*, ed. Raymond E. Brown, S.S., Joseph A. Fitzmyer, S.J., and Roland E. Murphy, O.Carm. (Englewood Cliffs, N.J.: Prentice Hall, 1990) 51:91, p. 855.
3. Kahlil Gibran, *The Prophet* (New York: Knopf, 1961) 15.
4. References to intellectual gifts, physical characteristics, and musical "loves" of Lisa and Marin.
5. Preachers should be aware that this consoling text refers not to our love of God but to God's love of us, as the following context makes clear; see Fitzmyer (n. 2 above) 51:51, p. 844.
6. For the facts and quotations in this paragraph, I am indebted to an article by Gregory Waldrop, " 'Grabbing Aholt of God,' " *America* 163, no. 15 (Nov. 17, 1990) 365.

Homily 18

1. Frederick Buechner, *Telling the Truth: The Gospel as Tragedy, Comedy, and Fairy Tale* (San Francisco: Harper & Row, 1977) 49–50.

2. Karl Rahner, "Following the Crucified," *Theological Investigations* 18: *God and Revelation* (New York: Crossroad, 1983) 157–70, at 169.
3. Richard Selzer, *Mortal Lessons: Notes on the Art of Surgery* (New York: Simon and Schuster, 1976) 45–46. I have used this story in the homily "That Their Kiss Still Works," in my collection *To Christ I Look: Homilies at Twilight* (New York/Mahwah: Paulist, 1989) 203–4.
4. The Church in the Modern World, no. 31.

Homily 19

1. William McNamara, O.C.D., *The Art of Being Human* (Garden City, N.Y.: Doubleday Echo Books, 1967) 72.
2. Richard Selzer, *Mortal Lessons: Notes on the Art of Surgery* (New York: Simon and Schuster, 1976) 19.
3. Ibid. 18.
4. I have taken this story from Gregory M. Corrigan, *Disciple Story: Every Christian's Journey* (Notre Dame, Ind.: Ave Maria, 1989) 99.
5. See Joseph A. Fitzmyer, S.J., *Paul and His Theology: A Brief Sketch* (2nd ed.; Englewood Cliffs, N.J.: Prentice Hall, 1989) 57–58, no. 64.
6. Tertullian, *To His Wife* 2.8 (tr. William P. Le Saint, S.J., Ancient Christian Writers 13 [New York/Ramsey: Newman, 1951] 35).

Homily 20

1. George W. Hunt, "The Fullness of Time," *America* 165, no. 19 (Dec. 14, 1991) 451.
2. Ibid.
3. Richard Selzer, *Mortal Lessons: Notes on the Art of Surgery* (New York: Simon and Schuster, 1976) 45–46.
4. See Editorial, "Christmas Present," *Commonweal* 118, no. 22 (Dec. 20, 1991) 739, using the U.S. bishops' report "Children and Families First."

Homily 21

1. Richard A. McCormick, S.J., "Notes on Moral Theology: The Abortion Dossier," *Theological Studies* 35 (1974) 312–59, at 313.
2. Hugo Rahner, S.J., *Ignatius the Theologian* (New York: Herder and Herder, 1968) 222.
3. Karl Rahner, *Ignatius of Loyola*, with an Historical Introduction by Paul Imhof, S.J. (London: Collins, 1979) 28. On the other hand, one must

recognize that for Ignatius "it was always the hierarchical Church which formed the yardstick of all spiritual authenticity" (Hugo Rahner, *Ignatius the Theologian* 228; the whole chapter "The Spirit and the Church" [214–38] is worth reading).

4. Letter from Catherine Benencasa to Pope Gregory XI, tr. in Colman J. Barry, O.S.B., ed., *Readings in Church History* 1: *From Pentecost to the Protestant Revolt* (Westminster, Md.: Newman, 1960) 473.

5. *Documents of the 31st and 32nd General Congregations of the Society of Jesus* (St. Louis: Institute of Jesuit Sources, 1977) 411, nos. 48–49.

6. Zacheus Maher, S.J., to George H. Dunne, S.J., as quoted in *King's Pawn: The Memoirs of George H. Dunne, S.J.* (Chicago: Loyola University, 1990) 69, 70.

7. See Dean Brackley, S.J., "Downward Mobility: Social Implications of St. Ignatius's Two Standards," *Studies in the Spirituality of Jesuits* 20/1 (January 1988).

8. From a homily delivered by Father Arrupe at the Ateneo de Manila, Quezon City, Philippines, on the feast of St. Ignatius, July 31, 1983; in *Recollections and Reflections of Pedro Arrupe, S.J.*, tr. Yolanda T. De Mola, S.C. (Wilmington, Del.: Michael Glazier, 1986) 128.

Homily 22

1. This homily was delivered on the feast of Our Lady's Birth, Sept. 8, 1991, to friends and relatives from various parts of the country gathered in Holy Trinity Church, Washington, D.C. For the record, the actual dates of my Jesuit entrance and priestly ordination were, respectively, February 10, 1931, and June 22, 1941.

2. Frederick Buechner, *The Faces of Jesus* (New York/San Francisco: Stearn/Harper & Row, 1989) 27.

3. On the interpretation of the Romans text, see Joseph A. Fitzmyer, S.J., "The Letter to the Romans," in *The New Jerome Biblical Commentary*, ed. Raymond E. Brown, S.S., Joseph A. Fitzmyer, S.J., and Roland E. Murphy, O.Carm. (Englewood Cliffs, N.J.: Prentice Hall, 1990) 51:90, p. 855.

4. I translate "*the* sinner" rather than "*a* sinner" because for years I have been affected (perhaps without sufficient biblical warrant) by the definite article in the Greek, *tō hamartōlō*.

5. Pierre Teilhard de Chardin, *The Divine Milieu* (San Francisco: Harper, 1960) 62–63.

6. For rich material on "the faces of Jesus," see the text and illustrations in Buechner, n. 2 above.

Homily 23

1. The occasion was the celebration, for priests currently in the Archdiocese of Baltimore, of 25, 40, 50, and 60 years in the priesthood.
2. John A. Coleman, S.J., "2001, A Priest's Odyssey," in *Exception and Promise: A Look at Catholic Vocations*, Proceedings of a symposium, Jan. 24, 1991, Palm Beach, Fla., cosponsored by Foundations and Donors Interested in Catholic Activities (FADICA), the Lilly Endowment, and Serra International Foundation, ed. Kerry Robinson (privately published by FADICA, Washington, D.C., 1991) 13–20, at 17.
3. Pastoral Constitution on the Church in the Modern World, no. 1.
4. *In Mysterious Ways: The Death and Life of a Parish Priest*; quoted from Coleman (n. 2 above) 18.
5. Dietrich Bonhoeffer, *Letters and Papers from Prison: The Enlarged Edition* (London: SCM, 1971) 371.
6. Ralph Waldo Emerson, "Divinity School Address," in *The World Treasury of Modern Religious Thought*, ed. Jaroslav Pelikan (Boston: Little, Brown, 1990) 252–53.

Homily 24

1. See Norman Cousins, *Anatomy of an Illness as Perceived by the Patient: Reflections on Healing and Regeneration* (New York: Norton, 1979).
2. Algernon Charles Swinburne, "Hymn to Proserpine."

Homily 25

1. For the record, 1491 marks the birth of Ignatius Loyola; 1540 saw the formal founding of the Society of Jesus; in 1840 the Jesuits arrived in Cincinnati; 1990 is the 450th anniversary of the Society; 1991 will see the 500th anniversary of Ignatius' birth.
2. I am aware that in this meditation Ignatius speaks explicitly of "God," not of Christ. But, as Hugo Rahner states emphatically, "In full accordance with Ignatian theology, the 'creator and Lord' of this contemplation is Christ, the incarnate Word, who in virtue of what he is and of what he does, dwells in all creatures and 'behaves as one who works' . . ." (*Ignatius the Theologian* [New York: Herder and Herder, 1968] 134).
3. A notable monument in Cincinnati.
4. John A. Coleman, S.J., "The Situation for Modern Faith," *Theological Studies* 39 (1978) 601–32, at 622.

5. A reference to the professional football team in Cincinnati.
6. Thea did indeed die, several months before this homily was delivered.
7. Second Vatican Council, Decree on the Apostolate of the Laity, no. 6.
8. Ibid. 5.

Homily 26

1. P. K. Rourke, "The Society of Jesus: The Modern Era," *Fenwick Review* (College of the Holy Cross, Worcester, Mass.) 2, no. 4 (February 1991) 7, 9, at 7.
2. Philip Caraman, *Ignatius Loyola* (London: Collins, 1990) 141.
3. Ibid.
4. Spiritual Exercises 95; tr. Louis J. Puhl, S.J., *The Spiritual Exercises of St. Ignatius* (Chicago: Loyola University, 1951) 44.
5. Ibid. 167 (Puhl 69).
6. Ibid. 234 (Puhl 102, with minor variations).
7. Here and in my second point I have borrowed liberally from a talk I gave to the Jesuit Guild in New York City 16 years ago, published in *The Jesuit*, New York Edition 50, no. 3 (autumn 1975) 1–3, reproduced in part in a 1981 homily celebrating my 50 years as a Jesuit; see "Let It Happen to Me," in my collection *Sir, We Would Like To See Jesus* (New York/Ramsey: Paulist, 1982) 203–9, at 207–8.
8. Henri de Lubac, S.J., "Meditation on the Church," in John H. Miller, C.S.C., ed., *Vatican II: An Interfaith Appraisal* (Notre Dame: University of Notre Dame, 1966) 258–66, at 259.
9. Spiritual Exercises 155 (Puhl 65).
10. Reference to a decision of Pope John Paul II committing the Society's care to a personal delegate, Paolo Dezza, S.J.

Homily 27

1. The liturgical feast "The Blessed Virgin Mary, Mother of the Society of Jesus" replaces the earlier feast "The Blessed Virgin Mary, Queen of the Society of Jesus." A communication (March 20, 1991) to Walter C. Deye, S.J., executive secretary of the U.S. Jesuit Conference, from Peter Gumpel, S.J., secretary of the Liturgical Commission of the Society of Jesus, informs us that "The question of the title of the feast celebrated on April 22 in honour of Our Lady was amply discussed by the Liturgical Commission of the Society before the new Calendar was published. With regard to the title of this feast (*Queen* or *Mother* of the Society) the opinions were divided." Some members favored change from Queen to Mother because "the title *Queen* had lost its meaning in today's demo-

cratic world." Others favored retention of Queen because "this title is closely linked to the Spiritual Exercises and the entire spirituality of St. Ignatius." The majority voted for Mother, and Father General Pedro Arrupe "decided that the title of the feast should be changed" from Queen to Mother. "Not all members of the Society were happy with this decision and we know that some continue to use the old title whereas others combine the two titles": Queen *and* Mother of the Society.

2. For details see Cándido de Dalmases, *Ignatius of Loyola, Founder of the Jesuits: His Life and Work* (St. Louis: Institute of Jesuit Sources, 1985) passim; also Harvey D. Egan, S.J., *Ignatius Loyola the Mystic* (Wilmington, Del.: Glazier, 1987) 114–18 ("A Marian Mysticism").

3. Autobiography, no. 10; see the fine introduction, translation, and commentary by Joseph N. Tylenda, S.J., *Ignatius: A Pilgrim's Journey. The Autobiography of Ignatius of Loyola* (Wilmington, Del.: Glazier, 1985).

4. Ibid. 239.

5. Exercises, no. 147; text from Louis J. Puhl, S.J., *The Spiritual Exercises of St. Ignatius* (Chicago: Loyola University, 1951) 62.

6. Hugo Rahner, S.J., *Ignatius the Theologian* (New York: Herder and Herder, 1968) 120.

7. Exercises, no. 299.

8. See, e.g., Raymond E. Brown, S.S., *The Gospel according to John (xiii–xxi)* (New York: Doubleday, 1970) 925–26.

9. Second Vatican Council, Dogmatic Constitution on the Church, no. 63.

10. Gerard Manley Hopkins, "The Blessed Virgin Compared to the Air We Breathe," in *The Poems of Gerard Manley Hopkins*, ed. W. H. Gardner and N. H. MacKenzie (4th ed.; London: Oxford University, 1970) 93–97, at 95. On the mother of Jesus and the arts, see the chapter "Madonna— Dei mater alma" in Andrew M. Greeley's informative and provocative *The Mary Myth: On the Femininity of God* (New York: Seabury, 1977) 105–27.

11. Elmer O'Brien, S.J., in *Theological Studies* 17 (1956) 214.

12. Avery Dulles, "The Symbolic Structure of Revelation," *Theological Studies* 41 (1980) 51–73, at 55–56.

13. *Osservatore romano*, Sept. 21, 1978, 2.

14. Elizabeth A. Johnson, C.S.J., "Mary and the Female Face of God," *Theological Studies* 50 (1989) 500–526, at 520.

Homily 28

1. Karl Rahner, *Schriften zur Theologie* 15: *Wissenschaft und christlicher Glaube* (Zurich: Benziger, 1983) 20.

2. Karl Rahner, "Following the Crucified," *Theological Investigations* 18: *God and Revelation* (New York: Crossroad, 1983) 157–70, at 165–66.

3. Ibid. 160–61.

4. Ibid. 169–70.
5. Quoted from *Recollections and Reflections of Pedro Arrupe, S.J.*, tr. Yolanda T. De Mola, S.C. (Wilmington, Del.: Michael Glazier, 1986) 52.
6. Exact figures are difficult to obtain. The number "about 75,000" as those who died instantly or soon after the bomb struck comes from an unsigned article on "Hiroshima" in the *New Encyclopaedia Britannica, Micropaedia* 5 (Chicago: Encyclopaedia Britannica Inc., 1976). The Japanese section of the Library of Congress estimates 202,000 as the number of those who died from Hiroshima's radiation as of 1990.
7. See *Recollections* 26–39.
8. Ibid. 53–54.
9. Ibid. 31.
10. Ibid. 54.
11. Cf. ibid.
12. I know this incident from "A Reprint from the 'Directors' Service' of the Apostleship of Prayer," Rome, January 1980, 13–14.
13. *Documents of the 31st and 32nd General Congregations of the Society of Jesus* (St. Louis: Institute of Jesuit Sources, 1977) 411, no. 48.
14. From a homily delivered by Father Arrupe at the Ateneo de Manila, Quezon City, Philippines, on the feast of St. Ignatius, July 31, 1983, commemorating the fourth centenary of the arrival of the Jesuits in the Philippines; in *Recollections* (n. 5 above) 128.
15. Address of Pope John Paul II opening the deliberations of the Third Assembly of Latin American Bishops, Puebla, Jan. 28, 1979, III, 2. A complete English version is available in *Origins* 8, no. 34 (Feb. 8, 1979) 530–38, though it translates the Spanish *indispensable* as "essential" (536), apparently unaware of a lively dispute on whether the struggle for justice is best denominated "essential" or "integral" to evangelization. What is beyond argument is that both the pope and the 1971 Synod of Bishops saw the search for justice as inseparable from the preaching of the gospel.
16. "Message of Fr. Pedro Arrupe to the Society," Sept. 3, 1983, *Documents of the 33rd General Congregation of the Society of Jesus* (St. Louis: Institute of Jesuit Sources, 1984) 93.
17. My translation from the original Spanish text, *Acta Romana Societatis Jesu* 18 (1983) 988.

Homily 29

1. For a recent brief treatment, see Zachary Hayes, O.F.M., "Limbo," in *The New Dictionary of Theology*, ed. Joseph A. Komonchak et al. (Wilmington, Del.: Glazier, 1987) 585–86.
2. See Gabriel Daly, O.S.A., "Original Sin," ibid. 727–31. I have deliberately couched "original sin" in a very general description, in the light of several contemporary efforts to cast new light on Gen 1–3, Rom 5:12–21,

and the Catholic tradition. For one engaging attempt at a synthesis appropriate to that tradition and to contemporary experience, see Stephen J. Duffy, "Our Hearts of Darkness: Original Sin Revisited," *Theological Studies* 49 (1988) 597–622.

Homily 30

1. The Gospel context is not quite ours. Jesus is telling his disciples what genuine greatness means: becoming childlike. I am focusing on the sheer fact that Jesus took a child in his arms.
2. For useful material on St. Paul and baptism, see Joseph A. Fitzmyer, S.J., *Paul and His Theology: A Brief Sketch* (2nd ed.; Englewood Cliffs, N.J.: Prentice Hall, 1987) esp. nos. 112–16.

Homily 31

1. I am quoting from the text released by the Vice President's office, p. 6. Mr. Quayle's questions should, in fairness, be taken in the context of the Report from the President's Council on Competitiveness (which he chairs), "Agenda for Civil Justice Reform in America," August 1991 (Washington, D.C.: U.S. Government Printing Office, 1991).
2. Richard Corliss, "Words of One Syllable," *Time* 138, no. 12 (Sept. 23, 1991) 68.
3. See William Shakespeare, *Julius Caesar*, Act 3, Scene 2, line 80.
4. In Wilfrid Ward, *The Life of John Henry Cardinal Newman* 2 (New York: Longmans, Green, 1912) 147.
5. Decree on the Apostolate of the Laity, nos. 5 and 7 (tr. *The Documents of Vatican II*, ed. Walter M. Abbott, S.J. [New York: Herder and Herder/Association, 1966] 495 and 498).
6. The ethical/legal downfall of evangelist Jim Bakker is well known. For the insider-trading "saga" of Ivan Boesky (and Michael Milken), see David A. Wise and Steve Coll, "The Two Faces of Greed," *Washington Post Magazine*, Sept. 29, 1991, 13–17, 28–31.

Homily 32

1. See *World Development Forum* (1300 19 St. NW, Suite 407, Washington, D.C. 20036), April 15, 1990.
2. Karl Rahner, *Schriften zur Theologie* 15: *Wissenschaft und christlicher Glaube* (Zurich: Benziger, 1983) 20.
3. See J. Bryan Hehir, "The Church in the World: Where Social and Pastoral Ministry Meet," *Church* 6, no. 4 (winter 1990) 17–22, 25.

4. Ibid. 21.
5. Lawrence S. Cunningham, *The Catholic Heritage* (New York: Crossroad, 1986) 1.
6. See Harvey Cox, *The Secular City* (New York: Macmillan, 1965); also Paul Lehmann, "Chalcedon in Technopolis," *Christianity and Crisis*, June 12, 1965, 149–51.
7. See my article "Intellectual and Catholic? Or Catholic Intellectual?" *America* 160, no. 17 (May 6, 1989) 420–25, specifically 424.
8. This homily was delivered at the close of a four-day workshop on "A Century of Social Teaching: A Common Heritage, A Continuing Challenge," sponsored by the United States Catholic Conference's Department of Social Development & World Peace and 11 other Catholic organizations concerned with social issues.
9. Constitution on the Sacred Liturgy, no. 10.
10. Hehir, "The Church in the World" 22.
11. See *Origins* 8, no. 34 (Feb. 8, 1979) 530–38, at 536; but note that this version translates the Spanish *indispensable* as "essential," a philosophical term which may go beyond the pope's exact meaning.
12. Hehir, "The Church in the World" 22.
13. Collect of the Mass for the Development of Peoples, *Missale romanum* (1975) 820.

Homily 33

1. Tissa Balasuriya, O.M.I., *The Eucharist and Human Liberation* (Maryknoll, N.Y.: Orbis, 1979).
2. "In the Greek text it is not clear whether 'to preach the good news' is to be taken with the preceding verb, 'he anointed me,' or with the following, 'he sent me.' My translation has followed the sense of the original Hebrew, 'to announce good news to the poor he sent me.' So too the LXX [Isa 61:1]" (Joseph A. Fitzmyer, S.J., *The Gospel according to Luke (I–IX)* [Garden City, N.Y.: Doubleday, 1981] 532).
3. James L. Empereur, S.J., and Christopher G. Kiesling, O.P., *The Liturgy That Does Justice* (Collegeville, Minn.: Liturgical, 1990) 123. This is a splendidly informative, inspiring book not only for the preacher but for the Christian community as a whole.
4. See *Time* 138, no. 26 (Dec. 30, 1991) 48. The poetry that heads the photo is from William Wordsworth's "We Are Seven."
5. See G. Carrière, "Oblates of Mary Immaculate," *New Catholic Encyclopedia* 10 (1967) 611–12, at 611.
6. See Vatican II's Decree on the Apostolate of the Laity, esp. nos. 5 ff.

Homily 34

1. "Unfriendly skies" was suggested by the United Airlines ad "the friendly skies of United."
2. In the Marcan text Jesus "takes Exod 3:6,15–16 as implying that Abraham, Isaac, and Jacob were still alive and continued their relationship with God" (Daniel J. Harrington, S.J., "The Gospel according to Mark," in *The New Jerome Biblical Commentary*, ed. Raymond E. Brown, S.S., Joseph A. Fitzmyer, S.J., and Roland E. Murphy, O.Carm. [Englewood Cliffs, N.J.: Prentice Hall, 1990] 41:78, p. 622). I am applying the statement more generally.
3. The baccalaureate homily was delivered on Trinity Sunday, Cycle B in the liturgical calendar.
4. See, e.g., Peregrine Worsthorne, "A Universe of Hospital Patients: Further Remarks on the British Condition," *Harpers* 251 (November 1975) 38, as quoted in Donald P. McNeill, Douglas A. Morrison, and Henri J. M. Nouwen, *Compassion: A Reflection on the Christian Life* (Garden City, N.Y.: Doubleday, 1982).

Homily 35

1. See Margot Hornblower, "Not in My Backyard, You Don't," *Time* 131, no. 26 (June 27, 1988) 44–45.
2. Ibid. 44.
3. Here I am applying to college graduates what I have preached more generally in a sermon specifically on the three servants; see "Only If You Risk," in my collection *Sir, We Would Like To See Jesus: Homilies from a Hilltop* (New York/Ramsey: Paulist, 1982) 137–42.

Homily 36

1. A popular soap opera.
2. Rod McKuen, *Listen to the Warm* (New York: Random House, 1969) 112.
3. *Washington Post*, May 22, 1990, A1.
4. "No Man Is an Island," *Union Theological Seminary Quarterly* 21 (1965–66) 121.
5. See the review by Richard Corliss, "Unlaced and Weird on Top," *Time* 135, no. 23 (June 4, 1990) 79.